Philosophies of Love

David L. Norton and Mary F. Kille

University of Delaware

A HELIX BOOK

Rowman & Allanheld
PUBLISHERS

To Tucker and Cory

© 1971 by Chandler Publishing Company

Reprinted 1983 as A HELIX BOOK
by Rowman & Allanheld, Publishers
81 Adams Drive, Totowa, New Jersey 07512

10   9   8   7   6   5   4   3   2

Printed in the United States of America

BOOK DESIGNED BY *R. Keith Richardson*

Contents

Introduction   3

PART I: ROMANTIC LOVE

Romantic Love: Madness of a Normal Man   11

José Ortega y Gasset
   Falling in Love / 14
   Love as Expression / 21

Stendhal (Marie-Henri Beyle)
   The "Crystallizations" of Passion-Love / 32

Søren Kierkegaard
   Don Juan's Secret / 42

Georg Simmel
   Coquetry / 50

Simone de Beauvoir
   Dependent Love in Women / 52

Max Scheler
   Love as Perfection of Differences / 64

Plato
   Aristophanes' Myth / 68

Arthur Schopenhauer
   Love as Illusion / 71

PART II: EROS

Eros: Love as Aspiration Toward the Ideal   81

Plato
   Eros / 85
   Man's Divided Soul / 96
   Divine Madness / 99

Aristotle
   Self-Love / 105

vi   Contents

José Ortega y Gasset
   Man's Vocation / *110*

Abraham H. Maslow
   Eudaimonia / *118*

George Santayana
   Philanthropy / *129*

Eric Neumann
   Love's Unmasking / *139*

Jean-Paul Sartre
   The Look / *146*

PART III: AGAPE

Agape: The Divine Bestowal   153

Anders Nygren
   The Content of Agape / *157*

Martin C. D'Arcy, S.J.
   Agape and Human Initiative / *162*

Friedrich Nietzsche
   Agape as Resentment and Suppression / *172*

Max Scheler
   *Agape as Superabundant Vitality: A Response to
   Nietzsche* / *176*

PART IV: TRISTANISM AND CHIVALRIC LOVE

Tristanism: Passion Chooses Death   187

Denis de Rougemont
   Tristanism: The Love of Love / *190*

Johan Huizinga
   The Conventions of Chivalric Love / *209*

John Jay Parry
   Courtly Love / *217*

PART V: FRIENDSHIP

Friendship: "Because It Was He, Because It Was I"   227

Aristotle
Three Kinds of Friendship / 230

Plato
The Congeniality of Excellences / 240

Ralph Waldo Emerson
Friendship at a Distance / 246

Arthur Schopenhauer
The Eagle's Lofty Solitude / 248

Martin Buber
The Friend as Thou / 253

PART VI: FELLOW FEELING

Fellow Feeling: Universal Bond of Humankind   263

Aristotle
Goodwill / 265

Herbert Spencer
Sympathy as a Social Emergent / 267

Max Scheler
Fellow-Feeling as Original Human Unity / 274

G. H. Mead
Sympathy and the Emergent Self / 283

Philosophies of Love

INTRODUCTION

If he chooses, the reader may use this collection casually, as the opportunity to see for himself what a number of experienced and thoughtful writers have found to be the real meaning of human love. To encourage this purpose the editors have chosen contributions which are concrete, expressive of diverse viewpoints, and written in compelling style. Included herein are practical men and visionaries, realists and idealists, skeptics and enthusiasts. Stylistically the adventure ranges from Socratic irony to the bite of Schopenhauer, the pyrotechnics of Ortega y Gasset and the prose poetry of Santayana, in which is to be heard the muted singing of the sea. Moreover, many of the questions which are dealt with are sure to have reared their hoary heads in the reader's own path—is love fugitive or enduring?; blind or clear-sighted?; possessive or liberating?; reserved for one alone or ideally universal?; elevating or degrading?

But in addition to casual perusal this collection affords a deeper opportunity which should be made explicit.

Love is a profound measure of human life, and a person's philosophy of love permeates his philosophy of life. Now developing a philosophy of life is not something we can relegate to others to do for us, like house building or plumbing repair, but something each of us must do for himself. There is no escaping it, each of us is required to be something of a philosopher. The practical man who scorns philosophers uses philosophical principles to justify himself for so doing. The typical "rugged individualism" of the self-made man is a philosophy. The prospective mother who opts for natural childbirth has her philosophical reasons. The teenage dropout is guided by philosophy in his rejection of established culture. The man or woman who raises his eyes from his daily tasks to question the meaning of what he does is behaving philosophically.

Philosophizing is the most human of activities and the most necessary. It consists in reflection upon experience in search of underlying meanings and principles which can afford guidance in life. The choice, then, is not between philosophizing or not, but between better philosophy and worse.

For the purposes of philosophy *any* experience whatever will be found to have afforded valuable material to someone, somewhere. But certain themes run so deep and spread so wide that they will be found to have provided philosophical material for everyone, everywhere; and among such themes love is paramount. Introduce it in dining hall or barracks or den and you will smoke out the hidden philosopher in all present, for no one alive lacks general hypotheses about love's nature, its conditions, and its consequences.

But much of the philosophy which you thus flush from cover will scarcely withstand the light of day. No one can help being struck, for example, by the haste with which a man leaps to general conclusions about "women" when he has known but two or three. The trouble is that his myopic conclusions shape his life. They will blind him to the reality of the next woman who stands before him, and the next, and the next.

What derives from insufficient experience, ill-considered, is bad philosophy; and bad philosophy impoverishes life by constricting one's vision and amputating his possibilities. Witness the selfish man who pronounces man's nature to be such and is thereafter blind both to the evidence of true altruism in others, and likewise to the possibility of it in himself. Conversely, good philosophy functions to enlarge our lives and transcend our limitations. It enriches our experience by sounding its depths and widening its horizons. It awakens us to possibilities within ourselves which, because of our special circumstances (that we are twentieth century Americans, for example, or white, or Protestant, and so forth) have gone unrecognized. In so doing it affords us opportunities of freedom and choice in the interest of meaningful living.

Admittedly, this kind of philosophical work goes largely undone today. Our leading American and British philosophical "schools"—logical empiricism and linguistic analysis—have openly renounced philosophy's ministry to life. One spokesman for this trend insists that he never got a philosophical problem from life but only from other philosophers (G. E. Moore). Another says that the problems with which philosophers should deal are theirs alone and do not concern the "plain man" (Gilbert Ryle). A third warns philosophers that to become involved in the problems of living endangers their objectivity (C. L. Stevenson).

Under such influence philosophy today lies remote from human concerns. It is a highly technical specialty requiring the Ph.D. for qualification, it employs language others cannot understand, and it works at problems which are such to no one but fellow specialists.

Of course these developments have been noticed by the wider community. Philosophy's retreat from living concerns has produced the widespread impression of her irrelevance and barrenness. She appears to much of the world as an ash-gray mortician to whom no one in his right mind would entrust a living thing. Under this opinion some readers may well recoil from the prospect of loosing philosophers upon the theme of love. Why must the embalming instruments be set to work here? Is there nothing *sacred* which requires to be preserved from the cold eye of analysis?

But this fear, appropriate as it may be when directed to contemporary British and American philosophy, becomes unwarranted in regard to Western philosophy as a whole. Seen in historical perspective, philosophy proves eminently humane, the skilled and devoted servant of human interests. Far from desacralizing life's deepest mysteries, it works continu-ously to reawaken us to wonder over those things which common sense conspires to cause us to take for granted. If philosophy's problems at present are remote, the themes of (for example) Plato's *Dialogues*—justice, courage, temperance, wisdom, love—are of vital interest to every living person.

In short, the man or woman who wishes to improve his personal philos-ophy of life can turn with confidence to a host of figures in the history of Western philosophy who have dedicated themselves to this aim. It is from the works of such figures that the selections included in these pages have been chosen. Plato, Aristotle, Santayana, Sartre—all are agreed upon philosophy's primary vocation as a ministry to life. Their thought arises from immediate experience and returns to it again. Behind the written words the perceptive reader will be able to see something of the man who writes and of the loves he has known. And he will find that the writers speak to him as to a fellow-philosopher, offering up their conclusions to the test of the reader's own experience and reflections.

Let the reader therefore approach with his own experience and phi-losophy well in hand. For it would be a travesty upon philosophy herself if in its name he were asked to dispense with what life has taught him in favor of someone else's offerings. This would constitute that fatal misstep which, as the Greeks knew, precludes all truth thereafter—untruth to one-self. By it one turns himself into another of those walking abstractions sociologist David Reismann called "other-directed" in *The Lonely Crowd*.

Let the reader begin where good philosophy must begin, in self-trust. Then the reflections he encounters in these pages will be used always as supplements to his own, never as substitutes. In this way he will be emulat-ing the great philosophers.

For good philosophy begins in scrupulous loyalty to one's own experi-ence—a trait the Greeks called *pistis*. Already this identifies the trait as a rarity, for humankind is notoriously careless in this regard. It is as if, on a trip to the zoo, we were to pass by the confines of our own species with scarcely a glance at the nameplate and identifying characteristics.

The mark of our carelessness with our own experience is that we let everybody including the corner newsboy tell us what it is. The art critic tells us we revere the paintings of Picasso, the newspapers point out to us our enemies among the nations, the psychologist informs us of our "alien-ation," the clock on the wall tells us when it is mealtime, the community tells us when to feel proud and when to feel ashamed.

In all of this we are living from the "outside in"; our selves are an im-port from foreign territory. The experience which we fund in this manner is borrowed capital which belongs to someone else. To whom, then?—the critic, the psychologist, the neighbor? But suppose they, too, are living on borrowed capital. In fact, it is largely the case that the opinions we imbibe are simply "in the air," they are "everyone's," and in being everyone's they belong to no one in particular. But this is to say they are anonymous, and by absorbing them we participate in their anonymity.

"Know thyself"—the imperative with which vital philosophy begins— will seem on the face of it to constitute the easiest of tasks, when in truth it is the most difficult because each of us makes his first appearance in the world as a dependent creature. If infants and young children were dependent upon others merely for the satisfaction of their physical needs the consequences would not be severe. But the child is dependent upon others to determine his needs for him (weaning, toilet training, starting school, and the like), and here we enter the innermost sanctum of personal identity. At bottom the child is dependent upon parents and community to tell him who and what he is. Likewise his first notions of such basic meanings as "fairness," "honesty," "freedom," are derived from external sources, and so are his early feelings. He is told that what he feels toward elders is "respect," toward brothers and sisters is "love," toward playmates is "friendship."

Especially is this true of love, for the American child is reared in a culture abounding with love's testimonials. Mother tells him he loves all members of his family and also the little foreign boy down the street. The church tells him that God loves him and that all people love one another. His teachers tell him he loves his country and its flag.

Later, as he approaches adolescence, he begins to hear more and more about a darkly mysterious kind of love, different from the others, which attaches to the opposite sex. Almost single-mindedly it is the subject of movies and popular songs; novels gyrate upon it; poets celebrate it or bemoan the loss of it; and everything from cars to hair tonic is advertised in conjunction with love's tokens and symbols. Such is the deluge that Erich Fromm is surely justified in calling our preoccupation with love an obsessional neurosis.

The result is that before the youth has had personal experience of love he possesses a headful of ideas about it and has marshalled a collection of feelings which are ready and waiting for its onset. At the first opportunity he will disgorge his stored contents upon the handiest object.

Childhood necessarily subsists on borrowed experience, but when the mode of dependence is prolonged, as it is in our culture, it can condition people to live on borrowings throughout their lifetime. Moreover, many of our institutions throw obstacles in the way of the individual's self-discovery. The institution of parenthood only grudgingly relinquishes its authority over the growing youth. American education, even at the college level, does little to encourage student initiative. And psychologist Carl Jung observes that by the church "people are effectively defended and shielded against immediate religious experience" (*Psychology and Religion*, The Terry Lectures, 1937).

But the onset of adolescence is announced by inner pricklings which make us aware of a being within—the Greeks called it one's *daimon*—which is noticeably at odds with the identities we have worn through childhood. For childhood identities are meant to be disposable garments, to be cast off when one's daimon—his authentic self—is ready for the light. Yet the daimon is at first a tentative thing, requiring to be found and nurtured; and the task of uncovering him is no child's work, for it requires that we make our way through the layers of borrowings which make up our child-identities. To shun the work, however, is to lose the possibility of discovering the life which is our own.

Vital philosophy begins in self-discovery. It derives its problems from experience that is authentically one's own, and it applies its tested methods to these problems. Its aim is the qualitative improvement of human experience.

In the interest of self-knowledge no better theme for investigation can be chosen than love, for of all human activities love is the most revelatory.

Normally we are slipshod in our observations of the life around us and within us, being preoccupied with our intentions of the moment. But to the clear eye every human act, even the most seemingly insignificant, is an expressive sign of the nature of the person whose act it is. The way a man walks, whether erect or slouching; his clothing, whether bright or drab; his gestures, whether ample or meager—these and all of his other acts signal something about the secret self within. Of course the sign reader must be canny. He learns very early, for example, that some signs are directly expressive while others express by inversion—e.g., bright clothing worn in a gray mood—and still others are compensatory, such as an excessive display of virility by the man who is insecure on this point. Moreover, every sign is ambiguous and must be referred to other signs as well as to the person making them. But this only suggests that the knowledge of persons requires cultivated skills on the order of any art or science. It is surely ironic that we readily acknowledge such prerequisites for the study of atoms, stars, or fossils, yet we do not dream of asking of ourselves a like effort toward the knowledge of persons.

Every human act is revelatory, but all are not equally so. Some express the fluid periphery of personality, while others divulge its core. Of those which run to the core it is acts of love which are most telling. For as Plato reminds us, love is life itself, and what a person loves and how he loves are the measure of himself—"Every one chooses his love from the ranks of beauty according to his own character" (*Phaedrus*). It is our love which unifies what otherwise would be a rag bag of unrelated events, making of it that whole which is a biography.

But if we begin with the investigation of our loves, are we not thrust immediately into that dilemma of which we spoke only a moment ago? In a culture saturated with the signs and tokens of love, is it not precisely here that self-discovery is thwarted?

Each of us steps from the circle of dependence into the world as the product of his time and place, but he is not bound to remain so. Suppose we were to ask the next person we meet whether he has ever been in love. Very likely he will answer yes, and in so doing he will in all probability be presupposing the dominant meaning of the word love in the United States today, a meaning steeped in the mystique of romance between the sexes. But let a third party be witness to this conversation, and let him be a European visitor to our shores. In short order this listener will express impatience with the American understanding of love between the sexes. "For love endures," he will argue, "while everyone knows that your romantic passion is but a fleeting seizure." And he will further suggest that in his eyes Americans are foolish to base their choice of partners in marriage, supposedly a lasting relationship, upon a clutch of passion which soon passes. If he proceeds thereafter to offer his own meaning of true love between the sexes it will most resemble what we will want to call companionship.

Hence as near as the nearest European lies, awaiting our discovery, an alternative meaning of love between the sexes. But how shall we respond to it? Unfortunately we typically react to such a discovery by digging ourselves deeper into our own trench, a procedure which the American philosopher C. S. Peirce called the "method of tenacity." It consists in precluding doubt by refusing to think, and by means of it we render ourselves radically ineducable. But if, instead, we will relate to the European in a manner which will here be termed "lending oneself," the enterprise of self-knowledge has much to gain.

Ordinarily we see other people through our own presuppositions and purposes. This mode of perception affords us external knowledge of them only, telling us what they are in relation to us, making of them grist for our personal mills. They thus appear as objects amid the multitude of other things within our perspective. But what this mode of perception precludes is what other people most essentially are—*other perspectives*. It was Emerson who observed that travel seldom broadens, for wherever we go we drag the same old self with us. It is not the addition of more facts, but the discovery of alternative perspectives which constitutes the true adventure of learning. The European of our previous illustration is now a resident of our home town. He sees what we see, but through different eyes. It is the discovery of the way he sees that constitutes our challenge. But in order to discover the way he sees it is first necessary to set aside our own way of seeing. We must temporarily exchange our perspective upon the world for his, in the process which we are calling "lending ourselves."

What C. S. Peirce called "tenacity" precludes "lending ourselves," and it is significant that Peirce believed tenacity to be the commonest human resort in the face of divergent beliefs. A familiar practitioner of tenacity is the individual who presumes that all men believe just what he himself does, or all "sane" men, or all "reasonable" men, or all "right-minded" men. Thus entrenched, no rumors of divergent beliefs can disturb his slumbers, for he has already pigeonholed them.

The passport which "lending oneself" requires is a secure sense of one's own identity. A person will not venture into foreign territory unless he is confident that his homeland remains where he left it, ready to receive him. And here is the rub; for it happens that our own time is characterized by a widespread "crisis of identity" in which no security of self exists, hence the ability to "lend ourselves" is severely diminished. But in this situation the prospect of finding ourselves vanishes, for it is through others that we discover the untapped potentialities within ourselves, and without such discovery we remain locked within our own mute presuppositions, victims of blind parochialism.

The release from parochialism lies in the discovery of life-styles different from our own, for each such discovery plucks the harp string of a potentiality hidden within ourselves. In the words of the Roman poet Terence, "Nihil humani a me alienum puto"—nothing human is alien to me. That *comradeship* in marriage which the European esteems is a potentiality within us as well. Don Juan and Tristan and Don Quixote and Prometheus and Faust are immortal because they are potentialities within every man. The ideals of exclusive love and of universal love are together within us, and to note their incompatability is simply to recognize that between them one must choose, for an individual cannot live all lives but only the one which is his own.

Through others we discover ourselves and our freedom, for each of the potentialities within us, once found, can be activated and lived. The discernment of alternatives within is thus the ground of *choice* concerning the kind of life which shall be our own. Having discovered alternatives by lending ourselves to others, we remain free to resume our living in its original terms, yet the change in us is immense, for now that original life-style has been made ours by decision. Moreover, because of the possibilities which have been touched within us in the course of our explorations we shall have gained the ability to enjoy life-styles different from our own, appreciating their distinctive virtues according to the principle which Socrates identified as the "congeniality of excellences." (*Lysis*—see the selection hereafter).

Each of the alternative meanings of love which form the headings of our table of contents has a profound place in Western history. Each is a subterranean stream, rising to the surface periodically to shape countless human lives, then giving way to another, but always present beside the human path. Among the major categories—Romantic Love, Eros, Agape, Sacred Love, Charitas, Friendship, Comradeship, Sympathy—the reader will be likely to encounter the mode and even the nuances which are his own, and by these contributions he may expect to be led to better knowledge of his home ground. At other times he is sure to find himself in territory which appears foreign and exotic, yet here no less than before his adventure is one of self-discovery—the discovery of potentials within himself which have thus far gone unactualized.

While the editors believe that the adventure afforded by these selections will prove both enticing and profound, by no means is it complete. Most notable among omissions are three vast perspectives upon love: that of the philosophies of the East; that which appears more or less problematically in studies of social bonding among lower animals; and that which promises to appear through the eyes of women (whose sole spokesman in this collection is Simone de Beauvoir).

Concerning the first two omissions the editors can only plead that while the exploration of love can go on endlessly, a single book cannot. The reader is therefore urged to overreach this collection in both of these directions. The great Hindu understanding of love, for example, opens a vast panorama of human possibility which every Westerner should traverse. And the study of sociality among primates, fascinating enough in itself, can be a needed corrective to certain human tendencies toward an over-spiritualization of love which robs it of its vigor and power. With such in mind, the present collection is offered as but the opening excursion in the larger adventure.

For the near absence of contributions by women, however, the editors are acutely regretful. Not only is the male perspective but half of the picture, it is a half which likes to think it is the whole, and by so doing it introduces severe distortions. The best that can be done, however, is to warn the reader to bear this deficiency continuously in mind, for it happens that Western philosophy has been a male prerogative, a "closed shop." Let us fervently hope that on some fine day very soon, women will cast off their dependence, cease to live definitions of themselves fabricated by men, and discover their authentic womanhood and its multiple modes. This event promises a sequence of discoveries which shall thoroughly eclipse the exploration of outer space lately begun with the landing on the moon.

PART *I*
Romantic Love

ROMANTIC LOVE: MADNESS OF A NORMAL MAN

The following scenario will be familiar to most readers as one in which they have played a part. It is presented from the male viewpoint, but women need only change the gender.

A friend pays us a surprise visit and we see at once that he is animated by a hectic spirit. "Come with me to dinner this evening," he begs—"I want you to meet the perfect incarnation of Beauty, Virtue, Wisdom, and Grace, in short, the loveliest woman in the world." The invitation is irresistible, and at the appointed hour we go forth to witness the revelation.

At the restaurant we find a table, and our friend fills the minutes of waiting with a feverish exposition of the lady's charms. Suddenly she is before us, and we struggle to conceal our astonishment. "*This*," we say to ourselves, "is the creature whose beauty outshines Venus, Helen, and Lady Hamilton?"

But patience, for it must be that what our friend has seen is the radiance of the spirit within, manifesting itself by soft and subtle emanations. Yet two hours' time confirms that the banalities which fall upon our ears are not prologue but the whole performance.

The affair leaves us with no choice. Since our friend has heretofore been of sound mind and eyesight, we must conclude that he has fallen victim to a temporary aberration, and we name his fit romantic love.

"Blindness," "madness," "a fit," "a rage," "a delusion"—the list of epithets directed against romantic love is endless. And here is the most obvious distinction between romantic love and loves of other kinds. Romantic love has high psychic temperature. It generates a heat which is piped into every discussion of it. Whether to praise or blame, no one speaks temperately about it. Here we discern romantic love's cardinal feature—intemperance. Romantic love and the "virtue" of moderation (we put the word in quotes in order not to prejudge the issue) cannot co-exist in the same world. By noting this rift we can anticipate some of the key points to be made by the selections which follow.

In the most emphatic terms, the lover celebrates qualities which he sees in his beloved. In virtue of these qualities the beloved appears to him as utterly unique, utterly above all others of her sex, a ray of dazzling sunlight in an undifferentiated field of twilight. Here is love's exclusivism; it chooses one and dismisses the rest.

But the non-lover's perception is very different. To him all women are rather more alike than different—a longer nose here, a shorter temper there, but what matter? Listening to the lover's ecstatic celebration of his beloved's qualities he may nod sympathetically, but he will find nothing exceptional in the virtues named. (Conversely the lover finds himself thoroughly frustrated in trying to find a friend who will "understand." He soon says to himself "What's the use," and retires with his beloved to a private bower.)

Thus from the world's viewpoint the first mark of love's intemperance is the exaggerated value it ascribes to the beloved, a value which distances her from her species. And this impertinence has an obverse in love's active *de*valuation of the daily world. As Socrates put it, the lover "is like a bird fluttering and looking upward and careless of the world below" (*Phaedrus*). Emerson observes that love "extrudes all other persons from his attention as cheap and unworthy" ("Love"). Nor is anyone exempt, for to Schopenhauer's keen displeasure love "sometimes embarrasses for awhile even the greatest minds, does not hesitate to intrude with its trash interfering with the negotiations of statesmen and the investigations of men of learning, knows how to slip its love letters and locks of hair even into ministerial portfolios and philosophical manuscripts. . . ." (See the selection hereafter.)

Think of it! Even the exalted stations of philosophy and ministry of state are trampled upon. Indeed, love has been known to seize a philosopher by the heels and shake him until his categories rattle and his postulates spill out upon the floor.

Intemperate love makes sport of the entire temperate world, the world of daily affairs; it is the implacable foe of the commonplace. Career, family, friends, obligations, duties—all are vaporized. But the ordinary world responds in kind. It first seeks to tame and domesticate love by throwing the weight of the world upon it—the institution of marriage serves the purpose. Those loves which remain untamed are excised, as the Greek philosopher Democritus is said to have plucked out his eye when it had fastened upon a passing woman. The world brands love "mad."

The antagonism between love and the world is responsible for most of the issues concerning romantic love. Partisans of the commonplace call love blind because it does not see what they see—duty, custom, propriety, law. Meanwhile a second group, smaller than the first, has no such faith in the commonplace. It regards "common sense" not as native wisdom but as shared prejudice, and it notes that conventional thinking is a contradiction in terms, and that habit dulls perception. To this group love is not blind but singularly clear-sighted. The non-lover cannot see the beloved's perfections? So much the worse for *him*. He needs an operation for cataract removal, for every person *is* unique if we could only for once truly see; yes, and every person is beautiful. These partisans of passion, our second group, are led by Plato, who termed love's madness *divine*.

Is passion but an arabesque upon animal sexuality? Then love's *exclu-*

sivism is illusion, for the sex drive is indiscriminate. Is passion transitory or enduring (and what are the implications of the answer)? Is it a free act or a determined one? A choice, or something which befalls us? Ennobling or demeaning? The attraction of like to like, or the magnetism of differences?

These are a few of the basic questions which the reader's own loves will have set before him. In the pages to follow he can test his reflections on the whetstones of worthy thinkers who have given these matters careful consideration.

FALLING IN LOVE

José Ortega y Gasset

What happens when we fall in love? According to this eminent philosopher of twentieth century Spain, falling in love is an "abnormal state of attention which occurs in a normal man." Our attention constricts to a single point—the beloved—banishing the rest of the world. Clearly this is in one respect an impoverishment of consciousness, and Ortega helps us see why love is called blind. But can it be that scope is here sacrificed for an utter concentration of attention which, by eliminating every distraction, penetrates deeper into its object, aiming at a kind of knowledge which ordinary attention cannot achieve?

Bear in mind that for Ortega passion's clutch is not the whole of love, but neither is it a dispensable aberration. It is the necessary first stage. Why necessary? Ortega hints but does not say, thus turning the reader to his own resources. And the second stage? Again, the careful reader of On Love *must collect hints. Ortega is no system-spinner; he is a peerless* provocateur.

"Falling in love" is a phenomenon of attention. No matter at what moment we examine the life of our consciousness, we will find its field engaged by a multitude of external and internal objects. These objects, which in each case fill the capacity of our minds, do not form a disorderly array. There is always a minimal order in them, an hierarchy. In fact, we always find that one of them stands out apart from the others, preferred and especially illuminated as if our mental focus, our preoccupation, might tone down its radiance by isolating it from the rest. It is natural for our consciousness to focus on something. But it is impossible for it to focus on something without disregarding other things which remain thereby as a secondary presence, in the manner of a chorus or a background.

Since the number of objects which compose the world of each of us is very large and the field of our consciousness very limited, there exists among them a sort of struggle to gain our attention. Properly speaking, our spiritual and mental life is merely that which takes place in the zone of maximum illumination. The rest—the zone of conscious inattention and,

Reprinted by permission of The World Publishing Company from *On Love, Aspects of a Single Theme* by José Ortega y Gasset, trans. Toby Talbot (New York: Meridian Books, 1957), pp. 48–60. Copyright 1957 by The World Publishing Company.

beyond that, the subconscious—is only potential life, a preparation, an arsenal or reserve. The attentive consciousness can be regarded as the very space of our personalities. We can just as well say that we are attentive to a thing as say that that thing dislodges a certain space in our personalities.

In the normal course, the focus of attention occupies this privileged center for a few moments and is soon driven out to leave its place to something else. To sum up, attention shifts from one object to another, remaining briefly or at length fixed upon each in accordance with its vital importance. Imagine what would happen if one fine day our attention became paralyzed, fixed upon one object. The rest of the world would be banished, removed, as though non-existent, and, lacking every possible comparison, the object of our abnormal attention would acquire enormous proportions for us. So much so that it would actually occupy the entire gamut of our minds and alone would be equivalent for us to that whole world which, thanks to our radical inattention, we left behind. The same thing happens, therefore, as when we bring our hand up to our eyes; though it is so small a body, it is enough to blot out the rest of the landscape and to fill our entire field of vision. What we fix our attention upon has for us *ipso facto* greater reality, a more vigorous existence than what we do not focus upon, an anemic and almost phantasmic background which lurks on the periphery of our minds. Since it has greater reality, it of course achieves greater esteem, merit, and importance and compensates for the obscured remainder of the universe.

When attention is fixed upon an object for a greater length of time or with greater frequency than normal, we speak about "mania." The maniac is a man with an abnormal attention-span. Almost all great men have been maniacs, except that the consequences of their mania, of their "fixed idea," seem useful or commendable to us. When Newton was asked how he had been able to discover his mechanical system of the universe, he answered: *Nocte dieque incubando* (By thinking about it day and night). This is a declaration of obsession. In truth, nothing characterizes us as much as our field of attention. It is differently modulated in every man. Thus, for the man given to contemplation, who follows every subject through to make it yield its innermost substance, the lightness with which the worldly man's attention skips from object to object is a cause of vexation. Conversely, the man of the world is wearied and distressed by the slowness with which the thinker's attention advances, moving as it does like a dragnet scratching the rough bottom of an abyss. Moreover, there are different preferences of attention which constitute the very basis of character. There are those who, if a fact of economics comes up in conversation, react as violently as if they had mentally fallen through a trap door. Another's attention will spontaneously descend toward art or sexual matters. This formula might well be accepted: tell me where your attention lies and I will tell you who you are.

I believe that "falling in love" is a phenomenon of attention, but of an abnormal state of attention which occurs in a normal man.

The initial stage of "falling in love" immediately reveals this. In society many men and women are confronted with each other. The·attention of each man—as of each woman—shifts indifferently from one representative of the opposite sex to another. Reasons based on former sentimental ties, greater proximity, etc., will cause the woman's attention to rest a bit longer upon one male than upon another; but the disproportion between attention to one and inattention to the rest is not great. To put it another way —and barring slight differences—every man that a woman knows is equidistant from her attention, in one straight line. One day, however, this equal division of attention ceases. The woman's attention of itself seems to rest upon one of those men, and soon it requires an effort for her to dismiss him from her thoughts, to mobilize her preoccupation toward other things. The straight line has been broken: one man stands out at a closer distance to the woman's attention.

"Falling in love," initially, is no more than this: attention abnormally fastened upon another person. If the latter knows how to utilize his privileged situation and ingeniously nourishes that attention, the rest follows with irremissible mechanism. Each day he will find himself further advanced before the line of those others, the indifferent ones; each day he will occupy more space in the mind of the attentive woman. She will begin to feel incapable of ignoring the privileged man. Other people and things will gradually be dislodged from her consciousness. Wherever "the woman in love," whatever her apparent occupation, her attention will gravitate by its own weight toward that man. And, vice versa, it will require a great effort on her part to tear her attention away from that direction for one moment and orient it toward life's obligations. St. Augustine wisely observed this spontaneous absorption in an object which is characteristic of love: *Amor meus, pondus meum: illo feror, quocumque feror.* (My love is my weight: because of it I move.)

It is not a question, then, of an enrichment of our mental lives. Quite the contrary. There is a progressive elimination of the things which formerly absorbed us. Consciousness contracts and is occupied by only one object. The attention remains paralyzed: it does not advance from one thing to another. It is fixed and rigid, the captive of one person alone. *Theia manía* (divine mania), said Plato. (We shall soon see where this surprising and excessive "divine" comes from.)

Nevertheless, the person in love has the impression that the life of his consciousness is very rich. His reduced world is more concentrated. All of his psychic forces converge to act upon one single point, and this gives a false aspect of superlative intensity to his existence.

At the same time, that exclusiveness of attention endows the favored object with portentous qualities. It is not that non-existent perfections are imagined in it. (I have already shown that this can happen; but it is neither essential nor necessary, as Stendhal erroneously supposes.) By overwhelming an object with attention and concentrating on it, the consciousness endows it with an incomparable force of reality. It exists for us at every moment; it is ever present, there alongside us, more real than anything else. The remainder of the world must be sought out, by laboriously deflecting our attention from the beloved.

Here is where we encounter a great similarity between falling in love and mystical ardor. The mystic frequently speaks of "the presence of God." It is not merely an expression. Behind it lies an authentic phenomenon. Through prayer, meditation, and addressing God, the latter acquires such objective solidity for the mystic that it is never permitted to vanish from the range of his thoughts. It is always there, precisely because attention does not let go of it. Every activity of the mystic's day brings him into contact with God, that is, makes him revert to his idea. This is not something peculiar to religious orders. There is nothing that can attain that everlasting presence which, according to the mystic, God enjoys. The sage who spends years at a time thinking about a problem and the novelist who is constantly harrowed by preoccupation with his imaginary character share the same phenomenon. And so Balzac winds up a business conversation by saying: "Well, let us return to reality! Let us talk about César Birotteau." For the lover his beloved also possesses a constant presence. It is as if the entire world is compressed in her. Actually, what happens is that the world does not exist for the lover. His beloved has dislodged and replaced it. That is why the lover in an Irish song says: "My darling, you are my share of the world!" Romantic poses aside, let us recognize that "falling in love"—I repeat that I am not talking about love *sensu stricto*—is an inferior state of mind, a form of transitory imbecility. Without a paralysis of consciousness and a reduction of our habitual world, we could never fall in love.

This description of "love" is, as you see, the reverse of the one used by Stendhal. Instead of heaping many things (perfections) upon an object, as the theory of crystallization presumes, what we do is to isolate one object to an abnormal degree and remain with it alone, fixed and paralyzed, like a rooster before a hypnotic white line.

By this I do not mean to disparage the great erotic episode which has created wondrous flashes of light in public and private history. Love is a work of high art, a magnificent transaction of minds and bodies. To occur, however, it undoubtedly needs the support of a number of mechanical, automatic processes possessed of little true spirituality. The aspects of love which are so estimable in aggregate are, when taken singly, quite gross and, as I said, mechanical.

There is no love, for example, without sexual instinct. Love uses it like a brute force, like a brig uses the wind. "Falling in love" is another gross mechanism, ready to be set off blindly, and love, good horseman that it is, merely utilizes and harnesses it. Do not forget that the lofty life of the spirit, so esteemed in our culture, is impossible without the contribution of innumerable and inferior automatisms.

When we have fallen into that state of mental contraction, of psychic angina, of which falling in love consists, we are lost. During the first few days we can still fight; but when the disproportion between the attention paid to a woman and that which we devote to other women and the rest of the universe exceeds a certain measure, it is no longer in our hands to restrain the process.

Attention is the supreme instrument of personality; it is the apparatus which regulates our mental lives. When paralyzed, it does not leave us any freedom of movement. In order to save ourselves, we would have to reopen the field of our consciousness, and to achieve that it would be necessary to introduce other objects into its focus to rupture the beloved's exclusiveness. If in the paroxysm of falling in love we could suddenly see the beloved in the normal perspective of our attention, her magic power would be destroyed. In order, however, to gain this perspective we would have to focus our attention upon other things, that is, we would have to emerge from our own consciousness, which is totally absorbed by the object that we love.

We have been entrapped in an hermetic enclosure that has no opening to the outside world. Nothing from the outside is able to penetrate and facilitate our escape. The soul of a man in love smells of the closed-up room of a sick man—its confined atmosphere is filled with stale breath.

Falling in love automatically tends toward madness. Left to itself, it goes to utter extremes. This is well known by the "conquistadors" of both sexes. Once a woman's attention is fixed upon a man, it is very easy for him to dominate her thoughts completely. A simple game of blowing hot and cold, of solicitousness and disdain, of presence and absence is all that is required. The rhythm of that technique acts upon a woman's attention like a pneumatic machine and ends by emptying her of all the rest of the world. How well our people put it: "to suck one's senses"![3] In fact: one *is* absorbed—absorbed by an object! Most "love affairs" are reduced to this mechanical play of the beloved upon the lover's attention.

The only thing that can save a lover is a violent shock from the outside, a treatment which is forced upon him. Many think that absence and long trips are a good cure for lovers. Observe that these are cures for one's attention. Distance from the beloved starves our attention toward him; it prevents anything further from rekindling the attention. Journeys, by physically obliging us to come out of ourselves and resolve hundreds of little problems, by uprooting us from our habitual setting and forcing hundreds of unexpected objects upon us, succeed in breaking down the maniac's haven and opening channels in his sealed consciousness, through which fresh air and normal perspective enter.

[3]*sorber los sesos* (Translator).

At this point in our discussion it would be well to purpose an objection which may have occurred to the reader while considering the previous chapter. When we define falling in love as a fixation of attention upon another person, we do not sufficiently draw a line between love and the thousands of situations in life in which serious and pressing political or economic affairs hold our attention to the utmost degree.

The difference, however, is radical. In falling in love, one's attention is voluntarily focused upon another person; whereas, in vital obligations, the fixation of attention is obligatory, against one's inclination. From a practical point of view, the most irritating thing about an annoying situation is being forced to attend to it. Wundt was the first—at least seventy years ago—to make the distinction between active and passive attention. Attention is passive when, for example, a shot is fired in the street. The unexpected noise imposes itself upon the spontaneous course of our consciousness and forces our attention. There is no such imposition upon the person who falls in love, for his attention is voluntarily given to the beloved.

A careful analysis of this phenomenon would reveal a curious two-sided situation in that we both willingly and unremittingly bestow our attention.

If understood in its finest implications, we can say that whoever falls in love does so because he wants to fall in love. This distinguishes falling in love, which is finally a normal phenomenon, from obsession, which is a pathological one. The obsessed man is not "fixed" upon his idea out of self-inclination. What is horrible about his condition is precisely this: that, though the idea is his, it presents itself to his mind in the form of a tenacious external imposition, which emanates from some anonymous, non-existent "other one."

There is only one case, other than falling in love, in which our attention is given voluntarily to another person. It is the case of hate. Hate and love are, in everything, hostile twins, identical and opposite. Just as there is the act of falling in love, so there is—and with no less frequency—an "act of falling in hate."

When we emerge from a period of falling in love we feel an impression similar to awakening and emerging from a narrow passage crammed with dreams. Then we realize that normal perspective is broader and airier, and we become aware of all the hermeticism and rarefaction from which our impassioned minds suffered. For a time we experience the moments of vacillation, weakness, and melancholy of convalescence.

Once begun, the process of falling in love proceeds with hopeless monotony. This is to say that all those who fall in love fall in love the same way —the clever man and the fool, the youth and the old man, the bourgeois and the artist. This confirms its mechanical nature. The only thing which is not purely mechanical about falling in love is its beginning. For that very reason we, as psychologists, are attracted by its beginning more than by any other phase of the phenomenon of love. What is it that draws the attention of a woman to a man and of a man to a woman? What qualities give one person the advantage over the indiscriminate array of others? There is no doubt that this is the most interesting subject of all; but, in turn, one of great complexity. Although all those who fall in love do so in the same way, not all fall in love for the same reason. There is no single quality which is universally loved.

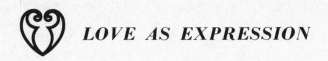

LOVE AS EXPRESSION

José Ortega y Gasset

The great question, Is love knowledge?, is ordinarily directed to the thing or person loved. Is the object of our love illuminated or concealed by our love? But Ortega gives the question a twist which turns us from the love object to the lover himself. It is he whom his love most of all illuminates, for of all possible human acts love is the most revelatory, rising from the depths to express the very "secret self" which much of daily behavior is designed to hide. We stand to learn most about a person not by listening to what he says, or reading his writings, or discovering his line of work, but by examining the quality of his loves. So, too, for the human race. And likewise for ourselves. In the ultimate imperative for self-knowledge the path is marked.

The essential core of our individuality is not fashioned from our opinions and experiences; it is not founded upon our temperament, but rather upon something more subtle, more ethereal and independent of these. We are, more than anything else, an innate system of preferences and distastes. Each of us bears within himself his own system, which to a greater or lesser degree is like that of the next fellow, and is always rigged and ready, like a battery of likes and dislikes, to set us in motion *pro* or *contra* something. The heart, an acceptance and rejection machine, is the foundation of our personality. Before knowing a total situation we find ourselves gravitating in one particular direction, toward certain particular values. Thanks to this, we are exceedingly wise about situations in which our preferred values are brought into play, and blind about others in which different, whether equal or superior, values exist which are alien to our sensibilities.

I wish to add to this idea, which is vigorously supported today by a whole group of philosophers, a second which I have not yet seen mentioned.

It is understandable that in living together with our fellow man nothing interests us so much as discovering what is his range of values, his system of preferences, for this constitutes the ultimate root of his being and the source of his character. Similarly, the historian who wishes to understand an epoch must, first of all, compile a list of the predominant values of the

Reprinted by permission of The World Publishing Company from *On Love, Aspects of a Single Theme*, by José Ortega y Gasset, trans. Toby Talbot (New York: Meridian Books, 1957), pp. 85–104 and 121–122. Copyright ℅ 1957 by The World Publishing Company.

men of that time. Otherwise, the facts and statements which the documents of that age reveal to him will be a dead letter, an enigma and a charade, as are the words and acts of our fellow man if we have not penetrated beneath them and caught a glimpse of what values they serve in his secret self. This self, this nucleus of the heart, is, in fact, concealed to a great extent, even from ourselves who bear it within us—or, rather, who are borne by it. It acts in the subterranean penumbra, in the cellar of one's personality, and it is as difficult for us to perceive as it is to see the span of ground upon which our feet step. Neither can the pupil of an eye view itself. A good part of our lives, moreover, consists in the best-intentioned comedy which we ourselves play for our own benefit. We feign temperaments which are not our own, and we feign them in all sincerity, not to deceive others, but to enhance ourselves in our own eyes. Impersonators of ourselves, we speak and act under the motivation of superficial influences which the social environment or our will exercises upon our organism and which for the moment supplant our authentic lives. If the reader devotes a while to analyzing himself, he will discover with surprise—perhaps with fright— that a great part of "his" opinions and feelings are not his own, that they have not sprung spontaneously from his own personal self, but are instead stray ones, dropped from the social environment into his innermost valley, as dust from the road falls upon the traveler.

Acts and words are not, then, the best clues for identifying a neighbor's intimate secrets. Both are capable of being controlled and feigned. The thief who has made his fortune through crime can one fine day perform a philanthropic act, but he is still a thief. Instead of analyzing words and acts, it is better to notice what seems less important: gesture and facial expression. For the very reason that they are unpremeditated, they reveal information about profound secrets and generally reflect them with exactness.[1]

There are situations, moments in life, in which, unawares, the human being confesses great portions of his ultimate personality, of his true nature. One of these situations is love. In their choice of lovers both the male and the female reveal their essential nature. The type of human being which we prefer reveals the contours of our heart. Love is an impulse which springs from the most profound depths of our beings, and upon reaching the visible surface of life carries with it an alluvium of shells and seaweed from the inner abyss. A skilled naturalist, by filing these materials, can reconstruct the oceanic depths from which they have been uprooted.

Someone may wish to refute this with the presumed experience that frequently a woman whom we consider to be of an eminent nature fixes her enthusiasm upon a stupid, vulgar man. But I suspect that those who make this judgment almost always suffer from an optical illusion: they speak from

[1]The arguments which expound this revealing power which gestures, facial expression, handwriting and the way of dressing possess, appear in the essay *"Sobre la expresión, fenómeno cósmico," El Espectador*, VII.

too great a distance, and love, being a gossamer of such delicate woof, can only be observed close up. In many instances, this enthusiasm is only apparent: in reality it does not exist. Genuine and false love comport themselves—when seen from afar—with similar movements. But let us imagine a case in which the enthusiasm is real: what ought we to think? One of two things: either that the man is not so contemptible as we think, or that the woman was not, really, of so select a temperament as we imagined.

In conversations and in university courses (when the occasion arises to define the meaning of what we call "character") I have repeatedly expounded this belief, and I have observed that it almost automatically provokes an initial reaction of protest and resistance. It is as if the idea itself contains some irritating or acid ingredient—why, as a general thesis, should we not flatter ourselves that our loves are a manifestation of our concealed beings?—and it is that automatic resistance which is tantamount to confirmation of its truth. The individual feels that he is caught by surprise, out in the open, because of a breach which he failed to close. We are always annoyed when someone judges us by some facet of our personality revealed by our negligence. They take us unawares, and this irritates us. We should like to be judged with forewarning and to pose, as for a photograph, with postures which we can control at will. (A terror of what is "instantaneous.") Of course, from the point of view of the investigator of the human heart, the most interesting adventure is to penetrate one's fellow man where he least expects it and to catch him *in flagranti*.

If man's will could completely supplant his spontaneity there would be no reason for delving into the recondite recesses of his personality. But the will can suspend the vigor of spontaneity only for a few moments at a time. In the course of a whole life, the intervention of will over character is practically nil. Our being tolerates a certain amount of falsification through the will: within this measure it is legitimate to say that, rather than falsify, it completes and perfects us. It is the finishing stroke which the mind—intelligence and will—gives to our primogenital clay. Long may this divine intervention of spiritual power remain in all its glory. It is necessary to modify one's illusions about it, however, and not believe that this marvelous influence can exceed a certain limit. Beyond this limit real falsification begins. The fact is that a man who goes against his instinctive inclinations during his entire life is as a consequence instinctively inclined to falseness. There are those who are sincerely hypocritical or naturally affected.

The more present-day psychology penetrates the mechanism of the human being, the more evident it becomes that the role of the will and, in general, of the mind, is not creative, but merely corrective. The will does not incite, but rather deters this or that involuntary impulse which animalistically rises from the subconscious. Its intervention is, then, negative. If it sometimes seems the contrary, it is for the following reason: it constantly occurs that, in the intricacy of our inclinations, appetites, and desires, one acts as a restraint upon the other. The will, when it defers to this restraint, allows the previously shackled inclination to flow and extend itself completely. It seems that our "wanting" has an active power when, actually, all that it has done is open the floodgates that restrained an already existing impulse.

The greatest error, from the Renaissance to our own day, lay in believing—with Descartes—that we live out of our consciousness, that slight portion of our being that we see clearly and upon which our will operates. To say that man is rational and free is, I think, a statement very close to being false. We actually do possess reason and freedom; but both powers form only a tenuous film which envelops our being, the interior of which is neither rational nor free. The ideas, of which reason is composed, come to us readymade from a vast, obscure source located beneath our consciousness. Likewise, desires appear upon the stage of our clear minds like actors who appear from the shadowy, mysterious wings, in their costumes, reciting their lines. And just as it would be incorrect to confuse the theater with the play performed upon its illuminated stage, so I think it is at least inaccurate to claim that man lives out of his consciousness, out of his spirit. The fact is that, except for the superficial intervention of our will, we live an irrational life, which empties into our consciousness and which originates from our hidden source, the invisible depths which really define us. For the preceding reasons, the psychologist must be transformed into a diver and submerge himself beneath the words, acts, and thoughts of his fellow being, for they are but the surface that conceals the deeps. The things which are important lie behind the things that are apparent. For the spectator it is enough to see Hamlet dragging his neurasthenia through the fictitious garden. The psychologist, however, waits for him when he leaves the stage, and, in the penumbra of the curtain and the stage riggings, he wishes to know who the *actor* is that plays Hamlet.

It is natural, then, for him to look for trap doors and crevices through which he can slip into the hidden aspect of an individual. Love is one of these trap doors. It is in vain for the lady, who is trying to appear so exquisite, to attempt to deceive us. We have seen that she once loved so-and-so. So-and-so is stupid and coarse, and worries only about the perfection of his tie and the shine of his Rolls-Royce . . .

There are innumerable objections to the idea that we reveal our most authentic inner selves by our choice of lovers. Possibly there are among them some which are strong enough to destroy the truth of the assertion. However, I think those which one usually hears are inoperative, inexact, and improvised by hasty judgment. It is forgotten that the psychology of eroticism can only proceed microscopically.

The more inward the psychological theme with which one deals, the greater will be the influence of detail. The need for love is one of the most inward. Probably, there is only one other theme more inward than love: that which may be called "metaphysical sentiment," or the essential, ultimate, and basic impression which we have of the universe. This acts as a foundation and support for our other activities, whatever they may be. No one lives without it, although its degree of clarity varies from person to person. It encompasses our primary, decisive attitude toward all of reality, the pleasure which the world and life hold for us. Our other feelings, thoughts, and desires are activated by this primary attitude and are sustained and colored by it. Of necessity, the complexion of our love affairs is one of the most telling symptoms of this primogenital sensation. By observing our neighbor in love we are able to deduce his vision or goal in life. And this is the most interesting thing to ascertain: not anecdotes about his existence, but the card upon which he stakes his life. We all realize to some extent that the kind of life to which we are committed is already determined in areas deeper than those in which our will is active. Turning experiences and arguments over and over in our minds is futile: our hearts, with the obstinacy of a star, are committed to a predetermined orbit, which will revolve by its own gravitation toward art, political ambition, sexual pleasure, or money. Many times, the surface existence of an individual rubs against the grain of his inner destiny, and surprising disguises are the result of this friction: the businessman who conceals a sensualist, or the writer whose only real ambition is political power.

The normal man "likes" almost every woman he encounters. This fact permits the nature of profound choice, which love possesses, to stand out all the more. It is necessary, however, that one not confuse liking and loving. The good-looking girl who passes by produces an excitation in the periphery of masculine sensibility, which is much more impressionable— let it be said to his credit—than that of a woman. This excitation automatically produces his first move in her direction. So automatic and mechanical is this reaction that not even the Church dares to consider it as a form of sin. In former times the Church was an excellent psychologist. It is a pity that it has fallen behind during the last two centuries. The fact is that the Church clairvoyantly recognized the innocence of "first moves." Thus it is that the male feels attracted and lured on by the woman who clicks along on high heels in front of him. Without these preliminaries there would be none of the rest—neither the good nor the bad, neither the virtue nor the vice. The expression "first move" does not say, however, all that it should. It is "first," because it emerges from the periphery where it has received the stimulus, without the person's inner self having participated in it.

The attraction which almost every woman exerts upon a man and which amounts to a sort of instinctual call to the profound core of our personality is, in fact, usually not followed by any response, or only by a negative response. The response would be positive if a feeling of involvement with what has just attracted our periphery burst forth from our utterly personal core. Such a feeling, when it arises, joins the core or axis of our souls to that external sensation; or, said in another way: we are not only attracted at our periphery, but, by ourselves, go toward that attraction, and put our whole being at its disposal. In sum: we are not only attracted, but we show interest. One is as different from the other as being dragged is different from moving voluntarily.

This interest is love. It acts upon the innumerable attractions which are experienced, eliminating most of them and focusing only upon one. Therefore, it produces selection in the extremely broad area of instinct, whose role is thereby recognized and at the same time limited. Nothing is more needed, in order to clarify the better the workings of love, than to define with some exactness the role which sexual instinct plays in them. If it is an absurdity to say that a man's or woman's true love for one another has nothing sexual about it, it is another absurdity to believe that love can be equated with sexuality. Among many characteristics which make the two different, is this fundamental one: instinct tends to amplify indefinitely the number of objects which satisfy it, whereas love tends toward exclusivism. These contrasting tendencies are clearly manifested in the fact that nothing immunizes a male against other sexual attractions so well as amorous enthusiasm for a *certain* woman.

Love, then, in its very essence, is choice. And since it springs from the personal core—the spiritual depths—the selective principles which determine it are at the same time the most intimate and mysterious preferences which form our individual character.

I have indicated that love, living on details, proceeds microscopically. Instinct, on the other hand, is macroscopic and is active in the presence of the whole. One could say that both operate from two different distances. The kind of beauty which attracts one is seldom the kind of beauty which makes one fall in love. If the indifferent man and the lover could compare what beauty means to each of them or what constitutes the charm of one and the same woman, they would be amazed at the incongruity. The indifferent man will find beauty in the broad lines of her face and figure— what, in fact, is usually called beauty. For the lover these sweeping lines— the architecture of the beloved person as seen from afar—do not exist; they have disappeared. If he is sincere, he will find beauty in separate little unrelated aspects: the color of her eyes, the way her mouth turns, the sound of her voice, etc.

When he analyzes his feeling and follows its course from within himself to his beloved, he notes that the thread of love is inextricably bound up with these little aspects, and constantly receives sustenance from them. There is no doubt that love is continually being fed; it derives nourishment from the beloved's charms, which it beholds either in reality or in imagination. It lives in the realm of ceaseless confirmation. (Love is monotonous, incessant, boring; no one would stand for anyone's repeating the most ingenious statement so many times and, yet, the lover demands unending reiteration that his beloved loves him. And vice versa: when someone is not in love, love bestowed upon him oppresses him and drives him mad by its utter plodding quality.)

It is important to emphasize the role which facial details and gesture play in love, because they are the most expressive means of revealing a person's true character, and hence are instrumental in our choice. That kind of beauty which, when viewed from a distance, reveals not only a personal character and a mode of being, but also an independent esthetic value—an objective plastic charm—is what we allude to by the noun *beauty*. It would be a mistake, I think, to believe that it is this plastic beauty which incites a man's ardor. I have always noticed that men seldom fall in love with the most plastically beautiful women. There are a few "official beauties" in every society, whom people point to with their fingers in theaters and at parties, as if they were public monuments; however, personal masculine ardor is rarely directed toward them. Such beauty is so decidedly esthetic that it converts the woman into an artistic object, and, by isolating her, places her at a distance. She is admired—a sentiment which implies distance—but she is not loved. The desire for intimacy, which acts as love's advance guard, is rendered impossible by mere admiration.

The expressive charm of a certain manner of being, and not correctness or plastic perfection, is, in my opinion, the quality which effectively inspires love. And vice versa: when an individual finds himself involved in a false instead of true love—whether for reasons of self-love, curiosity, or pigheadedness—the mute incompatibility which he feels with certain aspects of the other person is the first indication that he is not in love. On the other hand, a lack of correctness or perfection of appearance, from the point of view of pure beauty, is not an obstacle to love if it is not of grotesque proportions.

The idea of beauty, like a slab of magnificent marble, has crushed all possible refinement and vitality from the psychology of love. People think that in saying that a man has fallen in love with a woman whom he thinks good-looking they have said everything. This error has its origin in the Platonic inheritance. (No once can estimate the penetration of concepts of ancient philosophy into the ranks of western civilization. The most uneducated man uses words and concepts from Plato, Aristotle, and the Stoics.) It was Plato who made the everlasting connection between love and beauty; although by beauty he did not mean precisely physical perfection. Beauty was, rather, the name for all perfection, the form, to put it another way, in which anything worthy appeared to the Greeks. Beauty was superiority. This peculiarity in vocabulary has led subsequent thinking on eroticism astray.

Loving is something more serious and significant than being excited by the lines of a face and the color of a cheek; it is a decision on a certain type of human being, symbolically presented in the details of the face, voice and gestures.

"Love is a desire for generation and birth in beauty (*tiktein en tô kalô*)," Plato said. Generation is creation of a future. Beauty is the good life. Love implies an inner adherence to a certain type of humanity which to us seems the best and which we find preconceived, inherent in another being.

And this, my dear madame, probably sounds abstract, abstruse, and removed from concrete reality. Nevertheless, guided by this abstraction, I have just discovered in the look you gave to X what life means to you. Let's have another cocktail!

In most cases a man is in love several times during his lifetime. This fact raises a number of theoretical problems, in addition to the practical ones which the lover will have to solve on his own. For example: is this successive continuum of love affairs part of masculine nature, or is it a defect, a licentious remnant of primitivism and barbarism which still survives? Would a single love be the ideal, perfect and desirable thing? Is there any difference, in this matter, between the normal woman and the normal man?

For the moment we are going to avoid every attempt to answer such dangerous questions. Without allowing ourselves to take a stand on them, we accept, without much ado, the indisputable fact that the male is almost always pluralistic in love. Since we are discussing, however, the pure forms of this sentiment, the simultaneous existence of several love affairs is excluded and we are left with those which occur successively.

Does the fact of male pluralism present a serious objection to our thesis that choice in love reveals the essential nature of a person? Perhaps; but first it is worthwhile to remind the reader of the trivial observation that this diversity of love affairs can be of two classes. There are individuals who in the course of their lives love several women; but with clear persistency each one is a repetition of a single feminine type. Sometimes, the coincidence is so great that these women even share the same physical features. This kind of masked fidelity, in which actually a single generic woman is loved under the guise of many women, is exceedingly frequent and constitutes the most direct proof of the idea which we hold.

But in other cases, the women successively loved by a man, or the men preferred by a woman, are, in truth, very different types. If this fact is considered from the point of view of our previous idea, it would mean that the man's essential nature had changed from one time to another. Is such a change in the very roots of our being possible? The problem is of a crucial, and perhaps decisive, nature in any study of character. During the second half of the nineteenth century it was customary to think that the direction of character formation moved from the outside inwards. The experience of life, the habits they engender, the influences of the environment, the vicissitudes of fortune, physiological conditions, would, like a well, decant that essence which we call character. There would not be, then, an essential nature of an individual, there would not be any inner structure prior to and independent of the happenings of existence. We would be formed, like a snowball, from the dust on the road which we travel. According to this way of thinking, which obviates any radical nucleus in the personality, there does not exist, of course, the problem of radical changes. So-called character would be constantly modified: in the same way as it is being made it is also being unmade.

Arguments of sufficient weight, which this is not the time to enumerate, make me lean to the opposite belief: it seems more exact to say that we live from the inside outwards. The essential lines of our inner character are already formed prior to the occurrence of external contingencies, and although the events of one's existence do have some influence upon character, the influence which character exercises upon events is much greater. We are incredibly impervious to what befalls us when it is not in harmony with that innate "character" which, in the final analysis, we are. "In that case," you will say, "there is no point in even talking about fundamental character changes. What we were when we were born we will be at the hour of our death."

Indeed not. This opinion possesses enough flexibility to be adaptable to situations of every variety. It allows us to distinguish between the slight modifications which external events introduce into our mode of being and other deeper changes which are not founded on those grounds of chance, but on the very nature of character itself. I would say that character does change, if change is properly understood to be an evolution. And this evolution, like that of any organism, is induced and guided by internal reasons, inherent in the person himself and as innate as his character. The reader has most probably had betimes the impression that his neighbor's transformations are frivolous and unjustified, that they are foreign to his innermost self, but that in other instances the change possesses complete dignity and every visible sign of growth. It is like the seedling which becomes a tree; it is the naked tree before the leaves; it is the fruit which follows the foliage.

This is my answer to the former objection. There are people who do not develop, who, relatively speaking, are mentally stagnant (in general, those with little vitality: the prototype, the "good bourgeois"). They will persist in an invariable scheme of amorous choice. There are, however, individuals of a fertile nature, rich in possibilities and destinies, who patiently await their moment of blossoming. You can almost say that this is the normal case. A personality experiences in the course of its life two or three great transformations, which are like different stages of the same moral trajectory. Without losing solidarity, or even the fundamental homogeneity of yesterday's feelings, we notice one day that we have entered upon a new phase or modulation of our characters. Such modulation we call a fundamental change. It is nothing more, and nothing less.[2] Our innermost being seems, in each one of these two or three phases, to rotate a few degrees upon its axis, to shift toward another quadrant of the universe and to orient itself toward new constellations.

Is it not a meaningful coincidence that the number of true loves which the normal man usually experiences is almost always the same in number: two or three? And, moreover, that each of these loves appears chronologically localized in each of these stages in character? Therefore, I do not think it extravagant to see in the plurality of loves the sharpest confirmation of the doctrine I am suggesting. A new mode of reacting to life results in a vigorous change, and it is but a normal consequence that a different type of woman should be preferred. Our system of values has been altered to a greater or lesser degree—always in potential harmony with the old one; qualities which we previously did not value and of which we may not even have been aware, emerge into the foreground, and a new pattern of erotic selection is interposed between the man and passing woman.

Only the novel offers an adequate vehicle to illustrate this idea. I have read selections from one—which perhaps will never be published—whose theme is precisely this: the profound evolution of a masculine character seen through his loves. The author—and this is what is interesting—also insists on showing the continuity of the character in the course of his changes and the divergent contours which these changes possess, thus elucidating, with living logic, their inevitable genesis. At each step the rays of that evolving vitality are gathered and concentrated in the figure of one woman, like the images formed by light in a dense atmosphere. . . .

As does the individual, each generation reveals in the choice of its loves the undercurrents which give it form. This is true to such an extent that one of the most instructive avenues for assessing human evolution would be to attempt a history of the feminine types which have successively been preferred. Moreover, as does each generation, each race distills a prototype of femininity which is not produced spontaneously, but modeled in one long secular labor, by virtue of the majority of men coinciding in their preference for it. Thus, a careful, dispassionate outline of the nature of the archetypal Spanish woman would cast astounding light upon the secret recesses of the peninsular soul. To make her portrait stand out clearly she would have, of course, to be compared with the archetypal French woman, the archetypal Slavic woman, etc. The most fruitful aspect of this investigation, as of all such inquiries, lies in perceiving that things and peoples are what they are not merely because of sheer and spontaneous generation. No! Everything that is, everything in the world that has form, whatever it may be, is a product of some force, a vestige of some energy

---

[2]The most curious and extreme phenomenon is "conversion," the sudden tumultuous change which a person sometimes undergoes. Allow me to leave this difficult subject untouched for now.

and a symptom of some activity. In this sense, *everything has been made*, and it is always possible to inquire into the power that has forged each thing and in so doing, left its everlasting mark upon it. The acts of the entire history of Spain are preserved in the moral portrait of the Spanish woman, like the hammer blows struck in fashioning a chalice.

THE CRYSTALLIZATIONS OF PASSION-LOVE

Stendhal (Marie-Henri Beyle)

The great French novelist considered On Love *his most important work, and the book's focal point, the theory of "crystallization," has attained immortality no less than the characters of* The Charterhouse of Parma *and* The Red and the Black.

The theory's name derives from a practice popular with visitors to the salt mines of Salzburg, Germany. When a bare branch was thrown into the unused workings and allowed to remain there for a time, it was found upon recovery to be transformed into a thing of exquisite beauty by a coat of shimmering crystals. In like fashion, says Stendhal, the mind of the lover adorns with perfections the object of his love.

Stendhal's is a classic theory of blind love. The perfections which the lover attributes to the beloved are his own inventions. Having projected them upon her, the lover sees nothing of the plain twig beneath.

The process Stendhal describes is familiar to most of us through the experience of being loved. We are decked out in superlatives—"the best, kindest, handsomest, most intelligent." At first we glow in a welcome splendor, but when we try to live in accordance with the description we soon find that this life is not our own.

Moreover most of us have had the experience of falling out *of love, whereupon the sublime creature of just yesterday reverts to a plain twig.*

Such evidence suggests that crystallization indeed occurs, but the question remains: is Stendhal correct in identifying it with romantic love? Or is it instead a false substitute—albeit a prevalent one—which does not preclude the very different thing which is love itself?

A puzzle which goes to the very heart of the theory appears in Stendhal's unwavering celebration of passion-love. Of the four forms of love he identifies at the outset it is passion-love which prevails. But where lies its fascination? Where is the value which Stendhal unquestionably sees in it despite its blindness?

For Stendhal passion-love is deeply revelatory if one knows where to look. The imaginary perfections of crystallization tell us nothing about the beloved, but everything about the lover. Remember that Stendhal is a creative artist of the first rank. To him, what a person most essentially is is his imaginings. Here he is released from grubby necessity and fortui-

tous circumstance to freely fashion himself as he wants to be. He requires but a blank page on which to write, an empty canvas on which to paint. In the case of passion-love he requires a twig.

I am trying to account for that passion all of whose developments are inherently beautiful.

There are four different kinds of love:

1. Passion-love, that of the Portuguese Nun, of Héloise for Abélard, of Captain de Vesel, of the Cento man-at-arms[1].

2. Sympathy-love, such as was prevalent in Paris in 1760, and is found in the memoirs and romances of that period, in Crébillon, Lauzun, Duclos, Marmontel, Chamfort, Madame d'Épinay, etc., etc.

It is a picture in which everything, even to the shadows, must be rose coloured, and into which nothing unpleasant must intrude under any pretext whatever, at the risk of infringing custom, fashion, refinement, etc. A well-bred man knows in advance everything that he must do and expect in the various stages of this kind of love; as there is nothing passionate or unexpected about it, it is often more refined than real love, for it is always sprightly; it is like a cold and pretty miniature compared with a picture by the Caracci; and, whereas passion-love carries us away against all our interests, sympathy-love always knows how to adjust itself to them. It is true that if you strip this poor form of love of its vanity, very little remains; without its vanity, it is like a feeble convalescent who is scarcely able to drag himself along.

3. Sensual love.

Whilst out shooting, to meet a fresh, pretty country girl who darts away into a wood. Every one knows the love founded on pleasures of this kind; however unromantic and wretched one's character, it is there that one starts at the age of sixteen.

4. Vanity-love.

The great majority of men, especially in France, desire and possess a fashionable woman as they would possess a fine horse, as a necessary luxury for a young man. Their vanity, more or less flattered and more or less stimulated, gives rise to rapture. Sometimes sensual love is present also, but not always; often there is not even sensual pleasure. The Duchesse de Chaulnes used to say that a duchess is never more than thirty years old to a snob; and people who frequented the Court of that upright man, King Louis of Holland, still recall with amusement a pretty woman at the Hague who could never bring herself to think a man anything but charming if he was a Duke or a Prince. But, faithful to the monarchic principle, as soon as

[1]Monsieur Beyle's friends often asked him who this captain and this man-at-arms were; he always replied that he had forgotten their story. [Note in the first complete edition. Calmann-Levy, 1853.]

a Prince arrived at Court she dropped the Duke. She was a kind of insignia of the Corps Diplomatique.

The most agreeable form of this rather insipid relationship is the one in which sensual pleasure is increased by habit. In that case past memories make it seem something like real love; there is piqued vanity and sadness on being abandoned; and, becoming seized by romantic ideas, you begin to think you are in love and melancholy, for your vanity always aspires to have a great passion to its credit. The one thing certain is that to whatever kind of love one owes one's pleasures, so long as they are accompanied by mental exhilaration, they are very keen and their memory is entrancing; and in this passion, contrary to most others, the memory of what we have lost always seems sweeter than anything that we can hope for in the future.

Sometimes, in vanity-love, habit and the despair of finding anything better produces a kind of friendship, the least agreeable of all its kinds; it prides itself on its *security*, etc.

Sensual pleasure, being part of our nature, is within the grasp of every one, but it only holds a very low place in the eyes of tender and passionate beings. Although they may be ridiculous in drawing-rooms, although worldly people may often make them unhappy by their intrigues, on the other hand they taste pleasures utterly inaccessible to those hearts who only thrill to vanity or to gold.

Some virtuous and affectionate women have almost no idea at all of sensual pleasure; they have only very rarely laid themselves open to it, if I may put it so, and even then the raptures of passion-love have almost made them forget the pleasures of the body.

Some men are the victims and instruments of a satanic pride, a sort of Alfieri pride. These people, who are perhaps cruel because, like Nero, they live in constant fear, judging every one by their own heart, these people, I say, cannot obtain any sensual pleasure unless it is accompanied by circumstances which flatter their pride abnormally, that is to say, unless they can perpetrate some cruelty on the companion of their pleasures. Hence the horrors of *Justine*. These men cannot feel the emotion of security with anything less.

However, instead of distinguishing four different kinds of love, one could easily adopt eight or ten shades. There are perhaps as many different ways of feeling as of seeing amongst men; but these differences in terms do not affect the reasoning that follows. Every kind of love that one meets here below is born, lives, dies or becomes immortal, according to the same laws.[2]

---

[2]This first book is a free translation from an Italian manuscript of Lisio Visconti, a young man of the highest distinction, who died a short while ago at Volterra, his native town. On the day of his unexpected death he gave the translator permission to publish his essay on Love, if he could find some means of reducing it to a suitable form. Castel Fiorentino, 10 June, 1819.

THE BIRTH OF LOVE

This is what goes on in the mind:

1. Admiration.
2. One says to one's self: "How delightful to kiss her, to be kissed in return," etc.
3. Hope.

One studies her perfections. It is at this moment that a woman should surrender herself, to get the greatest possible sensual pleasure. The eyes of even the most modest women light up the moment hope is born; passion is so strong and pleasure is so acute that they betray themselves in the most obvious manner.

4. Love is born.

To love is to derive pleasure from seeing, touching and feeling through all one's senses and as closely as possible, a lovable person who loves us.

5. The first crystallization[3] begins.

We take a joy in attributing a thousand perfections to a woman of whose love we are sure; we analyze all our happiness with intense satisfaction. This reduces itself to giving ourselves an exaggerated idea of a magnificent possession which has just fallen to us from Heaven in some way we do not understand, and the continued possession of which is assured to us.

This is what you will find if you let a lover turn things over in his mind for twenty-four hours.

In the salt mines of Salzburg a bough stripped of its leaves by winter is thrown into the depths of the disused workings; two or three months later it is pulled out again, covered with brilliant crystals: even the tiniest twigs, no bigger than a tomtit's claw, are spangled with a vast number of shimmering, glittering diamonds, so that the original bough is no longer recognizable.

I call crystallization that process of the mind which discovers fresh perfections in its beloved at every turn of events.

For instance, should a traveller speak of the coolness of Genoese orange groves by the seashore on a scorching summer day, you immediately think how delightful it would be to enjoy this coolness in her company!

One of your friends breaks his arm out hunting: how sweet, you think, to be nursed by a woman you love! To be with her always and to revel in her constant love would almost make your pain blessèd; and you leave your friend's broken arm still more firmly convinced of the angelic sweetness of your mistress. In short, it is sufficient to think of a perfection in order to see it in the person you love.

This phenomenon which I have allowed myself to call *crystallization*, arises from the promptings of Nature which urge us to enjoy ourselves and

[3]For a fuller explanation of this word see *The Salzburg Bough*, page 42.

drive the blood to our brains, from the feeling that our delight increases with the perfections of the beloved, and from the thought: "She is mine." The savage has no time to get beyond the first step. He grasps his pleasures, but his brain is concentrated on following the buck fleeing from him through the forest, and with whose flesh he must repair his own strength as quickly as possible, at the risk of falling beneath the hatchet of his enemy.

At the other extreme of civilization, I have no doubt that a sensitive woman arrives at the point of experiencing no sensual pleasure except with the man she loves.[4] This is in direct opposition to the savage. But, amongst civilized communities woman has plenty of leisure, whilst the savage lives so close to essentials that he is obliged to treat his female as a beast of burden. If the females of many animals have an easier lot, it is only because the subsistence of the males is more assured.

But let us leave the forests and return to Paris. A passionate man sees nothing but perfection in the woman he loves; and yet his affections may still wander, for the spirit wearies of monotony, even in the case of the most perfect happiness.[5]

So what happens to rivet his attention is this:

6. Doubt is born.

When his hopes have first of all been raised and then confirmed by ten or a dozen glances, or a whole series of other actions which may be compressed into a moment or spread over several days, the lover, recovering from his first amazement and growing used to his happiness, or perhaps merely guided by theory which, based always on his most frequent experiences, is really only correct in the case of light women, the lover, I say, demands more positive proofs of love and wants to advance the moment of his happiness.

If he takes too much for granted he will be met with indifference,[6] coldness or even anger: in France there will be a suggestion of irony which seems to say: "You think you have made more progress than you really have." A woman behaves in this way either because she is recovering from a moment of intoxication and obeys the behests of modesty, which she is alarmed at having transgressed, or merely from prudence or coquettishness.

---

[4]If this peculiarity is not found in man, it is because he never has for one moment any modesty to sacrifice.

[5]That is to say that each shade of experience only gives one instant of perfect happiness, but the signs of passion in a man change ten times a day.

[6]What the seventeenth century romances called *love at first sight*, which decides once for all the destiny of the hero and his mistress, is an emotion of the heart which, in spite of having been abused by a vast number of scribblers, nonetheless exists in Nature; it arises from any such defensive manoeuvre becoming impossible. The woman who is in love finds too much happiness in the emotions she experiences to be able to succeed in dissembling; tired of prudence, she throws caution to the winds, and gives herself up blindly to the joy of loving. Caution makes love at first sight impossible.

The lover begins to be less sure of the happiness which he has promised himself; he begins to criticize the reasons he gave himself for hoping.

He tries to fall back on the other pleasures of life. *He finds they no longer exist*. He is seized with a dread of appalling misery, and his attention becomes concentrated.

7. Second crystallization.

Now begins the second crystallization, producing as its diamonds various confirmations of the following idea:

"She loves me."

Every quarter of an hour, during the night following the birth of doubt, after a moment of terrible misery, the lover says to himself: "Yes, she loves me"; and crystallization sets to work to discover fresh charms; then gaunt-eyed doubt grips him again and pulls him up with a jerk. His heart misses a beat; he says to himself: "But does she love me?" Through all these harrowing and delicious alternations the poor lover feels acutely: "With her I would experience joys which she alone in the world could give me."

It is the clearness of this truth and the path he treads between an appalling abyss and the most perfect happiness, that make the second crystallization appear to be so very much more important than the first.

The lover hovers incessantly amongst these three ideas:

1. She is perfect in every way.
2. She loves me.
3. How can I get the strongest possible proof of her love for me?

The most heartrending moment in love that is still young is when it finds that it has been wrong in its chain of reasoning and must destroy a whole agglomeration of crystals.

Even the fact of crystallization itself begins to appear doubtful.

HOPE

A very small degree of hope is sufficient to cause the birth of love.

Hope may subsequently fail at the end of two or three days, but love is none the less born.

In the case of a decided, bold and impetuous character and an imagination developed by the misfortunes of life:

The degree of hope may be smaller.

It may cease earlier, without destroying love.

If the lover has suffered misfortunes, if he has a sensitive and thoughtful nature, if other women have no further interest for him, if he has an intense admiration for the particular person in question, no ordinary pleasure can distract him from the second crystallization. He would rather dream of the most remote chance of attracting her in the future than receive from any ordinary woman everything she has to offer.

To put a stop to this, it would be necessary for the woman he loves to kill his hope at that precise moment (later, mark you, it would be useless), in the most cruel way, holding him up to that public contempt which makes it impossible ever to see people again.

The birth of love allows of much longer intervals between all these periods, but it requires much greater and much more sustained hope in the case of people who are temperamentally cold, phlegmatic and cautious. The same applies to people who have passed their first youth.

The thing that ensures the duration of love is the second crystallization, during which at every moment one realizes that one must either be loved or perish. How, with this conviction ever present in one's mind, and grown into a habit by several months of love, can one bear even the thought of ceasing to love? The more determined a man's character, the less liable is he to be inconstant.

This second crystallization is practically non-existent in love inspired by women who surrender themselves too quickly.

As soon as the crystallizations have taken place, especially the second one, which is much the stronger, indifferent eyes no longer recognize the bough:

For, 1. It is adorned by perfections or diamonds which they do not see;

2. It is adorned by perfections which are not perfections in their sight.

The perfection of certain charms which are commented on by an old friend of his mistress and a certain kindling in her eyes as he does so are a diamond in Del Rosso's crystallization.[7] These things noticed during the evening make him dream all night.

---

[7] I have called this book a book of ideology. My object in doing so was to point out that, although it was called *Love*, it was not a novel, and above all that it was not amusing in the way a novel is. I apologize to philosophers for having taken the word ideology; I certainly do not intend to usurp a title to which some one else has the right. If ideology is a minute description of ideas and of all their component parts, the present book is a minutely detailed description of all the emotions that go to make up the passion called *love*. Subsequently I draw certain conclusions from this description, as, for instance, the means of curing love. I know of no Greek word to describe a dissertation on emotions, in the way that ideology denotes a dissertation on ideas. I might have had a word invented for me by some of my learned friends, but I am already sufficiently vexed at having had to adopt the new word crystallization, and, very possibly, if this essay finds any readers, they will not even allow me this one. I confess that it would have shown much literary talent to have avoided it; I tried to do so, but without success. Without this word, which, to my idea, expresses the principal phenomenon of this folly called love, which folly nevertheless procures for mankind the greatest pleasures that their species is given to enjoy on earth, without the use of this word which I very nearly replaced by cumbersome periphrasis, the description which I give of what passes in a lover's head and heart would become obscure, dull and tedious, even for me who am the author: what would it have been like to the reader?
I invite the reader, therefore, who is shocked by this word *crystallization*, to close the book. It is not my desire, and this is probably fortunate for me, to have a lot of readers. It would be very pleasant to me really to delight thirty or forty people in Paris whom I shall never see, but whom I love madly, even though I do not know them. Some young Madame Roland, for instance, reading on the sly some book which she hides quickly, at the least sound, in her father's worktable, he being a watch case engraver. A soul like that of

An unexpected answer which gives me a clearer insight into a mind at once tender, generous, ardent, or, as it is commonly called, *romantic*,[8] and one which places above the happiness of kings the simple pleasure of strolling alone at midnight with one's lover in a lonely wood, makes me too dream all night.[9]

He may call my mistress a prude; I will call his a strumpet.

In the mind of a completely unbiased person, that, for instance, of a young girl living in a country house in an isolated part of the country—the most insignificant unexpected event may lead to a little admiration, and if this is followed by the slightest ray of hope, it causes the birth of love and crystallization.

In a case of this kind, the first attraction of love is that it is a distraction.

Surprise and hope are powerfully assisted by the need of love and the melancholy which one has at the age of sixteen. It is fairly clear that the main anxiety of that age is thirst for love, and it is characteristic of that thirst not to be unreasonably particular about the kind of draught that chance may offer to slake it.

Let us recapitulate the seven stages of love; these are:

1. Admiration;
2. One says to one's self, "What pleasure," etc.;
3. Hope;
4. Love is born;
5. The first crystallization;
6. Doubt is born;
7. Second crystallization.

A year may elapse between 1 and 2, a month between 2 and 3; if hope does not come quickly, one renounces 2 imperceptibly, as causing too much unhappiness.

Between 3 and 4 there is but the twinkling of an eye.

There is no interval between 4 and 5. Only the degree of intimacy separates them.

Madame Roland will forgive me, I hope, not only the word *crystallization* used to express that act of folly which makes us attribute every beauty and every kind of perfection to the woman we are beginning to love, but also many over-daring ellipses. She has only to take a pencil and to fill in the five or six missing words between the lines.

[8] All her actions had at first that heavenly quality about them that suddenly make a man a separate being, different from all others. I imagined I read in her eyes that thirst for a sublimer bliss, that unexpressed melancholy which yearns for something better than we find here below, and which, in every situation in which fortune or revolution can place a delicate soul,

.... Still prompts the celestial sight,
For which we wish to live or dare to die.

(Ultima lettera di Bianca a sua madre. Forli, 1817.)

[9] It is only in order to be brief, and to be able to depict the innermost feelings of the heart, that the author employs the first person in describing many sensations which are strange to him; nothing that ever happened to him personally is worth being mentioned.

A few days, more or less, in accordance with the degree of impetuosity and the boldness of the individual, may elapse between 5 and 6, and there is no interval between 6 and 7.

Man is not free to refuse to do the thing which gives him more pleasure than any other conceivable action.[10]

Love is like a fever; it comes and goes without the will having any part in the process. That is one of the principal differences between sympathy-love and passion-love, and one can only congratulate one's self on the fine qualities of the person one loves as on a lucky chance.

Love, indeed, belongs to every age: take, for instance, the passion of Madame du Deffand for the unattractive Horace Walpole. In Paris a more recent and above all a more pleasant example is perhaps still remembered.

I will only admit, as proofs of great passion, those of its consequences which are ridiculous; for example, shyness is a proof of love; I say nothing of the false shame of the boy who has just left school.

THE SALZBURG BOUGH

During love, crystallization hardly ever stops. This is its history: so long as you are on a distant footing with the person you love, crystallization takes place from an *imaginary solution*; it is only in your imagination that you are certain of the existence of any particular perfection in the woman you love. After you have arrived at terms of intimacy, constantly renewed fears are calmed by more real solutions. In this way, happiness is never uniform except in its source. Every day has a different flower.

If the loved woman surrenders to the passion she feels and falls into the grievous error of killing fear by the ardour of her transports, crystallization stops for a moment; but, when love loses its ardour, that is to say, its fears, it acquires the charm of complete unconstraint, of boundless confidence, and a sweet familiarity comes to deaden all the sorrows of life and bring fresh interest into one's pleasures.

If you are deserted, crystallization starts again; and the thought of every act of admiration and each delight which she can bestow on you and of which you had ceased to think, ends in this harrowing reflection: "That rapturous joy will *never* be mine again! And it is through my own fault that I have lost it!" If you try to find happiness in emotions of a different kind your heart refuses to react to them. Your imagination shows you clearly the physical aspect of the position, placing you on a swift hunter in Devonshire woods.[11] But you are quite aware that it would give you no pleasure. It is the sort of optical illusion produced by a pistol shot.

[10]Good education, from the standpoint of crime, consists in causing remorse which, when foreseen, weighs in the balance on the side of doing right.
[11]For, had you been able to imagine that happiness would lie in that direction, you would have bestowed on your mistress the exclusive privilege of conferring this happiness on you.

Gambling also produces its crystallization, stimulated by the thought of what you will do with the money you are going to win.

The chances of Court life, so regretted by the nobility, under the title of legitimism, were only attractive in the crystallizations which they produced. There was no courtier who did not dream of the rapid rise to fortune of a Luynes or a Lauzun, and no charming woman who did not dream of the duchy of Madame de Polignac. No rational government will ever be able to give that crystallization again. Nothing is so inimical to imagination as the government of the United States of America. We have seen that their savage neighbours know hardly anything of crystallization. The Romans had scarcely any idea of it at all, and only experienced it through sensual love.

Hatred has its crystallizations; as soon as one sees a chance of revenge, one begins to hate again.

That every creed in which there is anything absurd or unproven always tends to place the most ridiculous people at the head of its affairs, is but one more of the effects of crystallization. There is even crystallization in mathematics (*e. g.*, the Newtonians in 1740) in the minds of those who cannot visualize at the same moment all the steps of the processes in which they believe.

As a proof of this we may take the destiny of the great German philosophers, whose so often proclaimed immortality is never able to last for more than thirty or forty years.

It is because he cannot give an accurate account of the *reason* for his emotions that even the wisest man is fanatical on the subject of music.

One cannot at will convince one's self that one is right against any one who contradicts one.

DON JUAN'S SECRET

Søren Kierkegaard

If we can dispense with our hoots and sly winks, Don Juan emerges as an enticingly complex, enigmatic, and utterly fascinating figure in the annals of love. He is Molina's trickster, Moliere's philosopher of seduction, E. T. A. Hoffman's ideal-seeker and social rebel, Byron's refugee from women, Bernard Shaw's chaste anti-feminist, Camus's absurdist hero. He is all these things and more. But what is the essence from which all this springs? Kierkegaard believes that it is disclosed par excellence *in Mozart's music, for to Kierkegaard Don Juan's secret is a pure sensuousness which only music can express.*

What is Don Juan's attraction for women? Why are many of his past conquests overjoyed to meet him again? We shall only discover the answer when we look for a positive benefit which he confers upon those he seduces. Kierkegaard finds it in the power of sensuality to evoke the generic womanhood in every individual woman, be she country lass or grand dame.

In his total writings Kierkegaard sets forth three distinct modes of love, the sensuous, the "ethical" (or reflective), and the religious. Don Juan epitomizes the first; the second appears in Diary of a Seducer; *and the third lies in the Biblical story of Abraham and Isaac (see Kierkegaard's* Fear and Trembling *and* Works of Love).

It is relatively easy to mark the deficiencies of the Don Juan mode of love as Kierkegaard presents it. But let the reader try himself on its virtues. For example, sensuousness is pure presence, utterly devoid of reflection and anticipation (for Don Juan, "to see is to love"—not to see is not to love). Can the reader recall instances in which anticipation destroyed the pleasures of immediacy? Can he recall occasions in which this same result was brought about by the long anchor chain of memory?

Never before in the world has sensuousness been conceived as it is in *Don Juan*—as a principle: for this reason the erotic is here defined by another predicate: the erotic here is *seduction.* Strangely enough, the idea of a seducer was entirely wanting among the Greeks. It is by no means my intention, because of this, to wish to praise the Greeks, for, as every-

Reprinted from *Either/Or* by Søren Kierkegaard; trans. David F. Swenson and Lillian Marvin Swenson. Copyright 1944, 1972 by Howard A. Johnson and published by Princeton University Press. Reprinted by permission of the publisher.

body knows, gods as well as men were indiscreet in their love affairs; nor do I censure Christianity, for, after all, it has the idea only as something external to itself. The reason that the Greeks lacked this idea lay in the fact that the whole of the Greek life was posited as individuality. The psychical is thus the predominant or is always in harmony with the sensuous. Greek love, therefore, was psychical, not sensuous, and it is this which inspires the modesty which rests over all Greek love. They fell in love with a girl, they set heaven and earth in motion to get her; when they succeeded, then they perhaps tired of her, and sought a new love. In this instability they may, indeed, have had a certain resemblance to Don Juan. To mention only one instance, Hercules might surely produce a goodly list, when one considers that he sometimes took whole families numbering up to fifty daughters, and like a family son-in-law, according to some reports, had his way with all of them in a single night. Nevertheless, he is still essentially different from a Don Juan, he is no seducer. When one considers Greek love, it is, in accordance with its concept, essentially faithful, just because it is psychical; and it is some accidental factor in the particular individual that he loves many, and with regard to the many he loves, it is again accidental every time he loves a new one; when he is in love with one, he does not think of the next one. Don Juan, on the contrary, is a seducer from the ground up. His love is not psychical but sensuous, and sensuous love, in accordance with its concept, is not faithful, but absolutely faithless; it loves not one but all, that is to say, it seduces all. It exists only in the moment, but the moment, in terms of its concept, is the sum of moments, and so we have the seducer.

Chivalrous love is also psychical and, therefore, in accordance with its concept, is essentially faithful; only sensuous love, in terms of its very concept, is essentially faithless. But this, its faithlessness, appears also in another way; it becomes in fact only a constant repetition. Psychical love has the dialectic in it in a double sense. For partly it has the doubt and unrest in it, as to whether it will also be happy, see its desire fulfilled, and be requited. This anxiety sensuous love does not have. Even a Jupiter is doubtful about his victory, and this cannot be otherwise; moreover, he himself cannot desire it otherwise. With Don Juan this is not the case; he makes short work of it and must always be regarded as absolutely victorious. This might seem an advantage to him, but it is precisely poverty. On the other hand, psychical love has also another dialectic, it is in fact different in its relation to every single individual who is the object of love. Therein lies its wealth, its rich content. But such is not the case with Don Juan. For this, indeed, he has not time; everything for him is a matter of the moment only. To see her and to love her, that was one and the same. One may say this in a certain sense about psychical love, but in that there is only suggested a beginning. With regard to Don Juan it is valid in another way. To see her and to love her is the same thing; it is in the moment, in the same moment everything is over, and the same thing repeats itself endlessly. If one imagines a psychical love in Don Juan, it becomes at once ridiculous and a self-contradiction, which is not even in accord with the idea of positing 1,003 in Spain. It becomes an over-emphasis which acts disturbingly, even if one imagined oneself considering him ideally. Now if we had no other medium for describing this love than language, we should be up against it, for as soon as we have abandoned the naïveté which in all simplicity can insist that there were 1,003 in Spain, then we require something more, namely, the psychical individualization. The aesthetic is by no means satisfied that everything should thus be lumped together, and is astonished at the number. Psychical love does not exactly move in the rich manifold of the individual life, where the nuances are really significant. Sensuous love, on the other hand, can lump everything together. The essential for it is woman in the abstract, and at most is a more sensuous difference. Psychical love is a continuance in time, sensuous love a disappearance in time, but the medium which exactly expresses this is music. Music is excellently fitted to accomplish this, since it is far more abstract than language, and therefore does not express the individual but the general in all its generality, and yet it expresses the general not in reflective abstraction, but in the immediate concrete.

As an example of what I mean, I shall discuss a little more carefully the servant's second aria: the List of the Seduced. This number may be regarded as the real epic of Don Juan. Consequently, make this experiment, if you are sceptical about the truth of my assertion! Imagine a poet more happily endowed by nature than anyone before him; give him vigor of expression, give him mastery and authority over the power of language, let everything wherein there is the breath of life be obedient unto him, let his slightest suggestion be deferred to, let everything wait, ready and prepared for his word of command; let him be surrounded by a numerous band of light skirmishers, swift-footed messengers who overtake thought in its most hurried flight; let nothing escape him, not the least movement; let nothing secret, nothing unutterable be left behind him in the whole world—give him, after all this, the task of singing Don Juan as an epic, of unrolling the list of the seduced. What will the result be? He will never finish! The epic has the fault, if one wishes to call it that, of being able to go on as long as you will. His hero, the improviser, Don Juan, can go on indefinitely. The poet may now enter into the manifold, there will always be enough there which will give pleasure, but he will never achieve the effect which Mozart has obtained. For even if he finally finishes, he will still not have said half of what Mozart has expressed in this one number. Mozart has not even attempted the manifold; he deals only with certain great formations which are set in motion. This finds its sufficient explanation in the medium itself, in the music which is too abstract to express the differences. The musical epic thus becomes something comparatively short, and yet it has in an inimitable manner the epic quality that it can go on as long as it will, since one can constantly let it begin again from the beginning, and hear it over and over again, just because it expresses the general in the concreteness of immediacy. Here we do not hear Don Juan as a particular individual, nor his speech, but we hear a voice, the voice of sensuousness, and we hear it through the longing of womanhood. Only in this manner can Don Juan become epic, in that he constantly finishes, and constantly begins again from the beginning, for his life is the sum of repellent moments which have no coherence, his life as moment is the sum of the moments, as the sum of the moments is the moment.

In this generality, in this floating between being an individual and being a force of nature, lies Don Juan; as soon as he becomes individual the aesthetic acquires quite other categories. Therefore it is entirely proper, and it has a profound inner significance, that in the seduction which takes place in the play, Zerlina, the girl, should be a common peasant girl. Hypocritical aestheticists who, under the show of understanding poets and composers, contribute everything to their being misunderstood, will perhaps instruct us that Zerlina is an unusual girl. Anyone who believes this shows that he has totally misunderstood Mozart, and that he is using wrong categories. That he misunderstands Mozart is evident enough; for Mozart has purposely made Zerlina as insignificant as possible, something Hotho has also called attention to, yet without seeing the real reason for it. If, for instance, Don Juan's love were qualified as other than sensuous, if he were a seducer in an intellectual sense (a type which we shall consider presently), then it would have been a radical fault in the play for the heroine in the seduction which dramatically engages our attention to be only a little peasant girl. Then the aesthetic would require that Don Juan should have been set a more difficult task. To Don Juan, however, these differences mean nothing. If I could imagine him making such a speech about himself, he might perhaps say: "You are wrong. I am no husband who requires an unusual girl to make me happy; every girl has that which makes me happy, and therefore I take them all." In some such way we have to understand the saying I earlier referred to: "even sixty-year coquettes"—or in another place: *pur chè porti la gonella, voi sapete quel chè fà.** To Don Juan every girl is an ordinary girl, every love affair an everyday story. Zerlina is young and pretty, and she is a woman; this is the uncommon which she has in common with hundreds of others; but it is not the uncommon that Don Juan desires, but the common, and this she has in common with every woman. If this is not the case, then Don Juan ceases to be absolutely musical, and aesthetics requires speech, dialogue, while now, since it is the case, Don Juan is absolutely musical.

*Why are you wearing a skirt, you know what it does.

From another point of view I may throw some additional light upon this by analyzing the inner structure of the play. Elvira is Don Juan's mortal enemy; in the dialogue for which the Danish translator is responsible, this is frequently emphasized. That it is an error for Don Juan to make a speech is certain enough, but because of this it does not follow that the speech might not contain an occasional good observation. Well then, Don Juan fears Elvira. Now probably some aestheticist or other believes that he can profoundly explain this by coming forward with a long disquisition about Elvira's being a very unusual girl and so on. This altogether misses the mark. She is dangerous to him because she has been seduced. In the same sense, exactly in the same sense, Zerlina becomes dangerous to him when she is seduced. As soon as she is seduced, she is elevated to a higher sphere, to a consciousness which Don Juan does not have. Therefore, she is dangerous to him. Hence, it is not by means of the accidental but by means of the general that she is dangerous to him.

Don Juan, then, is a seducer; in him the erotic takes the form of seduction. Here much is well said when it is rightly understood, little when it is understood with a general lack of clarity. We have already noted that the concept, a seducer, is essentially modified with respect to Don Juan, as the object of his desire is the sensuous, and that alone. This is of importance in order to show the musical in Don Juan. In ancient times the sensuous found its expression in the silent stillness of plastic art; in the Christian world the sensuous must burst forth in all its impatient passion. Although one may say with truth that Don Juan is a seducer, this expression, which can work so disturbingly upon the weak brains of certain aestheticians, has often given rise to misunderstandings, as they have scraped this and that together that could be said about such a one, and have at once applied it to Don Juan. At times they have exposed their own cunning in tracking down Don Juan's, at times they talk themselves hoarse in explaining his intrigues and his subtlety; in short, the word *seducer* has given rise to the situation that everybody has been against him to the limit of his power, has contributed his mite to the total misunderstanding. Of Don Juan we must use the word *seducer* with great caution—assuming, that is, that it is more important to say something right than simply to say something. This is not because Don Juan is too good, but because he simply does not fall under ethical categories. Hence I should rather not call him a deceiver, since there is always something more ambiguous in that word. To be a seducer requires a certain amount of reflection and consciousness, and as soon as this is present, then it is proper to speak of cunning and intigues and crafty plans. This consciousness is lacking in Don Juan. Therefore, he does not seduce. He desires, and this desire acts seductively. To that extent he seduces. He enjoys the satisfaction of desire; as soon as he has enjoyed it, he seeks a new object, and so on endlessly. Therefore, I suppose he is a deceiver, but yet not so that he plans his deceptions in advance; it is the inherent power of sensuousness which deceives the seduced, and it is rather a kind of Nemesis. He desires, and is constantly desiring, and constantly enjoys the satisfaction of the desire. To be a seducer, he lacks time in advance in which to lay his plans, and time afterward in which to become conscious of his act. A seducer, therefore, ought to be in possession of a power Don Juan does not have, however well equipped he may otherwise be—the power of eloquence. As soon as we grant him eloquence he ceases to be musical, and the aesthetic interest becomes an entirely different matter.

Achim v. Arnim tells somewhere of a seducer of a very different style, a seducer who falls under ethical categories. About him he uses an expression which in truth, boldness, and conciseness is almost equal to Mozart's stroke of the bow. He says he could so talk with a woman that, if the devil caught him, he could wheedle himself out of it if he had a chance to talk with the devil's grandmother.[30] This is the real seducer; the aesthetic interest here is also different, namely: how, the method. There is evidently something very profound here, which has perhaps escaped the attention of most people, in that Faust, who reproduces Don Juan, seduces only one girl, while Don Juan seduces hundreds; but this one girl is also, in an intensive sense, seduced and crushed quite differently from all those Don Juan has deceived, simply because Faust, as reproduction, falls under the category of the intellectual. The power of such a seducer is speech, i.e., the lie. A few days ago I heard one soldier talking to another about a third who had betrayed a girl; he did not give a long-winded description, and yet his expression was very pithy: "He gets away with things like that by lies and things like that." Such a seducer is of quite a different sort from Don Juan, is essentially different from him, as one can see from the fact that he and his activities are extremely unmusical, and from the aesthetic standpoint come within the category of the interesting. The object of his desire is accordingly, when one rightly considers him aesthetically, something more than the merely sensuous.

But what is this force, then, by which Don Juan seduces? It is desire, the energy of sensuous desire. He desires in every woman the whole of womanhood, and therein lies the sensuously idealizing power with which he at once embellishes and overcomes his prey. The reaction to this gigantic passion beautifies and develops the one desired, who flushes in enhanced beauty by its reflection. As the enthusiast's fire with seductive splendor illumines even those who stand in a casual relation to him, so Don Juan transfigures in a far deeper sense every girl, since his relation to her is an essential one. Therefore all finite differences fade away before him in comparison with the main thing: being a woman. He rejuvenates the older woman into the beautiful middle age of womanhood; he matures the child almost instantly; everything which is woman is his prey (*pur chè porti la gonella, voi sapete quel chè fà*). On the other hand, we must by no means understand this as if his sensuousness were blind; instinctively he knows very well how to discriminate and, above all, he idealizes. If for a moment I here think back to the Page in a preceding stage, the reader will perhaps remember that once when we spoke of the Page, I compared a speech of his with one of Don Juan's. The mythical Page I left standing, the real one I sent away to the army. If I now imagined that the mythical Page had liberated himself, was free to move about, then I would recall here a speech of the Page which is appropriate to Don Juan. As Cherubino, light as a bird and daring, springs out of the window, it makes so strong an impression upon Susanne that she almost swoons, and when she recovers, she exclaims: "See how he runs! My, won't he make conquests among the girls!" This is quite correctly said by Susanne, and the reason for her swoon is not only the idea of the daring leap, but rather that he had already "got around her." The Page is really the future Don Juan, though without this being understood in a ridiculous way, as if the Page by becoming older became Don Juan. Now Don Juan can not only have his way with the girls, but he makes them happy and—unhappy, but, curiously enough, in such wise that that's the way they want it, and a foolish girl it would be who would not choose to be unhappy for the sake of having once been happy with Don Juan. If I still continue, therefore, to call him a seducer, I by no means imagine him slyly formulating his plans, craftily calculating the effect of his intrigues. His power to deceive lies in the essential genius of sensuousness, whose incarnation he really is. Shrewd sober-mindedness is lacking in him; his life is as effervescent as the wine with which he stimulates himself; his life is dramatic like the strains which accompany his joyous feast; always he is triumphant. He requires no preparation, no plan, no time; for he is always prepared. Energy is always in him and also desire, and only when he desires is he rightly in his element. He sits feasting, joyous as a god he swings his cup— he rises with his napkin in his hand, ready for attack. If Leporello rouses him in the middle of the night, he awakens, always certain of his victory. But this energy, this power, cannot be expressed in words, only music can give us a conception of it. It is inexpressible for reflection and thought. The cunning of an ethically determined seducer I can clearly set forth in words, and music will try in vain to solve this problem. With Don Juan, the converse holds true. What is this power?—No one can say. Even if I questioned Zerlina about it before she goes to the dance: "What is this power by which he captivates you?"—she would answer: "No one knows," and I would say: "Well said, my child! You speak more wisely than the sages of India; *richtig, das weiss man nicht;** and the unfortunate thing is that I can't tell you either."

This force in Don Juan, this omnipotence, this animation, only music

*Right, one does not know.

can express, and I know no other predicate to describe it than this: it is exuberant joy of life. When, therefore, Kruse lets his Don Juan say, as he comes upon the scene at Zerlina's wedding: "Cheer up, children, you are all of you dressed as for a wedding," he says something that is quite proper and also perhaps something more than he is aware of. He himself brings the gaiety with him, and no matter whose wedding it is, it is not unimportant that everyone be dressed as for a wedding; for Don Juan is not only husband to Zerlina, but he celebrates with sport and song the wedding of all the young girls in the parish. What wonder, then, that they crowd about him, the happy maidens! Nor are they disappointed, for he has enough for them all. Flattery, sighs, daring glances, soft handclasps, secret whispers, dangerous proximity, alluring withdrawal—and yet these are only the lesser mysteries, the gifts before the wedding. It is a pleasure to Don Juan to look out over so rich a harvest; he takes charge of the whole parish, and yet perhaps it does not cost him as much time as Leporello spends in his office.

By these considerations we are again brought to the main subject of this inquiry, that Don Juan is absolutely musical. He desires sensuously, he seduces with the daemonic power of sensuousness, he seduces everyone. Speech, dialogue, are not for him, for then he would be at once a reflective individual. Thus he does not have stable existence at all, but he hurries in a perpetual vanishing, precisely like music, about which it is true that it is over as soon as it has ceased to sound, and only comes into being again, when it again sounds.

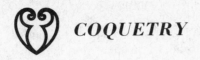 # COQUETRY

Georg Simmel

"Flirtation" is the game of blowing hot and cold, of invitation and re-pulse, of yes and no. As the foolproof means for capturing the other's entire attention for ourselves it finds its functional place in the first stage of romantic love.

According to German sociologist Georg Simmel (1858–1918), coquetry is what results when flirtation is severed from its natural consequences in love and sex and played as a game for its own sake. In Simmel's terms, coquetry is the "play-form" of flirtation. But why should that which is natively part of a process be disconnected from the process? Simmel answers: Because as part of the process it was burdened with heavy consequences in terms of human life. Released from these consequences it can kick up its heels, experiment, innovate, and realize the "play" values of joy, relief, and liveliness. And from this freedom to experiment, discoveries will follow which then can be introduced into the living process of love.

In the sociology of sex, we find a play-form: the play-form of eroticism is coquetry. In sociability, it finds its most facile, playful, and widely diffused realization.[1] Generally speaking, the erotic question between the sexes is that of offer and refusal. Its objects are, of course, infinitely varied and graduated, and by no means mere either-ors, much less exclusively physiological. The nature of feminine coquetry is to play up, alternately, allusive promises and allusive withdrawals—to attract the male but always to stop short of a decision, and to reject him but never to deprive him of all hope. The coquettish woman enormously enhances her attractiveness if she shows her consent as an almost immediate possibility but is ultimately not serious about it. Her behavior swings back and forth between "yes" and "no" without stopping at either. She playfully exhibits the pure and simple form of erotic decisions and manages to embody their polar opposites in a perfectly consistent behavior: its decisive, well-understood content, that would commit her to one of the two opposites, does not even enter.

This freedom from all gravity of immutable contents and permanent realities gives coquetry the character of suspension, distance, ideality, that

From *The Sociology of Georg Simmel*, trans. and ed. by Kurt H. Wolff (New York: The Free Press of Glencoe, 1950), pp. 50–51. Reprinted by permission of The Free Press of Glencoe.
[1]I have treated coquetry extensively in my book, *Philosophische Kultur* [Philosophic Culture].

has led one to speak, with a certain right, of its "art," not only of its "artifices." Yet in order for coquetry to grow on the soil of sociability, as we know from experience it does, it must meet with a specific behavior on the part of the male. As long as he rejects its attractions or, inversely, is its mere victim that without any will of his own is dragged along by its vacillations between a half "yes" and a half "no," coquetry has not yet assumed for him the form that is commensurate with sociability. For it lacks the free interaction and equivalence of elements that are the fundamental traits of sociability. It does not attain these until he asks for no more than this freely suspended play which only dimly reflects the erotically definitive as a remote symbol; until he is no longer attracted by the lust for the erotic element or by the fear of it which is all he can see in the coquettish allusions and preliminaries. Coquetry that unfolds its charms precisely at the height of sociable civilization has left far behind the reality of erotic desire, consent, or refusal; it is embodied in the interaction of the mere silhouettes, as it were, of their serious imports. Where they themselves enter or are constantly present in the background, the whole process becomes a private affair between two individuals: it takes place on the plane of reality. But under the sociological sign of sociability from which the center of the personality's concrete and complete life is barred, coquetry is the flirtatious, perhaps ironical play, in which eroticism has freed the bare outline of its interactions from their materials and contents and personal features. As sociability plays with the forms of society, so coquetry plays with those of eroticism, and this affinity of their natures predestines coquetry as an element of sociability.

DEPENDENT LOVE IN WOMEN

Simone de Beauvoir

Concerning relations between the sexes, probably the most widespread and deep-rooted presupposition is that of the dependent status of women. Man is autonomous, but woman is made of his substance (and the rib is scarcely the prime part of his anatomy) and has her being in reference to him. Shared alike by men and women, this belief introduces a significant difference in the meaning of love to the two sexes. Simone de Beauvoir here offers a description of the love of woman as the "inessential creature," together with her devious revenge for the "sterile hell" to which dependence condemns her.

The woman who appears here is the Psyche of the myth (see Eric Neumann under "Eros," Part II) before her "Amazonian" act of initiative releases her from imprisonment and darkness.

The selection ends with Mme. de Beauvoir's hope for emancipation, but she holds forth no Amazonian promise. Ideal love appears as the "mutual recognition of two liberties"; but within the present world this is available to men in friendships with other men. Is the emancipation of women to produce merely more of the same?

The question which goes unasked by Mme. de Beauvoir is, What is woman? Undeniably Western man has for centuries taken infinite pains to suppress the feminine, emptying its essence and substituting a variety of male-manufactured identities. Woman is weakness, insufficiency, the "eternal impediment," the source of irrationality, the corporeal as opposed to the spiritual (hence her identification in mythology and astrology with the earth, "earth mother"), the source of evil (Eve, Pandora). This elaborate effect by the male bespeaks his intuition of a feminine principle which is opposed to the masculine. On the other hand the enduring alienation theme in love (see "Aristophanes' Myth" hereafter) likewise divines a distinctive feminine essence, but sees it as the complement of the masculine rather than the antagonist.

Thus from the achievement of woman's autonomy we have ground to expect changes of a more dramatic sort than Mme. de Beauvoir forecasts. What remains highly meaningful in the selection however, is her presentation of the meaning of love to woman in her historical situation as the "second sex."

The word *love* has by no means the same sense for both sexes, and this is one cause of the serious misunderstandings that divide them. Byron well said: "Man's love is of man's life a thing apart; 'Tis woman's whole existence." Nietzsche expresses the same idea in *The Gay Science:*

The single word love in fact signifies two different things for man and woman. What woman understands by love is clear enough: it is not only devotion, it is a total gift of body and soul, without reservation, without regard for anything whatever. This unconditional nature of her love is what makes it a *faith*,[1] the only one she has. As for man, if he loves a woman, what he *wants*[1] is that love from her; he is in consequence far from postulating the same sentiment for himself as for woman; if there should be men who also felt that desire for complete abandonment, upon my word, they would not be men.

Men have found it possible to be passionate lovers at certain times in their lives, but there is not one of them who could be called "a great lover";[2] in their most violent transports, they never abdicate completely; even on their knees before a mistress, what they still want is to take possession of her; at the very heat of their lives they remain sovereign subjects; the beloved woman is only one value among others; they wish to integrate her into their existence and not to squander it entirely on her. For woman, on the contrary, to love is to relinquish everything for the benefit of a master. As Cecile Sauvage puts it: "Woman must forget her own personality when she is in love. It is a law of nature. A woman is nonexistent without a master. Without a master, she is a scattered bouquet."

The fact is that we have nothing to do here with laws of nature. It is the difference in their situations that is reflected in the difference men and women show in their conceptions of love. The individual who is a subject, who is himself, if he has the courageous inclination toward transcendence, endeavors to extend his grasp on the world: he is ambitious, he acts. But an inessential creature is incapable of sensing the absolute at the heart of her subjectivity; a being doomed to immanence cannot find self-realization in acts. Shut up in the sphere of the relative, destined to the male from childhood, habituated to seeing in him a superb being whom she cannot possibly equal, the woman who has not repressed her claim to humanity will dream of transcending her being toward one of these superior beings, of amalgamating herself with the sovereign subject. There is no other way out for her than to lose herself, body and soul, in him who is represented to her as the absolute, as the essential. Since she is anyway doomed to dependence, she will prefer to serve a god rather than obey tyrants—parents, husband, or protector. She chooses to desire her enslavement so ardently that it will seem to her the expression of her liberty; she will try to rise above her situation as inessential object by fully accepting it; through her flesh, her feelings, her behavior, she will enthrone him as supreme value

[1] Nietzsche's italics.
[2] In the sense that a woman may sometimes be called "*une grand amoureuse*."—Tr.

and reality: she will humble herself to nothingness before him. Love becomes for her a religion.

As we have seen, the adolescent girl wishes at first to identify herself with males; when she gives that up, she then seeks to share in their masculinity by having one of them in love with her; it is not the individuality of this one or that one which attracts her; she is in love with man in general. "And you, the men I shall love, how I await you!" writes Irène Reweliotty. "How I rejoice to think I shall know you soon: especially You, the first." Of course the male is to belong to the same class and race as hers, for sexual privilege is in play only within this frame. If man is to be a demigod, he must first of all be a human being, and to the colonial officer's daughter the native is not a man. If the young girl gives herself to an "inferior," it is for the reason that she wishes to degrade herself because she believes she is unworthy of love; but normally she is looking for a man who represents male superiority. She is soon to ascertain that many individuals of the favored sex are sadly contingent and earthbound, but at first her presumption is favorable to them; they are called on less to prove their worth than to avoid too gross a disproof of it—which accounts for many mistakes, some of them serious. A naive young girl is caught by the gleam of virility, and in her eyes male worth is shown, according to circumstances, by physical strength, distinction of manner, wealth, cultivation, intelligence, authority, social status, a military uniform; but what she always wants is for her lover to represent the essence of manhood.

Familiarity if often sufficient to destroy his prestige; it may collapse at the first kiss, or in daily association, or during the wedding night. Love at a distance, however, is only a fantasy, not a real experience. The desire for love becomes a passionate love only when it is carnally realized. Inversely, love can arise as a result of physical intercourse; in this case the sexually dominated woman acquires an exalted view of a man who at first seemed to here quite insignificant.

But it often happens that a woman succeeds in deifying none of the men she knows. Love has a smaller place in woman's life than has often been supposed. Husband, children, home, amusements, social duties, vanity, sexuality, career, are much more important. Most women dream of a *grand amour*, a soul-searing love. They have known substitutes, they have been close to it; it has come to them in partial, bruised, ridiculous, imperfect, mendacious forms; but very few have truly dedicated their lives to it. The *grandes amoureuses* are most often women who have not frittered themselves away in juvenile affairs; they have first accepted the traditional feminine destiny: husband, home, children; or they have known pitiless solitude; or they have banked on some enterprise that has been more or less a failure. And when they glimpse the opportunity to salvage a disappointing life by dedicating it to some superior person, they desperately give themselves up to this hope. Mlle Aïsse, Juliette Drouet, and Mme d'Agoult were almost thirty when their love-life began, Julie de Lespinasse not far from forty. No other aim in life which seemed worth while was open to them, love was their only way out.

Even if they can choose independence, this road seems the most attractive to a majority of women: it is agonizing for a woman to assume responsibility for her life. Even the male, when adolescent, is quite willing to turn to older women for guidance, education, mothering, but customary attitudes, the boy's training, and his own inner imperatives forbid him to content himself in the end with the easy solution of abdication; to him such affairs with older women are only a stage through which he passes. It is man's good fortune—in adulthood as in early childhood—to be obliged to take the most arduous roads, but the surest; it is woman's misfortune to be surrounded by almost irresistible temptations; everything incites her to follow the easy slopes; instead of being invited to fight her own way up, she is told that she has only to let herself slide and she will attain paradises of enchantment. When she perceives that she has been duped by a mirage, it is too late; her strength has been exhausted in a losing venture.

The psychoanalysts are wont to assert that woman seeks the father image in her lover; but it is because he is a man, not because he is a father, that he dazzles the girl child, and every man shares in this magical power. Woman does not long to reincarnate one individual in another, but to reconstruct a situation: that which she experienced as a little girl, under adult protection. She was deeply integrated with home and family, she knew the peace of quasi-passivity. Love will give her back her mother as well as her father, it will give her back her childhood. What she wants to recover is a roof over her head, walls that prevent her from feeling her abandonment in the wide world, authority that protects her against her liberty. This childish drama haunts the love of many women; they are happy to be called "my little girl, my dear child"; men know that the words: "you're just like a little girl" are among those that most surely touch a woman's heart. We have seen that many women suffer in becoming adults; and so a great number remain obstinately "babyish," prolonging their childhood indefinitely in manner and dress. To become like a child again in a man's arms fills their cup with joy. The hackneyed theme: "To feel so little in your arms, my love," recurs again and again in amorous dialogue and in love letters. "Baby mine," croons the lover, the woman calls herself "your little one," and so on. A young woman will write: "When will he come, he who can dominate me?" And when he comes, she will love to sense his manly superiority. A neurotic studied by Janet illustrates this attitude quite clearly:

All my foolish acts and all the good things I have done have the same cause: an aspiration for a perfect and ideal love in which I can give myself completely, entrust my being to another, God, man, or woman, so superior to me that I will no longer need to think what to do in life or to watch over myself. . . . Someone to obey blindly and with confidence . . . who will bear me up and lead me gently and lovingly toward perfection. How I envy the ideal love of Mary Magdalen and Jesus: to be the ardent disciple of an adored and worthy master; to live and die for him, my idol, to win at last the victory of the Angel over the beast, to rest in his protecting arms, so small, so lost in his loving care, so wholly his that I exist no longer.

Many examples have already shown us that this dream of annihilation is in fact an avid will to exist. In all religions the adoration of God is combined with the devotee's concern with personal salvation; when woman gives herself completely to her idol, she hopes that he will give her at once possession of herself and of the universe he represents. In most cases she asks her lover first of all for the justification, the exaltation, of her ego. Many women do not abandon themselves to love unless they are loved in return; and sometimes the love shown them is enough to arouse their love. The young girl dreamed of herself as seen through men's eyes, and it is in men's eyes that the woman believes she has finally found herself. Cécile Sauvage writes:

To walk by your side, to step forward with my little feet that you love, to feel them so tiny in their high-heeled shoes with felt tops, makes me love all the love you throw around me. The least movements of my hands in my muff, of my arms, of my face, the tones of my voice, fill me with happiness.

The woman in love feels endowed with a high and undeniable value; she is at last allowed to idolize herself through the love she inspires. She is overjoyed to find in her lover a witness. This is what Colette's *Vagabonde* declares:

I admit I yielded, in permitting this man to come back the next day, to the desire to keep in him not a lover, not a friend, but an eager spectator of my life and my person. . . . One must be terribly old, Margot said to me one day, to renounce the vanity of living under someone's gaze.

In one of her letters to Middleton Murry, Katherine Mansfield wrote that she had just bought a ravishing mauve corset; she at once added: "Too bad there is no one to *see* it!" There is nothing more bitter than to feel oneself but the flower, the perfume, the treasure, which is the object of no desire: what kind of wealth is it that does not enrich myself and the gift of which no one wants? Love is the developer that brings out in clear, positive detail the dim negative, otherwise as useless as a blank exposure. Through love, woman's face, the curves of her body, her childhood memories, her former tears, her gowns, her accustomed ways, her universe, everything she is, all that belongs to her, escape contingency and become essential: she is a wondrous offering at the foot of the altar of her god. . . .

The supreme happiness of the woman in love is to be recognized by the loved man as a part of himself; when he says "we," she is associated and identified with him, she shares his prestige and reigns with him over the rest of the world; she never tires of repeating—even to excess—this delectable "we." As one necessary to a being who is absolute necessity, who stands forth in the world seeking necessary goals and who gives her back the world in necessary form, the woman in love acquires in her submission that magnificent possession, the absolute. It is this certitude that gives her lofty joys; she feels exalted to a place at the right hand of God. Small matter to her to have only second place if she has *her* place, forever, in a most wonderfully ordered world. So long as she is in love and is loved by and necessary to her loved one, she feels herself wholly justified: she knows peace and happiness. Such was perhaps the lot of Mlle Aïsse[3] with the Chevalier d'Aydie before religious scruples troubled his soul, or that of Juliette Drouet in the mighty shadow of Victor Hugo.

But this glorious felicity rarely lasts. No man really is God. The relations sustained by the mystic with the divine Absence depend on her fervor alone; but the deified man, who is not God, is present. And from this fact are to come the torments of the woman in love. Her most common fate is summed up in the famous words of Julie de Lespinasse:[4] "Always, my dear friend, I love you, I suffer and I await you." To be sure, suffering is linked with love for men also; but their pangs are either of short duration or not overly severe. Benjamin Constant wanted to die on account of Mme Rècamier: he was cured in a twelvemonth. Stendhal regretted Métilde for years, but it was a regret that perfumed his life without destroying it. Whereas woman, in assuming her role as the inessential, accepting a total dependence, creates a hell for herself. Every woman in love recognizes herself in Hans Andersen's little mermaid who exchanged her fishtail for feminine legs through love and then found herself walking on needles and live coals. It is not true that the loved man is absolutely necessary, above chance and circumstance, and the woman is not necessary to him; he is not really in a position to justify the feminine being who is consecrated to his worship, and he does not permit himself to be possessed by her.

An authentic love should assume the contingence of the other; that is to say, his lacks, his limitations, and his basic gratuitousness. It would not pretend to be a mode of salvation, but a human interrelation. Idolatrous love attributes an absolute value to the loved one, a first falsity that is brilliantly apparent to all outsiders. "*He* isn't worth all that love," is whispered around the woman in love, and posterity wears a pitying smile at the thought of certain pallid heroes, like Count Guibert. It is a searing disappointment to the woman to discover the faults, the mediocrity of her idol. Novelists, like Colette, have often depicted this bitter anguish. The disillusion is still more cruel than that of the child who sees the father's

[3] An account of her life, with her letters, will be found in *Lettres du XVIIe et du XVIIIe Siècle*, by Eugène Asse (Paris, 1873).—Tr.
[4] Famous intellectual woman of the eighteenth century, noted for her salon and her fervid correspondence with the rather undistinguished military officer and writer Count Guibert, mentioned below.—Tr.

prestige crumble, because the woman has herself selected the one to whom she has given over her entire being.

Even if the chosen one is worthy of the profoundest affection, his truth is of the earth, earthy, and it is no longer this mere man whom the woman loves as she kneels before a supreme being; she is duped by that spirit of seriousness which declines to take values as incidental—that is to say, declines to recognize that they have their source in human existence. Her bad faith[5] raises barriers between her and the man she adores. She offers him incense, she bows down, but she is not a friend to him since she does not realize that he is in danger in the world, that his projects and his aims are as fragile as he is; regarding him as the Faith, the Truth, she misunderstands his freedom—his hesitancy and anguish of spirit. This refusal to apply a human measuring scale to the lover explains many feminine paradoxes. The woman asks a favor from her lover. Is it granted? Then he is generous, rich, magnificent; he is kingly, he is divine. Is it refused? Then he is avaricious, mean, cruel; he is a devilish or a bestial creature. One might be tempted to object: if a "yes" is such an astounding and superb extravagance, should one be surprised at a "no"? If the "no" discloses such abject selfishness, why wonder so much at the "yes"? Between the superhuman and the inhuman is there no place for the human?

A fallen god is not a man: he is a fraud; the lover has no other alternative than to prove that he really is this king accepting adulation—or to confess himself a usurper. If he is no longer adored, he must be trampled on. In virtue of that glory with which she has haloed the brow of her beloved, the woman in love forbids him any weakness; she is disappointed and vexed if he does not live up to the image she has put in his place. If he gets tired or careless, if he gets hungry or thirsty at the wrong time, if he makes a mistake or contradicts himself, she asserts that he is "not himself" and she makes a grievance of it. In this indirect way she will go so far as to take him to task for any of his ventures that she disapproves; she judges her judge, and she denies him his liberty so that he may deserve to remain her master. Her worship sometimes finds better satisfaction in his absence than in his presence; as we have seen, there are women who devote themselves to dead or otherwise inaccessible heroes, so that they may never have to face them in person, for beings of flesh and blood would be fatally contrary to their dreams. Hence such disillusioned sayings as: "One must not believe in Prince Charming. Men are only poor creatures," and the like. They would not seem to be dwarfs if they had not been asked to be giants.

It is one of the curses afflicting the passionate woman that her generosity is soon converted into exigence. Having become identified with another, she wants to make up for her loss; she must take possession of

---

[5]In Sartre's existentialist terminology, "bad faith" means abdication of the human self with its hard duty of choice, the wish therefore to become a thing, the flight from the anguish of liberty.—TR.

that other person who has captured her. She gives herself to him entirely; but he must be completely available to receive this gift. She dedicates every moment to him, but he must be present at all times; she wants to live only in him—but she wants to live, and he must therefore devote himself to making her live. Mme d'Agoult writes to Liszt:

I love you sometimes foolishly, and at those moments I do not understand that I could not, would not, and should not be so absorbing a thought for you as you are for me.

She is trying to curb her spontaneous wish to be everything to him. The same plaintive appeal sounds in the words of Mlle de Lespinasse:

Ah, God! If you only knew the emptiness of my days, my life, deprived of the interest and pleasure of seeing you! Dear friend, for you amusements, occupation, action, are enough; as for me, my happiness is you, only you; I would not care to live if I were not to see you and to love you every day of my life.

At first the woman in love takes delight in gratifying her lover's desire to the full; later on—like the legendary fireman who for love of his profession started fires everywhere—she applies herself to awakening this desire so that she may have it to gratify. If she does not succeed in this enterprise, she feels so humiliated and useless that her lover will feign ardors he does not feel. In making herself a slave, she has found the surest means of enchaining him. Here we come upon another falsity of love which many men—for example, Lawrence and Montherlant—have resentfully exposed: it comes in the form of a gift, when it is really a tyranny. In *Adolphe*, Benjamin Constant describes in bitter terms the chains that the too generous passion of a woman forges around a man. "She was not circumspect in her sacrifices because she was concerned with making me accept them," he says cruelly of Eléonore.

Acceptance is in fact an obligation that is binding on the lover, without his having even the benefit of seeming to be a giver; the woman requires him to accept gratefully the burdens with which she crushes him. And her tyranny is insatiable. The man in love is tyrannical, but when he has obtained what he wants he is satisfied; whereas there are no limits to woman's exigent devotion. A lover who has confidence in his mistress feels no displeasure if she absents herself, is occupied at a distance from him; sure that she is his, he prefers to possess a free being than to own a thing. For the woman, on the contrary, the absence of her lover is always torture; he is an eye, a judge, and as soon as he looks at anything other than herself, he frustrates her; whatever he sees, he robs her of; away from him, she is dispossessed, at once of herself and of the world; even when seated at her side reading or writing or whatever, he is abandoning her, betraying her. She hates his sleep. But Baudelaire grew tender over woman in sleep: "Your beautiful eyes are weary, my poor loved one"; and Proust is enchanted in watching Albertine[6] asleep. The point is that male jealousy is simply the will to exclusive possession; the loved woman, when sleep restores the disarmed candor of childhood, belongs to no one: that certitude is enough. But the god, the master, should not give himself up to the repose of immanence; the woman views this blasted transcendence with a hostile eye; she detests the animal inertia of this body which exists no longer *for her* but *in itself*, abandoned to a contingence of which her contingence is the price.[7] Violette Leduc has given strong expression to this feeling in *Je hais les dormeurs*:

> I hate sleepers. I bend over them with evil intent. Their submissiveness irritates me. I hate the unconscious calm, the blind studious face. . . . My sleeper is hard to awaken, he has made a clean sweep of everything. . . . I hate his power to create through loss of consciousness a calm which I do not share. . . . We were in swift flight from earth . . . we took off, soared, waited, came to it, moaned, won, and lost, together. We played truant in earnest. We found a new nothingness. Now you sleep . . . I hate you when you sleep.

The god must not sleep lest he become clay, flesh; he must not cease to be present, lest his creature sink into nothingness. For woman, man's sleep is selfishness and treason. The lover sometimes awakens his mistress: it is to embrace her; she wakes him up simply to keep him from sleeping, to keep him there, in the room, in the bed, in her arms—like God in the tabernacle. That is what woman wants: she is a jailer.

And yet she is not willing for him to be nothing but her prisoner. This is one of the painful paradoxes of love: a captive, the god is shorn of his divinity. Woman preserves her transcendence by transferring it to him; but he must bring it to bear upon the whole world. If two lovers sink together in the absolute of passion, all their liberty is degraded into immanence; death is then the only solution. That is one of the meanings of the *Tristan and Isolde* myth. Two lovers destined solely for each other are already dead: they die of ennui, of the slow agony of a love that feeds on itself.

Woman is aware of this danger. Save in crises of jealous frenzy, she herself demands that man be all project, all action, for he is no more a hero if he engages in no exploits. The knight departing for new adventures offends his lady, yet she has nothing but contempt for him if he remains at her feet. This is the torture of the impossible love; the woman wants to possess the man wholly, but she demands that he transcend any gift that could possibly be possessed: a free being cannot be *had*. She wants to imprison *here* an existent who is, as Heidegger puts it, "a creature of far distances," but she knows very well that this attempt is foredoomed to failure.

[6]If Albertine were Albert it would be the same; Proust's attitude here is masculine in either case.
[7]That is, when he loses his independent powers, his transcendence, even in sleep, it costs her hers, because she lives in and by him.—TR.

"My dear friend, I love you as one should love, excessively, madly, with transport and despair," writes Julie de Lespinasse. Idolatrous love, if clear-sighted, must partake of desperation. For the loving woman who asks her lover to be a hero, a giant, a demigod, also is asking not to be all the world to him, even though she cannot have happiness unless she possesses him completely. Says Nietzsche in *The Gay Science*:

> Woman's passion, a total renunciation of all rights of her own, postulates precisely that the same feeling, the same desire for renunciation, does exist also in the other sex, for if both severally made this renunciation for love, there would result, on my word I do not know just what, shall we say, perhaps, the horror of nothingness? The woman wishes to be taken . . . she demands, therefore, someone to *take* her, someone who does not give himself, who does not abandon himself, but who wishes, on the contrary, to enrich his ego through love. . . . The woman gives herself, the man adds to himself by taking her.

At the least the woman will be able to find her joy in this enrichment which she brings to her beloved; she is not Everything to him, to be sure, but she will try to believe herself indispensable; there are no degrees in necessity. If he "cannot get along without her," she considers herself the foundation of her precious existence, and she derives her own value from that. Her joy is to serve him—but he must gratefully recognize this service; the gift becomes a demand in accordance with the usual dialectic of devotion.[8] And a woman with a scrupulous mind is bound to ask herself: does he really need *me*? The man is fond of her, desires her, with a personal tenderness and desire; but would he not have an equally personal feeling for someone else in her place? Many women in love permit themselves to be deluded; they would like to ignore the fact that the general is involved in the particular, and man furthers the illusion because he shares it at first; his desire often has a fire that seems to defy time; at the moment when he wants that woman, he wants her passionately, he wants her only. And, to be sure, that moment is an absolute—but a momentary absolute. Not realizing this, duped, the woman goes on to the eternal. Deified by the master's embrace, she believes she has always been divine and destined for the god—she and nobody else. But male desire is as ephemeral as it is imperious; once allayed, it dies rather quickly, whereas it is most often afterward that woman becomes love's captive. This is the burden of a whole fluent literature and of many facile songs. "A young man passed her way, a girl sang. . . . A young man sang, a girl wept."

And if the man is lastingly attached to the woman, that is still no sign that she is necessary to him. What she claims, however, is this: her abdication of self saves her only on condition that it restores her empire; reciprocity cannot be evaded. So she must either suffer or lie to herself. Most often she clutches at the straw of falsehood. She fancies that the man's

---

[8]Which I have attempted to set forth in my essay *Pyrrhus et Cinéas*.

love is the exact counterpart of the love she brings to him; in bad faith she takes desire for love, erection for desire, love for a religion. She compels the man to lie to her: "Do you love me? As much as yesterday? Will you always love me?" and so on. She cleverly poses her questions 'at a moment when there is not time enough to give properly qualified and sincere answers, or more especially when circumstances prevent any response; she asks her insistent questions in the course of a sexual embrace, at the verge of a convalescence, in the midst of sobs, or on a railroad platform. She makes trophies of the extorted replies; and if there are no replies, she takes silence to mean what she wishes; every woman in love is more or less a paranoiac. I recall a friend who said in reference to a long silence on the part of her distant lover: "When one wants to break off, one writes to announce the break"; then, having finally received a quite unambiguous letter: "When one really wants to break off, one doesn't write." . . .

Genuine love ought to be founded on the mutual recognition of two liberties; the lovers would then experience themselves both as self and as other: neither would give up transcendence, neither would be mutilated; together they would manifest values and aims in the world. For the one and the other, love would be .revelation of self by the gift of self and enrichment of the world. In his work on self-knowledge[9] George Gusdorf sums up very exactly what *man* demands of love.

Love reveals us to ourselves by making us come out of ourselves. We affirm ourselves by contact with what is foreign and complementary to us. . . . Love as a form of perception brings to light new skies and a new earth even in the landscape where we have always lived. Here is the great secret: the world is different, I myself *am different*. And I am no longer alone in knowing it. Even better: someone has apprised me of the fact. Woman therefore plays an indispensable and leading role in man's gaining knowledge of himself.

This accounts for the importance to the young man of his apprenticeship in love; we have seen how astonished Stendhal, Malraux, were at the miracle expressed in the phrase: "I myself, I am different." But Gusdorf is wrong when he writes: "And *similarly* man represents for woman an indispensable intermediary between herself and herself," for today her situation is not *similar*; man is revealed in a different aspect but he remains himself, and his new aspect is integrated with the sum total of his personality. It would be the same with woman only if she existed no less essentially than man as *pour-soi*; this would imply that she had economic independence, that she moved toward ends of her own and transcended herself, without using man as an agent, toward the social whole. Under these circumstances, love in equality is possible, as Malraux depicts it between Kyo and May in *Man's Fate*. Woman may even play the virile and dominating role, as did Mme de Warens with Rousseau, and, in Colette's *Chéri*, Léa with Chéri.

[9]*La Découverte de soi* (Paris, 1948), pp. 421, 425.—Tr.

But most often woman knows herself only as different, relative; her *pour-autrui*, relation to others, is confused with her very being; for her, love is not an intermediary "between herself and herself" because she does not attain her subjective existence; she remains engulfed in this loving woman whom man has not only revealed, but created. Her salvation depends on this despotic free being that has made her and can instantly destroy her. She lives in fear and trembling before this man who holds her destiny in his hands without quite knowing it, without quite wishing to. She is in danger through an other, an anguished and powerless onlooker at her own fate. Involuntary tyrant, involuntary executioner, this other wears a hostile visage in spite of her and of himself. And so, instead of the union sought for, the woman in love knows the most bitter solitude there is; instead of cooperation, she knows struggle and not seldom hate. For woman, love is a supreme effort to survive by accepting the dependence to which she is condemned; but even with consent a life of dependency can be lived only in fear and servility.

Men have vied with one another in proclaiming that love is woman's supreme accomplishment. "A woman who loves as a woman becomes only the more feminine," says Nietzsche; and Balzac: "Among the first-rate, man's life is fame, woman's life is love. Woman is man's equal only when she makes her life a perpetual offering, as that of man is perpetual action." But therein, again, is a cruel deception, since what she offers, men are in no wise anxious to accept. Man has no need of the unconditional devotion he claims, nor of the idolatrous love that flatters his vanity; he accepts them only on condition that he need not satisfy the reciprocal demands these attitudes imply. He preaches to woman that she should give—and her gifts bore him to distraction; she is left in embarrassment with her useless offerings, her empty life. On the day when it will be possible for woman to love not in her weakness but in her strength, not to escape herself but to find herself, not to abase herself but to assert herself—on that day love will become for her, as for man, a source of life and not of mortal danger. In the meantime, love represents in its most touching form the curse that lies heavily upon woman confined in the feminine universe, woman mutilated, insufficient unto herself. The innumerable martyrs to love bear witness against the injustice of a fate that offers a sterile hell as ultimate salvation.

 **LOVE AS PERFECTION OF DIFFERENCES**

Max Scheler

The belief that romantic love aims at the union of two people is so wide-spread that it qualifies under the rubric of common sense. But common sense is by no means exempt from philosophical scrutiny—quite the contrary. Common sense we take for granted, which is to say it goes un-questioned. And that which for a long time has gone unquestioned is apt to be badly in need of scrutiny.

Philosopher Max Scheler (twentieth century, German) interrogates the union-ideal of love (he begins by attacking the underlying "meta-physical monism"—the doctrine that in reality all things are one) and finds it wanting. Instead, the ideal of love is two free and distinct in-dividuals who by their love become more free and distinct. Love thus functions to realize the person as the unique and irreplaceable individual he is.

The roots of Scheler's thesis lie in the self-realization ethics of classical Greece, according to which it is each person's first responsibility to fulfill the ideal possibility within him (his "daimon"—see under Eros in Part II). We can sense the depth of the Greek opposition to the unity-ideal by recalling that even their gods were many, and distinctively individual.

Although we shall deal with love and hate at a later stage, we pro-pose, for the sake of continuity, to ask at this point whether the phenom-enon of *love* either requires or permits of interpretation in terms of metaphysical monism.

We may take vön Hartmann as a typical representative: 'We have al-ready[1] seen that love in its deepest sense involves treating the beloved as if his being were identical with our own: but if this instinctive premiss of love is an illusion, then the whole of love, being based upon it, is likewise illusory. If on the other hand, love is to be ranked as the highest, noblest and most god-like of all our moral instincts, there can be nothing illusory about it or about its fundamental premiss (whether this be conscious or un-conscious), and we must recognize, in its emotional anticipation and partial realization of the principle of the essential Identity of individuals, an un-

From *The Nature of Sympathy*, trans. by Peter Heath, with a general introduction to Max Scheler's works by W. Stark (Yale University Press, 1954), pp. 68–71. Reprinted by per-mission of Routledge and Kegan Paul, Ltd., London.
[1]See *Phänomenologie des sittlichen Bewusstseins*, pp. 266–97, in the chapter headed 'Das Moralprinzip der Liebe', in which the lover's yearning to identify the beloved with himself is described as an 'extension of self-love' by incorporation of the other person into oneself.

conscious intimation pointing prophetically to the absolute basis of morality and bearing witness to its truth.' Farther on he says: 'Love exhibits in an emotional and partial fashion what is theoretically and universally established by insight into the essential Identity of individuals. Though love may restrict its application of this absolute moral principle of the Identity of Being to a few persons, it does hold out to them an emotional guarantee of practical fulfilment; whereas theoretical insight into this universal Identity of Being must first strive, with the help of reason or religious feeling, to acquire the power of influencing practice. A (merely theoretical)[2] insight into the Identity of Being may show egoism to be theoretically an illusion, but meanwhile leave it unaffected in practice; so that we are still left with the task of resisting and crushing the power it exercises, wherever it may find an outlet. Love on the other hand is normally quite unconscious of its metaphysical basis, yet it represents an instinctive and genuine conquest of egoism in regard to the loved one, its superiority being all the greater in proportion to its strength. The absolute moral principle of the Identity of Being imposes a common ethical obligation (the repression of egoism by virtue of the One Being which is in all individuals alike): love already provides the required solution, though only in a particularized sense, for it is unaware of the universal nature of the obligation, and perhaps of its very existence'. On the relationship between love and fellow-feeling von Hartmann says: "In fellow-feeling the sense of the universal unity of Being merely flickers up, only to be quickly stifled again in the dismal vapours of egoism; but in love it bursts out into a calm and steady flame whose radiance gives warmth to life. Fellow-feeling is a passive affection received through the observation of passive states of emotion in others; love is an active spontaneous yearning to give practical effect to the feeling of identity.'

Now von Hartmann's predecessor in this view is Hegel, whose opinions on love are most fully expressed in those early fragments on theology and history of which W. Dilthey has recently given a detailed account in his admirable study entitled 'Die Jugendgeschichte Hegels'. Love, for Hegel, is 'the sense of the whole': 'It is a feeling peculiar to the living, and it is as living beings that those who love are one.' 'From this one feeling life breaks forth, to lose itself in dissipation among a diversity of emotions, and in the whole of this diversity to find itself again. This whole is not contained in love as a multitude of separate items in an aggregate; life finds its own self therein, reduplicated in its own image, and again merged in unity.' Even the love of God, for Hegel, rests on the essential identity of the human and the divine spirit, which in man attains to self-awareness only in religion. 'To love God is to feel oneself in all things living, to infinity, and without restraint.' The gospel's injunction, 'love thy neighbour as

[2]The bracketed expression is an insertion of my own.

thyself', does not tell us 'to love him as much as oneself (in degree), for to love oneself is an expression without meaning; it says, love him as if he *were* yourself; a feeling of being neither stronger nor weaker, but on a level'. Thus Hegel's rejection of the theistic interpretation of love is no less clear-cut and decisive than von Hartmann's; or than that of Spinoza, for whom men's love for one another and for God is merely part of that love with which God eternally loves himself, and who holds that though man is certainly able to love God, in *amor intellectualis Dei*, there can be no such love of God for man.

Our case against such theories, and all those like them is that so far from 'saving' the phenomenon of love, they simply *abolish* it. For love "in its deepest sense' does not consist in taking the other person and treating him as if he were identical with oneself. It is not a mere quantitative 'extension of self-love', nor is it a relationship of parts within a whole, whose collective exertions are devoted merely to its own (egoistic) self-maintenance, self-aggrandisement or growth. This is nothing less than a palpable *misrepresentation of the phenomenon*. It is the utterly and essentially different facts of emotional identification, and of what we have called the idiopathic variety at that, which would answer more nearly to the description of love furnished by Hegel and von Hartmann. If I take hold of someone and treat him 'as if' he were essentially identical with myself, this means that I am mistaken, firstly about his status in reality, and secondly about his nature. The first point is obvious enough. Since, at that very moment, his reality as another person would have been extinguished in the *phenomenon* itself, there could really be no such thing as an other-regading love here at all; it would simply have to be explained psychogenetically as a fortuitous instance of *self*-love—as a case of selfishness, indeed, since there is no thought or recognition here of love as an act by nature independent of its target ('myself' or 'another'), unaffected by changes therein, and totally different from any sort of hatred, for instance (though this can also be hatred of self or of others). Now it is just such an attitude of emotional outrage upon one's neighbour that we do actually find in idiopathic identification. The second point is no less obvious. Love calls explicitly for an understanding entry into the individuality of *another* person *distinct in character* from the entering self, by him accepted as such, and coupled, indeed, with a warm and whole-hearted endorsement of 'his' reality as an individual, and 'his' being what he is. This is profoundly and beautifully expressed by the Indian poet Rabindranath Tagore, when he depicts the sudden revulsion from (erotic) subjection and the yearning for the willing self-devotion of love:

> Free me from the bonds of your sweetness, my love!
> No more of this wine of kisses.
>   This mist of heavy incense stifles my heart.

Open the doors, make room for the morning light.
I am lost in you, wrapped in the folds of your caresses.
Free me from your spells, and give me back the manhood to
offer you my freed heart.

The Gardener, xlviii.

This giving and receiving of freedom, independence and individuality is of the essence of love. And in love, as it gradually re-emerges from the state of identification, there is built up, within the phenomenon itself, a clear-cut consciousness of two *distinct* persons. This consciousness is not merely a starting-point of love, for it only reaches full maturity as love pursues its course. It is the point at which psychical and spiritual love, as found in man at least, is, as the poet says, at its farthest remove from subjection, i.e. from the archetypal forms of suggestion and hypnosis. This *freedom* of love has nothing to do with arbitrary decision or freedom of choice or with free-will in any form, for it springs rather from the freedom of personality as against the sway of impulse in general; yet it is completely annihilated in metaphysical monism. What has obviously happened here is that in concentrating on the phenomena of identification at the vital level, an entire *range of love-emotions* has been passed over and misunderstood. Nor, finally, is there any regard whatever here for those limits of *absolute personal privacy*, our marginal awareness of which is first quickened and made clear in the fullness and depth of love, and there alone. For by the very fact that no man can have knowledge of this privacy in another, there can be no talk, in such a connection, of being or becoming or apprehending oneself as one and the same. So to von Hartmann's assertion: 'If the instinctive premiss of love—the essential identity of the persons—were an illusion, the whole of love would also be illusion', I oppose its converse: 'If the difference of the persons were an illusion, and if the consciousness of this which accompanies love in its increasing reverence and delicacy of approach to the absolute intimacy of the other's self —if this consciousness of personal diversity, greatest when love is deepest, were likewise an illusion, then love itself would indeed be illusion too.'

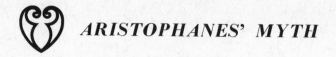

ARISTOPHANES' MYTH

Plato

East or West, poet or philosopher, love as the product of alienation is a deathless hypothesis. In Western literature its locus classicus is the charming myth told by Aristophanes in Plato's Symposium. *According to the story original man was complete and self-sufficient, containing both sexes within himself. But by his arrogance he angered Zesus, who for punishment split man in half. Ever afterward the resulting creatures were condemned to roam the earth in search of their other halves, and the moving force of their search is love.*

Broadly, alienation means separation from what was originally or by nature part of oneself. Within this meaning love characterizes incomplete creatures who yearn to become whole. Aristophanes' myth (much older than Aristophanes and Plato) is the source of the common expression, "better half," and also of the "soul mate" idea, according to which each person has but one ideal love partner whom he must search the earth in order to discover. (If this idea is dismaying today, remember that for the Greek the significant world was confined to his city-state, outside of which were only barbaroi.)

For the current vogue of the alienation theme Karl Marx is largely responsible. Marx referred not to the alienation of man from woman, but in the first instance to the alienation of man from the product of his labor. Marx saw this as man's alienation from himself, and sought to restore wholeness. This introduction of Marx under the myth of Aristophanes is not gratuitous, but affords a glimpse of Marx's roots in the self-realization ethics of classical Greece, roots which Marx translated into the terms of economics.

Aristophanes professed to open another vein of discourse; he had a mind to praise Love in another way, unlike that either of Pausanias or Eryximachus. Mankind, he said, judging by their neglect of him, have never, as I think, at all understood the power of Love. For if they had understood him they would surely have built noble temples and altars, and offered solemn sacrifices in his honour; but this is not done, and most certainly ought to be done: since of all the gods he is the best friend of men, the helper and the healer of the ills which are the great impediment to the

From the *Symposium. The Dialogues of Plato*, trans. B. Jowett, 3rd ed. (Oxford University Press, 1892), Vol. 1, pp. 9–61. Reprinted by permission of Oxford University Press.

happiness of the race. I will try to describe this power to you, and you shall teach the rest of the world what I am teaching you. In the first place, let me treat of the nature of man and what has happened to it; for the original human nature was not like the present, but different. The sexes were not two as they are now, but originally three in number; there was man, woman, and the union of the two, having a name corresponding to this double nature, which had once a real existence, but is now lost, and the word 'Androgynous' is only preserved as a term of reproach. In the second place, the primeval man was round, his back and sides forming a circle; and he had four hands and four feet, one head with two faces, looking opposite ways, set on a round neck and precisely alike; also four ears, two privy members, and the remainder to correspond. He could walk upright as men now do, backwards or forwards as he pleased, and he could also roll over and over at a great pace, turning on his four hands and four feet, eight in all, like tumblers going over and over with their legs in the air; this was when he wanted to run fast. Now the sexes were three, and such as I have described them; because the sun, moon, and earth are three; and the man was originally the child of the sun, the woman of the earth, and the man-woman of the moon, which is made up of sun and earth, and they were all round and moved round and round like their parents. Terrible was their might and strength, and the thoughts of their hearts were great, and they made an attack upon the gods; of them is told the tale of Otys and Ephialtes who, as Homer says, dared to scale heaven, and would have laid hands upon the gods. Doubt reigned in the celestial councils. Should they kill them and annihilate the race with thunderbolts, as they had done the giants, then there would be an end of the sacrifices and worship which men offered to them; but, on the other hand, the gods could not suffer their insolence to be unrestrained. At last, after a good deal of reflection, Zeus discovered a way. He said: 'Methinks I have a plan which will humble their pride and improve their manners; men shall continue to exist, but I will cut them in two and then they will be diminished in strength and increased in numbers; this will have the advantage of making them more profitable to us. They shall walk upright on two legs, and if they continue insolent and will not be quiet, I will split them again and they shall hop about on a single leg.' He spoke and cut men in two, like a sorb-apple which is halved for pickling, or as you might divide an egg with a hair; and as he cut them one after another, he bade Apollo give the face and the half of the neck a turn in order that the man might contemplate the section of himself: he would thus learn a lesson of humility. Apollo was also bidden to heal their wounds and compose their forms. So he gave a turn to the face and pulled the skin from the sides all over that which in our language is called the belly, like the purses which draw in, and he made one mouth at the centre, which he fastened in a knot (the same which is called the navel); he also moulded the breast and took out most of the wrinkles, much as a shoemaker might smooth leather upon a last; he left a few, however, in the region of the belly and navel, as a memorial of the primeval state. After the division the two parts of man, each desiring his other half, came together, and throwing their arms about one another, entwined in mutual embraces, longing to grow into one, they were on the point of dying from hunger and self-neglect, because they did not like to do anything apart; and when one of the halves died and the other survived, the surviror sought another mate, man or woman as we call them,—being the sections of entire men or women,—and clung to that. They were being destroyed, when Zeus in pity of them invented a new plan: he turned the parts of generation round to the front, for this had not been always their position, and they sowed the seed no longer as hitherto like grasshoppers in the ground, but in one another; and after the transposition the male generated in the female in order that by the mutual embraces of man and woman they might breed, and the race might continue; or if man came to man they might be satisfied, and rest, and go their ways to the business of life: so ancient is the desire of one another which is implanted in us, reuniting our original nature, making one of two, and healing the state of man. Each of us when separated, having one side only, like a flat fish, is but the indenture of a man, and he is always looking for his other half. Men who are a section of that double nature which was once called Androgynous are lovers of women; adulterers are generally of this breed, and also adulterous women who lust after men: the women who are a section of the woman do not care for men, but have female attachments; the female companions are of this sort. But they who are a section of the male follow the male, and while they are young, being slices of the original man, they hang about men and embrace them, and they are themselves the best of boys and youths, because they have the most manly nature. Some indeed assert that they are shameless, but this not true; for they do not act thus from any want of shame, but because they are valiant and manly, and have a manly countenance, and they embrace that which is like them. And these when they grow up become our statesmen, and these only, which is a great proof of the truth of what I am saying.

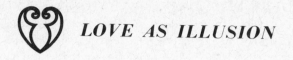

LOVE AS ILLUSION

Arthur Schopenhauer

In the literatures of the world sexual orgasm is known as the "little death," a name Schopenhauer finds well deserved. Orgasm ends sexual desire, which in turn ends the illusion of love. Under the thrust of desire we imagine that the other is an exceptional individual, the one person in the world with whom we can attain the heights. But consummation brings "wonder that after such a high, heroic, and infinite effort nothing has resulted for [our] pleasure but what every sexual gratification affords." This is because love is a trick played upon us by the subterranean Will of the species. It makes us think that we act freely and in our own interest, when in truth we are puppets of the species-Will. When Will has achieved its purpose (reproduction) illusion is no longer needed and love disappears. "Hence, then, every lover, after the ultimate consummation of the great work, finds himself cheated; for the illusion has vanished by means of which the individual was here the dupe of the species."

A great shaper of nineteenth century European thought, Schopenhauer exerts substantial influence today in continental existentialism and in Freudian psychoanalysis. His theory of love echoes in Freud's thesis on the "over-valuation" produced by romantic love (Three Essays on Sexuality).

... For all love, however ethereally it may bear itself, is rooted in the sexual impulse alone, nay, it absolutely is only a more definitely determined, specialised, and indeed in the strictest sense individualised sexual impulse. If now, keeping this in view, one considers the important part which the sexual impulse in all its degrees and nuances plays not only on the stage and in novels, but also in the real world, where, next to the love of life, it shows itself the strongest and most powerful of motives, constantly lays claim to half the powers and thoughts of the younger portion of mankind, is the ultimate goal of almost all human effort, exerts an adverse influence on the most important events, interrupts the most serious occupations every hour, sometimes embarrasses for a while even the greatest minds, does not hesitate to intrude with its trash interfering with the negotiations of statesmen and the investigations of men of learning, knows how to slip its love letters and locks of hair even into ministerial

From *The World as Will and Idea*, trans. R. B. Haldane and J. Kemp (New York: Charles Scribner's Sons, 1883), Vol. III, pp. 339–349 and p. 370. Reprinted by permission of Routledge and Kegan Paul, Ltd.

portfolios and philosophical manuscripts, and no less devises daily the most entangled and the worst actions, destroys the most valuable relationships, breaks the firmest bonds, demands the sacrifice sometimes of life or health, sometimes of wealth, rank, and happiness, nay, robs those who are otherwise honest of all conscience, makes those who have hitherto been faithful, traitors; accordingly, on the whole, appears as a malevolent demon that strives to pervert, confuse, and overthrow everything;—then one will be forced to cry, Wherefore all this noise? Wherefore the straining and storming, the anxiety and want? It is merely a question of every Hans finding his Grethe.[1] Why should such a trifle play so important a part, and constantly introduce disturbance and confusion into the well-regulated life of man? But to the earnest investigator the spirit of truth gradually reveals the answer. It is no trifle that is in question here; on the contrary, the importance of the matter is quite proportionate to the seriousness and ardour of the effort. The ultimate end of all love affairs, whether they are played in sock or cothurnus, is really more important than all other ends of human life, and is therefore quite worthy of the profound seriousness with which every one pursues it. That which is decided by it is nothing less than *the composition of the next generation.* The *dramatis personae* who shall appear when we are withdrawn are here determined, both as regards their existence and their nature, by these frivolous love affairs. As the being, the *existentia*, of these future persons is absolutely conditioned by our sexual impulse generally, so their nature, *essentia*, is determined by the individual selection in its satisfaction, *i.e.*, by sexual love, and is in every respect irrevocably fixed by this. This is the key of the problem: we shall arrive at a more accurate knowledge of it in its application if we go through the degrees of love, from the passing inclination to the vehement passion, when we shall also recognise that the difference of these grades arises from the degree of the individualisation of the choice.

The collective love affairs of the present generation taken together are accordingly, of the whole human race, the serious *meditatio compositionis generationis futurae, e qua iterum pendent innumaroe generationes.** This high importance of the matter, in which it is not a question of individual weal or woe, as in all other matters, but of the existence and special nature of the human race in future times, and therefore the will of the individual appears at a higher power as the will of the species;—this it is on which the pathetic and sublime elements in affairs of love depend, which for thousands of years poets have never wearied of representing in innumerable examples; because no theme can equal in interest this one, which stands to all others which only concern the welfare of individuals as the

---

[1] I have not ventured to express myself distinctly here: the courteous reader must therefore translate the phrase into Aristophanic language.

*meditation on the composition of a future generation, from which, again, innumerable generations follow.

solid body to the surface, because it concerns the weal and woe of the species. Just on this account, then, is it so difficult to impart interest to a drama without the element of love, and, on the other hand, this theme is never worn out even by daily use.

That which presents itself in the individual consciousness as sexual impulse in general, without being directed towards a definite individual of the other sex, is in itself, and apart from the phenomenon, simply the will to live. But what appears in consciousness as a sexual impulse directed to a definite individual is in itself the will to live as a definitely determined individual. Now in this case the sexual impulse, although in itself a subjective need, knows how to assume very skilfully the mask of an objective admiration, and thus to deceive our consciousness; for nature requires this strategem to attain its ends. But yet that in every case of falling in love, however objective and sublime this admiration may appear, what alone is looked to is the production of an individual of a definite nature is primarily confirmed by the fact that the essential matter is not the reciprocation of love, but possession, *i.e.*, the physical enjoyment. The certainty of the former can therefore by no means console us for the want of the latter; on the contrary, in such a situation many a man has shot himself. On the other hand, persons who are deeply in love, and can obtain no return of it, are contented with possession, *i.e.*, with the physical enjoyment. This is proved by all forced marriages, and also by the frequent purchase of the favour of a woman, in spite of her dislike, by large presents or other sacrifices, nay, even by cases of rape. That this particular child shall be begotten is, although unknown to the parties concerned, the true end of the whole love story; the manner in which it is attained is a secondary consideration. Now, however loudly persons of lofty and sentimental soul, and especially those who are in love, may cry out here about the gross realism of my view, they are yet in error. For is not the definite determination of the individualities of the next generation a much higher and more worthy end than those exuberant feelings and supersensible soap bubbles of theirs? Nay, among earthly aims, can there be one which is greater or more important? It alone corresponds to the profoundness with which passionate love is felt, to the seriousness with which it appears, and the importance which it attributes even to the trifling details of its sphere and occasion. Only so far as this end is assumed as the true one do the difficulties encountered, the infinite exertions and annoyances made and endured for the attainment of the loved object, appear proportionate to the matter. For it is the future generation, in its whole individual determinateness, that presses into existence by means of those efforts and toils. Nay, it is itself already active in that careful, definite, and arbitrary choice for the satisfaction of the sexual impulse which we call love. The growing inclination of two lovers is really already the will to live of the new individual which they can and desire to produce; nay, even in the meeting of their longing glances its new life breaks out, and announces itself as a future individuality harmoniously and well composed. They feel the longing for an actual union and fusing together into a single being, in order to live on only as this; and this longing receives its fulfilment in the child which is produced by them, as that in which the qualities transmitted by them both, fused and united in one being, live on. Conversely, the mutual, decided and persistent aversion between a man and a maid is a sign that what they could produce would only be a badly organised, in itself inharmonious and unhappy being. Hence there lies a deeper meaning in the fact that Calderon, though he calls the atrocious Semiramis the daughter of the air, yet introduces her as the daughter of rape followed by the murder of the husband.

But, finally, what draws two individuals of different sex exclusively to each other with such power is the will to live, which exhibits itself in the whole species, and which here anticipates in the individual which these two can produce an objectification of its nature answering to its aims. This individual will have the will, or character, from the father, the intellect from the mother, and the corporisation from both; yet, for the most part, the figure will take more after the father, the size after the mother,—according to the law which comes óut in the breeding of hybrids among the brutes, and principally depends upon the fact that the size of the foetus must conform to the size of the uterus. Just as inexplicable as the quite special individuality of any man, which is exclusively peculiar to him, is also the quite special and individual passion of two lovers; indeed at bottom the two are one and the same: the former is *explicite* what the latter was *implicite*. The moment at which the parents begin to love each other— to fancy each other, as the very happy English expression has it—is really to be regarded as the first appearance of a new individual and the true *punctum saliens* of its life, and, as has been said, in the meeting and fixing of their longing glances there appears the first germ of the new being, which certainly, like all germs, is generally crushed out. This new individual is to a certain extent a new (Platonic) Idea; and now, as all Ideas strive with the greatest vehemence to enter the phenomenal world, eagerly seizing for this end upon the matter which the law of causality divides among them all, so also does this particular Idea of a human individuality strive with the greatest eagerness and vehemence towards its realisation in the phenomenon. This eagerness and vehemence is just the passion of the two future parents for each other. It has innumerable degrees, the two extremes of which may at any rate be described as $A\phi\rho o\delta\iota\tau\eta$ $\pi\alpha\nu\delta\eta\mu os$ and $o\nu\rho\alpha\nu\iota\alpha$*; in its nature, however, it is everywhere the same. On the other hand, it will be in degree so much the more powerful the more *individualised* it is; that is, the more the loved individual is ex-

*heavenly and earthly Aphrodite

clusively suited, by virtue of all his or her parts and qualities, to satisfy the desire of the lover and the need established by his or her own individuality. What is really in question here will become clear in the future course of our exposition. Primarily and essentially the inclination of love is directed to health, strength, and beauty, consequently also to youth; because the will first of all seeks to exhibit the specific character of the human species as the basis of all individuality: ordinary amorousness ($A\phi\rho o\delta\iota\tau\eta$ $\pi\alpha\nu\delta\eta\mu os$)* does not go much further. To these, then, more special claims link themselves on, which we shall investigate in detail further on, and with which, when they see satisfaction before them, the passion increases. But the highest degrees of this passion spring from that suitableness of two individualities to each other on account of which the will, *i.e.*, the character, of the father and the intellect of the mother, in their connection, make up precisely that individual towards which the will to live in general which exhibits itself in the whole species feels a longing proportionate to this its magnitude, and which therefore exceeds the measure of a mortal heart, and the motives of which, in the same way, lie beyond the sphere of the individual intellect. This is thus the soul of a true and great passion. Now the more perfect is the mutual adaptation of two individuals to each other in each of the many respects which have further to be considered, the stronger will be their mutual passion. Since there do not exist two individuals exactly alike, there must be for each particular man a particular woman—always with reference to what is to be produced—who corresponds most perfectly. A really passionate love is as rare as the accident of these two meeting. Since, however, the possibility of such a love is present in every one, the representations of it in the works of the poets are comprehensible to us. Just because the passion of love really turns about that which is to be produced, and its qualities, and because its kernel lies here, a friendship without any admixture of sexual love can exist between two young and good-looking persons of different sex, on account of the agreement of their disposition, character, and mental tendencies; nay, as regards sexual love there may even be a certain aversion between them. The reason of this is to be sought in the fact that a child produced by them would have physical or mental qualities which were inharmonious; in short, its existence and nature would not answer the ends of the will to live as it exhibits itself in the species. On the other hand, in the case of difference of disposition, character, and mental tendency, and the dislike, nay, enmity, proceeding from this, sexual love may yet arise and exist; when it then blinds us to all that; and if it here leads to marriage it will be a very unhappy one.

Let us now set about the more thorough investigation of the matter. Egoism is so deeply rooted a quality of all individuals in general, that in

*earthly Aphrodite

order to rouse the activity of an individual being egoistical ends are the only ones upon which we can count with certainty. Certainly the species has an earlier, closer, and greater claim upon the individual than the perishable individuality itself. Yet when the individual has to act, and even make sacrifices for the continuance and quality of the species, the importance of the matter cannot be made so comprehensible to his intellect, which is calculated merely with regard to individual ends, as to have its proportionate effect. Therefore in such a case nature can only attain its ends by implanting a certain illusion in the individual, on account of which that which is only a good for the species appears to him as a good for himself, so that when he serves the species he imagines he is serving himself; in which process a mere chimera, which vanishes immediately afterwards, floats before him, and takes the place of a real thing as a motive. This illusion is instinct. In the great majority of cases this is to be regarded as the sense of the species, which presents what is of benefit to *it* to the will. Since, however, the will has here become individual, it must be so deluded that it apprehends through the sense of the individual what the sense of the species presents to it, thus imagines it is following individual ends while in truth it is pursuing ends which are merely general (taking this word in its strictest sense). The external phenomenon of instinct we can best observe in the brutes where its rôle is most important; but it is in ourselves alone that we arrive at a knowledge of its internal process, as of everything internal. Now it is certainly supposed that man has almost no instinct; at any rate only this, that the new-born babe seeks for and seizes the breast of its mother. But, in fact, we have a very definite, distinct, and complicated instinct, that of the selection of another individual for the satisfaction of the sexual impulse, a selection which is so fine, so serious, and so arbitrary. With this satisfaction in itself, *i.e.*, so far as it is a sensual pleasure resting upon a pressing want of the individual, the beauty or ugliness of the other individual has nothing to do. Thus the regard for this which is yet pursued with such ardour, together with the careful selection which springs from it, is evidently connected, not with the chooser himself—although he imagines it is so—but with the true end, that which is to be produced, which is to receive the type of the species as purely and correctly as possible. Through a thousand physical accidents and moral aberrations there arise a great variety of deteriorations of the human form; yet its true type, in all its parts, is always again established: and this takes place under the guidance of the sense of beauty, which always directs the sexual impulse, and without which this sinks to the level of a disgusting necessity. Accordingly, in the first place, every one will decidedly prefer and eagerly desire the most beautiful individuals, *i.e.*, those in whom the character of the species is most purely impressed; but, secondly, each one will specially regard as beautiful in another individual those perfections which he himself lacks, nay, even those imperfections which are the opposite of his own. Hence, for example, little men love big women, fair persons like dark, &c. &c. The delusive ecstasy which seizes a man at the sight of a woman whose beauty is suited to him, and pictures to him a union with her as the highest good, is just the *sense of the species*, which, recognising the distinctly expressed stamp of the same, desires to perpetuate it with this individual. Upon this decided inclination to beauty depends the maintenance of the type of the species: hence it acts with such great power. We shall examine specially further on the considerations which it follows. Thus what guides man here is really an instinct which is directed to doing the best for the species, while the man himself imagines that he only seeks the heightening of his own pleasure. In fact, we have in this an instructive lesson concerning the inner nature of all instinct, which, as here, almost always sets the individual in motion for the good of the species. For clearly the pains with which an insect seeks out a particular flower, or fruit, or dung, or flesh, or, as in the case of the ichneumonidae, the larva of another insect, in order to deposit its eggs there only, and to attain this end shrinks neither from trouble nor danger, is thoroughly analogous to the pains with which for his sexual satisfaction a man carefully chooses a woman with definite qualities which appeal to him individually, and strives so eagerly after her that in order to attain this end he often sacrifices his own happiness in life, contrary to all reason, by a foolish marriage, by love affairs which cost him wealth, honour, and life, even by crimes such as adultery or rape, all merely in order to serve the species in the most efficient way, although at the cost of the individual, in accordance with the will no nature which is everywhere sovereign. Instinct, in fact, is always an act which seems to be in accordance with the conception of an end, and yet is entirely without such a conception. Nature implants it wherever the acting individual is incapable of understanding the end, or would be unwilling to pursue it. Therefore, as a rule, it is given only to the brutes, and indeed especially to the lowest of them which have least understanding; but almost only in the case we are here considering it is also given to man, who certainly could understand the end, but would not pursue it with the necessary ardour, that is, even at the expense of his individual welfare. Thus here, as in the case of all instinct, the truth assumes the form of an illusion, in order to act upon the will. It is a voluptuous illusion which leads the man to believe he will find a greater pleasure in the arms of a woman whose beauty appeals to him than in those of any other; or which indeed, exclusively directed to a single individual, firmly convinces him that the possession of her will ensure him excessive happiness. Therefore he imagines he is taking trouble and making sacrifices for his own pleasure, while he does so merely for the maintenance of the regular type of the species, or else a quite special individuality, which can only come from these parents, is to attain to existence. The character of instinct is here so perfectly present, thus an action which seems to be in accordance with the conception of an end, and yet is entirely without such a conception, that he who is drawn by that illusion often abhors the end which alone guides it, procreation, and would like to hinder it; thus it is in the case of almost all illicit love affairs. In accordance with the character of the matter which has been explained, every lover will experience a marvellous disillusion after the pleasure he has at last attained, and will wonder that what was so longingly desired accomplishes nothing more than every other sexual satisfaction; so that he does not see himself much benefited by it. That wish was related to all his other wishes as the species is related to the individual, thus as the infinite to the finite. The satisfaction, on the other hand, is really only for the benefit of the species, and thus does not come within the consciousness of the individual, who, inspired by the will of the species, here served an end with every kind of sacrifice, which was not his own end at all. Hence, then, every lover, after the ultimate consummation of the great work, finds himself cheated; for the illusion has vanished by means of which the individual was here the dupe of the species. . . .

Because the passion depended upon an illusion, which represented that which has only value for the species as valuable for the individual, the deception must vanish after the attainment of the end of the species. The spirit of the species which took possession of the individual sets it free again. Forsaken by this spirit, the individual falls back into its original limitation and narrowness, and sees with wonder that after such a high, heroic, and infinite effort nothing has resulted for its pleasure but what every sexual gratification affords. Contrary to expectation, it finds itself no happier than before. It observes that it has been the dupe of the will of the species. Therefore, as a rule, a Theseus who has been made happy will forsake his Ariadne. If Petrarch's passion had been satisfied, his song would have been silenced from that time forth, like that of the bird as soon as the eggs are laid.

PART *II*
Eros

EROS: LOVE AS ASPIRATION TOWARD THE IDEAL

"What can he possibly see in her?" is the question put by the world to the lover.

Eros answers that love sees something which the non-lover can never see—the ideal possibility within the beloved which it is his or her destiny to fulfill. So different is this perception from our normal way of seeing other people that Plato called love "divine madness." The abnormality will scarcely be contested, for the lover's perception appears abnormal even to himself. Last week all women appeared to him as much alike, but meanwhile one among them has stepped so far forth from the ranks of her sex as to utterly banish the rest from consideration. From the world's viewpoint it is just the conviction of the beloved's singularity which constitutes love's delusion. But Plato employed the term "divine" because he took love's perception of singularity to be the highest truth.

In ancient Greece, sculptors made busts of the semi-deity Silenus which had a trick to them. Inside the hollow clay likeness lay hidden a little gold figurine which was revealed when the bust was opened. According to the Greeks, Eros is the power which discerns the golden figure within the clay.

For each human being can be likened to a bust by Silenus. The clay is his appearance to the world, which is always to some degree flawed and misshapen. It is his *actuality*, and as such it includes the mole on his cheek, the phobias in his psyche, and his penchant for saying more than he knows. But within his actuality is the golden figurine which love discerns—his *possibility*.

The Greeks called one's ideal possibility his *daimon*, and ascribed to it several important characteristics. First of all it is inborn and constitutes an individual's true self; hence when one acts in obedience to the great Greek imperative, "Know Thyself," it is his daimon he seeks. Secondly, as noted, the daimon subsists within him not as an actuality but as a possibility, and this means that what he discovers by the enterprise of self-knowledge is not a *fait accompli*, a finished product, but is instead a job of work and a direction of growth. It is our responsibility to progressively *actualize* our ideal possibility, living in truth to it along the line of growth which stretches to it from the place where we presently are, a direction the Greeks called one's *destiny*. And finally, each person's daimon is unique, it is a form of perfection differing from every other (as perfection of the apple differs from that of the pear, the Jonathan from the Winesap, and so on). This means that to the degree to which an individual fails to know himself or to live in truth to himself, to the degree to which he is distracted from his destiny by external enticements, or deflected from it by external pressures, or barred from it by his own fears and self-doubts—to this degree that unique value which he represents will be lacking in the world.

Within this understanding all things begin at home, notably knowledge, truth, and love. Integrity, which means living in truth to oneself, is the precondition of truthfulness to others, for the man whose own life is untruth will exhale deception at every breath. Similarly self-love is the precondition of loving others, and the individual who negates the humanity within himself is no friend of man. But self-love within Eros must be carefully distinguished from egoism. The egoist's love is for his own *actuality*, hence this poor fool presents himself as entirely satisfied with what the world readily perceives to be flawed goods. Moreover the prognosis is certain. Because the egoist and his love are one and the same, his love has no dynamic and he will not grow. Finally, the egoist loves himself to the exclusion of others, thereby proving himself blind to his kinship with the race.

By contrast, what Eros loves is the indwelling *ideal*; hence this love is a constant reminder of the actual self's insufficiency and an enduring dynamic of growth. And because the self is but a particular expression of the larger humanity, self-love is by no means exclusive of the love of others but the ground of such love.

Some critics of Eros contend that love of ideals is not love of persons (see, e.g., Irving Singer, *The Nature of Love, Plato to Luther*, Chap. 3). Acknowledging the distinction between possibility and actuality, they identify the person with his actuality. But Eros responds that a love which centers upon the other's actuality serves to imprison him in it, making of him a depersonalized object. His actuality is his past and present, and to define him in these terms is to deprive him of his freedom and his future. Has he failed in his schoolwork?; then he *is* a Non-achiever. Has he deceived us repeatedly?; then he *is* Untrustworthy. Has she forgotten appointments?; then she *is* Thoughtless. The past is precisely that which we can do nothing about, hence to identify the person with his past is to say that he can do nothing about himself. What this identification ignores is the person's own *attitude* toward his past. (Did his lie please or distress him?) By the inclusion of his attitude we allow to him a future which is not a simple extrapolation of his past; we grant him his freedom. In the words of psychologist Abraham Maslow, we must recognize that "man has his future within him, dynamically active at the present moment." (*Toward a Psychology of Being*, Chap. 2.) Eros loves the ideal future which the other most essentially is, including his actuality as that future's foreshadowing. Without this living future, love is not of persons but of things. It is a possessiveness which amputates human freedom.

Other critics of Eros suppose that self-love precludes the love of others, thus identifying Eros with egoism. But Eros is love of the ideal humanity *which all men share.* To love it in oneself is the *precondition* of loving it in others, by no means the preclusion. More concretely, through self-knowledge we discover our need for the special excellences of others, for these cannot be realized by us but only by them. In Socrates' words, "Every one chooses his love from the ranks of beauty according to his own character." (*Phaedrus*) In virtue of this "division of labor," to love human exellence is necessarily to love others no less than ourselves. It consists in the discernment and appreciation of excellences different from our own, and as such it is our need. But it is a need which is fulfilled by the other becoming *himself,* by his living in truth to his *daimon.*

A weightier charge against Eros is that this mode of love affords no *consolation* to human distress, whether this be another's or one's own. For Eros is an arrow aiming ever aloft and heedless of what lies beneath; as love of excellence it can never turn downward in pity, commiseration, or charity.

Eros responds to the charge by pointing to two ways by which it treats adversity. It ministers to despair and loss of the sense of self-worth in the other by reminding him always of the golden figurine within his bust of clay. Rather than descending to him in his lack, it serves to elevate him from it by its love for the perfection within him which he himself cannot see. It holds before him a mirror in which to rediscover his daimon. And secondly, it ministers to distress and disadvantage by the pedagogical principle of the emulation of example. Here is the function of the Greek hero upon the tragic stage. He exemplifies human integrity and encourages individuals to live in like fashion. No less in life, the great man or woman is an inducement to greatness in others.

In sum, according to the psychology of the Eros tradition, better than pity in our distress is the reminder of the ultimate worth within us and the exemplification of human worth by individuals from whom we can draw inspiration.

But what of the hero, the man who is living in truth to himself? Is he not caught in what Robert Frost called "a pursuit of a pursuit forever"? His destiny is to grow toward an ideal which can never be fully actualized. Is he not doomed to ultimate frustration, and is his life style not rendered harsh by this ceaseless striving, this relentless tension between the ideal and the actual? Where, in this mode of living, is peace? Where is respite? Where is Taoism's Wu-wei, namely, "not-doing, letting be?"

Eros responds by holding forth a special attitude which is not the *outcome* of a process, as with "happiness," but attends the process throughout. The man who is living in truth with himself experiences the feeling of *eudaimonia.* We must leave detailed consideration of this feeling to the selection from Abraham Maslow which appears hereafter. Put succinctly, it is the feeling of being at one with oneself, as against being "at odds" with oneself, divided against oneself. In the end, the judgment of Eros' adequacy on this score must be the reader's own.

The wellspring of Eros is ancient Greece, but current spokesmen are numerous and prominent. In the United States for the first half of our century George Santayana and John Dewey were leading voices (see, e.g., Santayana'a *The Life of Reason* and Dewey's *A Common Faith*). In Europe philosophical Existentialism enunciates a pure Eros in such partisans as Max Scheler, José Ortega y Gasset, Jean-Paul Sartre, Albert Camus, and Maurice Merleau-Ponty, while existential theologians— notable among them Martin Buber, Gabriel Marcel, and Paul Tillich— attempt a reconciliation between Eros and Agape. And Eros undergirds the emerging humanistic psychology of Abraham Maslow (*Toward a Psychology of Being*), Erich Fromm (*Man for Himself*), Rollo May (*Man's Search for Himself*), and Viktor Frankl (*Man's Search for Meaning*).

 *EROS*

Plato

Love is a form of desire, says Socrates, and to desire something means that we presently lack it, hence love marks deficient beings. Gods do not love, but only men.

Yet what we love is also part of us in virtue of our love; it is ours as that which would complete us and make us whole. Here we confront an apparent paradox in the nature of love. What we love, it seems, we both lack and possess.

The seeming paradox dissolves with the introduction of the key distinction between actuality *and* ideality. *A man is both actuality and potentiality, he has his future active within him. What he loves is lacked by his present (actual) self, being part of that ideal, fulfilled self which it is his responsibility to realize. Thus love is the connection between ideality and actuality. In Plato's words it is the desire for "generation and of birth in beauty." Generation means growth, and beauty means for Socrates the good life. Our love leads us to the ideal which constitutes our special excellence, our potential perfection.*

In the magnificent oration which you have just uttered, I think that you were right, my dear Agathon, in proposing to speak of the nature of Love first and afterwards of his works—that is a way of beginning which I very much approve. And as you have spoken so eloquently of his nature, may I ask you further, Whether love is the love of something or of nothing? And here I must explain myself: I do not want you to say that love is the love of a father or the love of a mother—that would be ridiculous; but to answer as you would, if I asked is a father a father of something? to which you would find no difficulty in replying, of a son or daughter: and the answer would be right.

Very true, said Agathon.

And you would say the same of a mother?

He assented.

Yet let me ask you one more question in order to illustrate my meaning: Is not a brother to be regarded essentially as a brother of something?

Certainly, he replied.

That is, of a brother or sister?

From the *Symposium. The Dialogues of Plato*, trans. B. Jowett, 3rd ed. (Oxford University Press, 1892), Vol. 1, pp. 569–582. Reprinted by permission of Oxford University Press.

Yes, he said.

And now, said Socrates, I will ask about Love:—Is Love of something or of nothing?

Of something, surely, he replied.

Keep in mind what this is, and tell me what I want to know—whether Love desires that of which love is.

Yes, surely.

And does he possess, or does he not possess, that which he loves and desires?

Probably not, I should say.

Nay, replied Socrates, I would have you consider whether 'necessarily' is not rather the word. The inference that he who desires something is in want of something, and that he who desires nothing is in want of nothing, is in my judgment, Agathon, absolutely and necessarily true. What do you think?

I agree with you, said Agathon.

Very good. Would he who is great, desire to be great, or he who is strong, desire to be strong?

That would be inconsistent with our previous admissions.

True. For he who is anything cannot want to be that which he is?

Very true.

And yet, added Socrates, if a man being strong desired to be strong, or being swift desired to be swift, or being healthy desired to be healthy, in that case he might be thought to desire something which he already has or is. I give the example in order that we may avoid misconception. For the possessors of these qualities, Agathon, must be supposed to have their respective advantages at the time, whether they choose or not; and who can desire that which he has? Therefore, when a person says, I am well and wish to be well, or I am rich and wish to be rich, and I desire simply to have what I have—to him we shall reply: 'You, my friend, having wealth and health and strength, want to have the continuance of them; for at this moment, whether you choose or no, you have them. And when you say, I desire that which I have and nothing else, is not your meaning that you want to have what you now have in the future?' He must agree with us— must he not?

He must, replied Agathon.

Then, said Socrates, he desires that what he has at present may be preserved to him in the future, which is equivalent to saying that he desires something which is non-existent to him, and which as yet he has not got:

Very true, he said.

Then he and every one who desires, desires that which he has not already, and which is future and not present, and which he has not, and is not, and of which he is in want;—these are the sort of things which love and desire seek?

Very true, he said.

Then now, said Socrates, let us recapitulate the argument. First, is not love of something, and of something too which is wanting to a man?

Yes, he replied.

Remember further what you said in your speech, or if you do not remember I will remind you: you said that the love of the beautiful set in order the empire of the gods, for that of deformed things there is no love— did you not say something of that kind?

Yes, said Agathon.

Yes, my friend, and the remark was a just one. And if this is true, Love is the love of beauty and not of deformity?

He assented.

And the admission has been already made that Love is of something which a man wants and has not?

True, he said.

Then Love wants and has not beauty?

Certainly, he replied.

And would you call that beautiful which wants and does not possess beauty?

Certainly not.

Then would you still say that love is beautiful?

Agathon replied: I fear that I did not understand what I was saying.

You made a very good speech, Agathon, replied Socrates; but there is yet one small question which I would fain ask:—Is not the good also the beautiful?

Yes.

Then in wanting the beautiful, love wants also the good?

I cannot refute you, Socrates, said Agathon:—Let us assume that what you say is true.

Say rather, beloved Agathon, that you cannot refute the truth; for Socrates is easily refuted.

And now, taking my leave of you, I will rehearse a tale of love which I heard from Diotima of Mantineia, a woman wise in this and in many other kinds of knowledge, who in the days of old, when the Athenians offered sacrifice before the coming of the plague, delayed the disease ten years. She was my instructress in the art of love, and I shall repeat to you what she said to me, beginning with the admissions made by Agathon, which are nearly if not quite the same which I made to the wise woman when she questioned me: I think that this will be the easiest way, and I shall take both parts myself as well as I can. As you, Agathon, suggested, I must speak first of the being and nature of Love, and then of his works. First I said to her in nearly the same words which he used to me, that Love was a mighty god, and like-wise fair; and she proved to me as I proved to him that, by my own showing, Love was neither fair nor good. 'What do you mean, Diotima,' I said, 'is love then evil and foul?' 'Hush,' she cried; 'must that be foul which is not fair?' 'Certainly,' I said. 'And is that which is not wise, ignorant? do you not see that there is a mean between wisdom and ignorance?' 'And what may that be?' I said. 'Right opinion,' she replied; 'which, as you know, being incapable of giving a reason, is not knowledge (for how can knowledge be devoid of reason? nor again, ignorance, for neither can ignorance attain the truth), but is clearly something which is a mean between ignorance and wisdom.' 'Quite true,' I replied. 'Do not then insist,' she said, 'that what is not fair is of necessity foul, or what is not good evil; or infer that because love is not fair and good he is therefore foul and evil; for he is in a mean between them.' 'Well,' I said, 'Love is surely admitted by all to be a great god.' 'By those who know or by those who do not know?' 'By all.' 'And how, Socrates,' she said with a smile, 'can Love be acknowledged to be a great god by those who say that he is not a god at all?' 'And who are they?' I said. 'You and I are two of them,' she replied. 'How can that be?' I said. 'It is quite intelligible,' she replied; 'for you yourself would acknowledge that the gods are happy and fair—of course you would—would you dare to say that any god was not?' 'Certainly not,' I replied. 'And you mean by the happy, those who are the possessors of things good or fair?' 'Yes.' 'And you admitted that Love, because he was in want, desires those good and fair things of which he is in want?' 'Yes, I did.' 'But how can he be a god who has no portion in what is either good or fair?' 'Impossible.' 'Then you see that you also deny the divinity of Love.'

'What then is Love?' I asked; 'Is he mortal?' 'No.' 'What then?' 'As in the former instance, he is neither mortal nor immortal, but in a mean between the two.' 'What is he, Diotima?' 'He is a great spirit ($\delta\alpha\iota\mu\omega\nu$), and like all spirits he is intermediate between the divine and the mortal.' 'And what,' I said, 'is his power?' 'He interprets,' she replied, 'between gods and men, conveying and taking across to the gods the prayers and sacrifices of men, and to men the commands and replies of the gods; he is the mediator who spans the chasm which divides them, and therefore in him all is bound together, and through him the arts of the prophet and the priest, their sacrifices and mysteries and charms, and all prophecy and incantation, find their way. For God mingles not with man; but through Love all the intercourse and converse of God with man, whether awake or asleep, is carried on. The wisdom which understands this is spiritual; all other wisdom, such as that of arts and handicrafts, is mean and vulgar. Now these spirits or intermediate powers are many and diverse, and one of them is Love.' 'And who,' I said, 'was his father, and who his mother?' 'The tale,' she said, 'will take time; nevertheless I will tell you. On the birthday of Aphrodite there was a feast of the gods, at which the god Poros or Plenty, who is the son of Metis or Discretion, was one of the guests. When the feast was over, Penia or Poverty, as the manner is on such occasions, came about the doors to beg. Now Plenty, who was the worse for nectar (there was no wine in those days), went into the garden of Zeus and fell into a heavy sleep; and Poverty considering her own straitened circumstances, plotted to have a child by him, and accordingly she lay down at his side and conceived Love, who partly because he is naturally a lover of the beautiful, and because Aphrodite is herself beautiful, and also because he was born on her birthday, is her follower and attendant. And as his parentage is, so also are his fortunes. In the first place he is always poor, and anything but tender and fair, as the many imagine him; and he is rough and squalid, and has no shoes, nor a house to dwell in; on the bare earth exposed he lies under the open heaven, in the streets, or at the doors of houses, taking his rest; and like his mother he is always in distress. Like his father too, whom he also partly resembles, he is always plotting against the fair and good; he is bold, enterprising, strong, a mighty hunter, always weaving some intrigue or other, keen in the pursuit of wisdom, fertile in resources; a philosopher at all times, terrible as an enchanter, sorcerer, sophist. He is by nature neither mortal nor immortal, but alive and flourishing at one moment when he is in plenty, and dead at another moment, and again alive by reason of his father's nature. But that which is always flowing in is always flowing out, and so he is never in want and never in wealth; and, further, he is in a mean between ignorance and knowledge. The truth of the matter is this: No god is a philosopher or seeker after wisdom, for he is wise already; nor does any man who is wise seek after wisdom. Neither do the ignorant seek after wisdom. For herein is the evil of ignorance, that he who is neither good nor wise is nevertheless satisfied with himself: he has no desire for that of which he feels no want.' 'But who then, Diotima,' I said, 'are the lovers of wisdom, if they are neither the wise nor the foolish?' 'A child may answer that question,' she replied; 'they are those who are in a mean between the two; Love is one of them. For wisdom is a most beautiful thing, and Love is of the beautiful; and therefore Love is also a philosopher or lover of wisdom, and being a lover of wisdom is in a mean between the wise and the ignorant. And of this too his birth is the cause; for his father is wealthy and wise, and his mother poor and foolish. Such, my dear Socrates, is the nature of the spirit Love. The error in your conception of him was very natural, and as I imagine from what you say, has arisen out of a confusion of love and the beloved, which made you think that love was all beautiful. For the beloved is the truly beautiful, and delicate, and perfect, and blessed; but the principle of love is of another nature, and is such as I have described.'

I said: 'O thou stranger woman, thou sayest well; but, assuming Love to be such as you say, what is the use of him to men?' 'That, Socrates,' she replied, 'I will attempt to unfold: of his nature and birth I have already spoken; and you acknowledge that love is of the beautiful. But some one will say: Of the beautiful in what, Socrates and Diotima?—or rather let me put the question more clearly, and ask: When a man loves the beautiful, what does he desire?' I answered her 'That the beautiful may be his.' 'Still,' she said, 'the answer suggests a further question: What is given by the possession of beauty?' 'To what you have asked,' I replied, 'I have no answer ready.' 'Then,' she said, 'let me put the word "good" in the place of the beautiful, and repeat the question once more: If he who loves loves the good, what is it then that he loves?' 'The possession of the good,' I said. 'And what does he gain who possesses the good?' 'Happiness,' I replied; 'there is less difficulty in answering that question.' 'Yes,' she said, 'the happy are made happy by the acquisition of good things. Nor is there any need to ask why a man desires happiness; the answer is already final.' 'You are right,' I said. 'And is this wish and this desire common to all? and do all men always desire their own good, or only some men?—what say you?' 'All men,' I replied; 'the desire is common to all.' 'Why, then,' she rejoined, 'are not all men, Socrates, said to love, but only some of them? whereas you say that all men are always loving the same things.' 'I myself wonder,' I said, 'why this is.' 'There is nothing to wonder at,' she replied; 'the reason is that one part of love is separated off and receives the name of the whole, but the other parts have other names.' 'Give an illustration,' I said. She answered me as follows: 'There is poetry, which, as you know, is complex and manifold. All creation or passage of non-being into being is poetry or making, and the processes of all art are creative; and the masters of arts are all poets or makers.' 'Very true.' 'Still,' she said, 'you know that they are not called poets, but have other names; only that portion of the art which is separated off from the rest, and is concerned with music and metre, is termed poetry, and they who possess poetry in this sense of the word are called poets.' 'Very true,' I said. 'And the same holds of love. For you may say generally that all desire of good and happiness is only the great and subtle power of love; but they who are drawn towards him by any other path, whether the path of money-making or gymnastics or philosophy, are not called lovers—the name of the whole is appropriated to those whose affection takes one form only—they alone are said to love, or to be lovers.' 'I dare say,' I replied, 'that you are right.' 'Yes,' she added, 'and you hear people say that lovers are seeking for their other half; but I say that they are seeking neither for the half of themselves, nor for the whole, unless the half or the whole be also a good. And they will cut off their own hands and feet and cast them away, if they are evil; for they love not what is their own, unless perchance there be some one who calls what belongs to him the good, and what belongs to another the evil. For there is nothing which men love but the good. Is there anything?' 'Certainly, I should say, that there is nothing.' 'Then,' she said, 'the simple truth is, that men love the good.' 'Yes,' I said. 'To which must be added that they love the possession of the good?' 'Yes, that must be added.' 'And not only the possession, but the everlasting possession of the good?' 'That must be added too.' 'Then love,' she said, 'may be described generally as the love of the everlasting possession of the good?' 'That is most true.'

'Then if this be the nature of love, can you tell me further,' she said, 'what is the manner of the pursuit? what are they doing who show all this eagerness and heat which is called love? and what is the object which they have in view? Answer me.' 'Nay, Diotima,' I replied, 'if I had known, I should not have wondered at your wisdom, neither should I have come to learn from you about this very matter.' 'Well,' she said, 'I will teach you: —The object which they have in view is birth in beauty, whether of body or soul.' 'I do not understand you,' I said; 'the oracle requires an explanation.' 'I will make my meaning clearer,' she replied. 'I mean to say, that all men are bringing to the birth in their bodies and in their souls. There is a certain age at which human nature is desirous of procreation—procreation which must be in beauty and not in deformity; and this procreation is the union of man and woman, and is a divine thing; for conception and generation are an immortal principle in the mortal creature, and in the inharmonious they can never be. But the deformed is always inharmonious with the divine, and the beautiful harmonious. Beauty, then, is the destiny or goddess of parturition who presides at birth, and therefore, when approaching beauty, the conceiving power is propitious, and diffusive, and benign, and begets and bears fruit: at the sight of ugliness she frowns and contracts and has a sense of pain, and turns away, and shrivels up, and not without a pang refrains from conception. And this is the reason why, when the hour of conception arrives, and the teeming nature is full, there is such a flutter and ecstacy about beauty whose approach is the alleviation of the pain of travail. For love, Socrates, is not, as you imagine, the love of the beautiful only.' 'What then?' 'The love of generation and of birth in beauty.' 'Yes,' I said. 'Yes, indeed,' she replied. 'But why of generation?' 'Because to the mortal creature, generation is a sort of eternity and immortality,' she replied; 'and if, as has been already admitted, love is of the everlasting possession of the good, all men will necessarily desire immortality together with good: Wherefore love is of immortality.'

All this she taught me at various times when she spoke of love. And I remember her once saying to me, 'What is the cause, Socrates, of love, and the attendant desire? See you not how all animals, birds, as well as beasts, in their desire of procreation, are in agony when they take the infection of love, which begins with the desire of union; whereto is added the care of offspring, on whose behalf the weakest are ready to battle against the strongest even to the uttermost, and to die for them, and will let themselves be tormented with hunger or suffer anything in order to maintain their young. Man may be supposed to act thus from reason; but why should animals have these passionate feelings? Can you tell me why?' Again I replied that I did not know. She said to me: 'And do you expect ever to become a master in the art of love, if you do not know this?' 'But I have told you already, Diotima, that my ignorance is the reason why I come to you; for I am conscious that I want a teacher; tell me then the cause of this and of the other mysteries of love.' 'Marvel not,' she said, 'if you believe that love is of the immortal, as we have several times acknowledged; for here again, and on the same principle too, the mortal nature is seeking as far as is possible to be everlasting and immortal: and this is only to be attained by generation, because generation always leaves behind a new existence in the place of the old. Nay even in the life of the same individual there is succession and not absolute unity: a man is called the same, and yet in the short interval which elapses between youth and age, and in which every animal is said to have life and identity, he is undergoing a perpetual process of loss and reparation—hair, flesh, bones, blood, and the whole body are always changing. Which is true not only of the body, but also of the soul, whose habits, tempers, opinions, desires, pleasures, pains, fears, never remain the same in any one of us, but are always coming and going; and equally true of knowledge, and what is still more surprising to us mortals, not only do the sciences in general spring up and decay, so that in respect of them we are never the same; but each of them individually experiences a like change. For what is implied in the word "recollection," but the departure of knowledge, which is ever being forgotten, and is renewed and preserved by recollection, and appears to be the same although in reality new, according to that law of succession by which all mortal things are preserved, not absolutely the same, but by substitution, the old worn-out mortality leaving another new and similar existence behind—unlike the divine, which is always the same and not another? And in this way, Socrates, the mortal body, or mortal anything, partakes of immortality; but the immortal in another way. Marvel not then at the love which all men have of their offspring; for that universal love and interest is for the sake of immortality.'

I was astonished at her words, and said: 'Is this really true, O thou wise Diotima?' And she answered with all the authority of an accomplished sophist: 'Of that, Socrates, you may be assured;—think only of the ambition of men, and you will wonder at the senselessness of their ways, unless you consider how they are stirred by the love of an immortality of fame. They are ready to run all risks greater far than they would have run for their children, and to spend money and undergo any sort of toil, and even to die, for the sake of leaving behind them a name which shall be eternal. Do you imagine that Alcestis would have died to save Admetus, or Achilles to avenge Patroclus, or your own Codrus in order to preserve the kingdom for his sons, if they had not imagined that the memory of their virtues, which still survives among us, would be immortal? Nay,' she said, 'I am persuaded that all men do all things, and the better they are the more they do them, in hope of the glorious fame of immortal virtue; for they desire the immortal.

'Those who are pregnant in the body only, betake themselves to women and beget children—this is the character of their love; their offspring, as they hope, will preserve their memory and give them the blessedness and immortality which they desire in the future. But souls which are pregnant —for there certainly are men who are more creative in their souls than in their bodies—conceive that which is proper for the soul to conceive or contain. And what are these conceptions?—wisdom and virtue in general. And such creators are poets and all artists who are deserving of the name inventor. But the greatest and fairest sort of wisdom by far is that which is concerned with the ordering of states and families, and which is called temperance and justice. And he who in youth has the seed of these implanted in him and is himself inspired, when he comes to maturity desires to beget and generate. He wanders about seeking beauty that he may beget offspring—for in deformity he will beget nothing—and naturally embraces the beautiful rather than the deformed body; above all when he finds a fair and noble and well-nurtured soul, he embraces the two in one person, and to such an one he is full of speech about virtue and the nature and pursuits of a good man; and he tries to educate him; and at the touch of the beautiful which is ever present to his memory, even when absent, he brings forth that which he had conceived long before, and in company with him tends that which he brings forth; and they are married by a far nearer tie and have a closer friendship than those who beget mortal children, for the children who are their common offspring are fairer and more immortal. Who, when he thinks of Homer and Hesiod and other great poets, would not rather have their children than ordinary human ones? Who would not emulate them in the creation of children such as theirs, which have preserved their memory and given them everlasting glory? Or who would not have such children as Lycurgus left behind him to be the saviours, not only of Lacedaemon, but of Hellas, as one may say? There is Solon, too, who is the revered father of Athenian laws; and many others there are in many other places, both among Hellenes and barbarians, who have given to the world many noble works, and have been the parents of virtue of every kind; and many temples have been raised in their honour for the sake of children such as theirs; which were never raised in honour of any one, for the sake of his mortal children.

'These are the lesser mysteries of love, into which even you, Socrates, may enter; to the greater and more hidden ones which are the crown of these, and to which, if you pursue them in a right spirit, they will lead, I know not whether you will be able to attain. But I will do my utmost to inform you, and do you follow if you can. For he who would proceed aright in this matter should begin in youth to visit beautiful forms; and first, if he be guided by his instructor aright, to love one such form only—out of that he should create fair thoughts; and soon he will of himself perceive that the beauty of one form is akin to the beauty of another; and then if beauty of form in general is his pursuit, how foolish would he be not to recognize that the beauty in every form is one and the same! And when he perceives this he will abate his violent love of the one, which he will despise and deem a small thing, and will become a lover of all beautiful forms; in the next stage he will consider that the beauty of the mind is more honourable than the beauty of the outward form. So that if a virtuous soul have but a little comeliness, he will be content to love and tend him, and will search out and bring to the birth thoughts which may improve the young, until he is compelled to contemplate and see the beauty of institutions and laws, and to understand that the beauty of them all is of one family, and that personal beauty is a trifle; and after laws and institutions he will go on to the sciences, that he may see their beauty, being not like a servant in love with the beauty of one youth or man or institution, himself a slave mean and narrow-minded, but drawing towards and contemplating the vast sea of beauty, he will create many fair and noble thoughts and notions in boundless love of wisdom; until on that shore he grows and waxes strong, and at last the vision is revealed to him of a single science, which is the science of beauty everywhere. To this I will proceed; please to give me your very best attention:

'He who has been instructed thus far in the things of love, and who has learned to see the beautiful in due order and succession, when he comes toward the end will suddenly perceive a nature of wondrous beauty (and this, Socrates, is the final cause of all our former toils)—a nature which in the first place is everlasting, not growing and decaying, or waxing and waning; secondly, not fair in one point of view and foul in another, or at one time or in one relation or at one place fair, at another time or in another relation or at another place foul, as if fair to some and foul to others, or in the likeness of a face or hands or any other part of the bodily frame, or in any form of speech or knowledge, or existing in any other being, as for example, in an animal, or in heaven, or in earth, or in any other place; but beauty absolute, separate, simple, and everlasting, which without diminution and without increase, or any change, is imparted to the ever-growing and perishing beauties of all other things. He who from these ascending under the influence of true love, begins to perceive that beauty, is not far from the end. And the true order of going, or being led by another, to the things of love, is to begin from the beauties of earth and mount upwards for the sake of that other beauty, using these as steps only, and from one going on to two, and from two to all fair forms, and from fair forms to fair practices, and from fair practices to fair notions, until from fair notions he arrives at the notion of absolute beauty, and at last knows what the essence of beauty is. This, my dear Socrates,' said the stranger of Mantineia, 'is that life above all others which man should live, in the contemplation of beauty absolute; a beauty which if you once beheld, you would see not to be after the measure of gold, and garments, and fair boys and youths, whose presence now entrances you; and you and many a one would be content to live seeing them only and conversing with them without meat or drink, if that were possible—you only want to look at them and to be with them. But what if man had eyes to see the true beauty—the divine beauty, I mean, pure and clear and unalloyed, not clogged with the pollutions of mortality and all the colours and vanities of human life—thither looking, and holding converse with the true beauty simple and divine? Remember how in that communion only, beholding beauty with the eye of the mind, he will be enabled to bring forth, not images of beauty, but realities (for he has hold not of an image but of a reality), and bringing forth and nourishing true virtue to become the friend of God and be immortal, if mortal man may. Would that be an ignoble life?'

Such, Phaedrus—and I speak not only to you, but to all of you—were the words of Diotima; and I am persuaded of their truth. And being persuaded of them, I try to persuade others, that in the attainment of this end human nature will not easily find a helper better than love. And therefore, also, I say that every man ought to honour him as I myself honour him, and walk in his ways, and exhort others to do the same, and praise the power and spirit of love according to the measure of my ability now and ever.

The words which I have spoken, you, Phaedrus, may call an encomium of love, or anything else which you please.

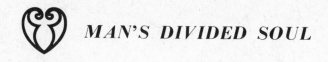

Plato

At first sight what is most puzzling about Eros is its call upon man for self-love. Isn't self-love man's natural condition and one which demands therapy? Isn't self-love the evidence of his "perversity of will" and the cause of much human suffering? So says Christianity; and here looms a severe problem of understanding for the reader whose background is Christian. For if he wishes to grasp Eros he must be able to set aside Christian presuppositions for very different ones. At the very core of Eros is a conception of man which is at odds with the Christian, a conception which appears in Plato's image of the human soul as a charioteer with two horses, the white one aiming aloft while the black one tries to plunge below.

By no means, the image tells us, is man simple and unidirectional (as egoistical doctrines present him). Instead he is a divided being, a radical equivocation, an argument with himself. He is torn between impulses of self-affirmation and self-negation, self-love and self-hatred. Only thus do the blockages and convolutions of human history, whether of mankind or of the individual, become intelligible.

The obstacle to the realization of full humanness comes not from the outside, but from within. Nor can anything outside of man relieve him of his essential task—becoming himself. The work will only be begun in earnest when the impulses to self-negation (the black horse) are checked, harnessed, and turned to the upward direction of the white horse.

Moreover each individual must first affirm the humanity within himself before he can be capable of affirming it in others. Self-love is the precondition of the love of others. Let the world beware of the man who hates himself, for he will perpetually revenge himself upon his neighbors.

. . . Of the nature of the soul, though her true form be ever a theme of large and more than mortal discourse, let me speak briefly, and in a figure. And let the figure be composite—a pair of winged horses and a charioteer. Now the winged horses and the charioteers of the gods are all of them noble and of noble descent, but those of other races are mixed; the human charioteer drives his in a pair; and one of them is noble and of noble breed, and the other is ignoble and of ignoble breed; and the driving of them of necessity gives a great deal of trouble to him. I will endeavour to explain

From the *Phaedrus. The Dialogues of Plato,* trans. B. Jowett, 3rd ed. (Oxford University Press, 1892), Vol. 1, pp. 452–453 and 460–461. Reprinted by permission of Oxford University Press.

to you in what way the mortal differs from the immortal creature. The soul in her totality has the care of inanimate being everywhere, and traverses the whole heaven in divers forms appearing;—when perfect and fully winged she soars upward, and orders the whole world; whereas the imperfect soul, losing her wings and drooping in her flight at last settles on the solid ground—there, finding a home, she receives an earthly frame which appears to be self-moved, but is really moved by her power; and this composition of soul and body is called a living and mortal creature. For immortal no such union can be reasonably believed to be; although fancy, not having seen nor surely known the nature of God, may imagine an immortal creature having both a body and also a soul which are united throughout all time. Let that, however, be as God wills, and be spoken of acceptably to him. And now let us ask the reason why the soul loses her wings!

The wing is the corporeal element which is most akin to the divine, and which by nature tends to soar aloft and carry that which gravitates downwards into the upper region, which is the habitation of the gods. The divine is beauty, wisdom, goodness, and the like; and by these the wing of the soul is nourished, and grows apace; but when fed upon evil and foulness and the opposite of good, wastes and falls away. Zeus, the mighty lord, holding the reins of a winged chariot, leads the way in heaven, ordering all and taking care of all; and there follows him the array of gods and demi-gods, marshalled in eleven bands; Hestia alone abides at home in the house of heaven; of the rest they who are reckoned among the princely twelve march in their appointed order. They see many blessed sights in the inner heaven, and there are many ways to and fro, along which the blessed gods are passing, every one doing his own work; he may follow who will and can, for jealousy has no place in the celestial choir. But when they go to banquet and festival, then they move up the steep to the top of the vault of heaven. The chariots of the gods in even poise, obeying the rein, glide rapidly; but the others labour, for the vicious steed goes heavily, weighing down the charioteer to the earth when his steed has not been thoroughly trained: —and this is the hour of agony and extremest conflict for the soul. For the immortals when they are at the end of their course, go forth and stand upon the outside of heaven, and the revolution of the spheres carries them round, and they behold the things beyond. . . .

As I said at the beginning of this tale, I divided each soul into three— two horses and a charioteer; and one of the horses was good and the other bad: the division may remain, but I have not yet explained in what the goodness or badness of either consists, and to that I will now proceed. The right-hand horse is upright and cleanly made; he has a lofty neck and an aquiline nose; his colour is white, and his eyes dark; he is a lover of honour and modesty and temperance, and the follower of true glory; he needs no touch of the whip, but is guided by word and admonition only. The other is a crooked lumbering animal, put together anyhow; he has a short thick neck; he is flat-faced and of a dark colour, with grey eyes and blood-red complexion; the mate of insolence and pride, shag-eared and deaf, hardly yielding to whip and spur. Now when the charioteer beholds the vision of love, and has his whole soul warmed through sense, and is full of the prickings and ticklings of desire, the obedient steed, then as always under the government of shame, refrains from leaping on the beloved; but the other, heedless of the pricks and of the blows of the whip, plunges and runs away, giving all manner of trouble to his companion and the charioteer, whom he forces to approach the beloved and to remember the joys of love. They at first indignantly oppose him and will not be urged on to do terrible and unlawful deeds; but at last, when he persists in plaguing them, they yield and agree to do as he bids them. And now they are at the spot and behold the flashing beauty of the beloved; which when the charioteer sees, his memory is carried to the true beauty, whom he beholds in company with Modesty like an image placed upon a holy pedestal. He sees her, but he is afraid and falls backwards in adoration, and by his fall is compelled to pull back the reins with such violence as to bring both the steeds on their haunches, the one willing and unresisting, the unruly one very unwilling; and when they have gone back a little, the one is overcome with shame and wonder, and his whole soul is bathed in perspiration; the other, when the pain is over which the bridle and the fall had given him, having with difficulty taken breath, is full of wrath and reproaches, which he heaps upon the charioteer and his fellow-steed, for want of courage and manhood, declaring that they have been false to their agreement and guilty of desertion. Again they refuse, and again he urges them on, and will scarce yield to their prayer that he would wait until another time. When the appointed hour comes, they make as if they had forgotten, and he reminds them, fighting and neighing and dragging them on, until at length he on the same thoughts intent, forces them to draw near again. And when they are near he stoops his head and puts up his tail, and takes the bit in his teeth and pulls shamelessly. Then the charioteer is worse off than ever; he falls back like a racer at the barrier, and with a still more violent wrench drags the bit out of the teeth of the wild steed and covers his abusive tongue and jaws with blood, and forces his legs and haunches to the ground and punishes him sorely. And when this has happened several times and the villain has ceased from his wanton way, he is tamed and humbled, and follows the will of the charioteer, and when he sees the beautiful one he is ready to die of fear. And from that time forward the soul of the lover follows the beloved in modesty and holy fear.

 **DIVINE MADNESS**

Plato

The popular notion of "scientific objectivity" in matters of knowledge (deriving from John Locke and the early empiricists) banishes emotion from the domain of inquiry. But is it safe to say that emotion per se is detrimental to inquiry, or must we proceed more carefully, distinguishing emotions of various kinds and interrogating them separately?

For Plato one emotion is inseparable from the enterprise of knowledge and utterly essential to it—the emotion of love in the mode of Eros. Eros is the movement of the lover to the object of his love. In love he goes to it, into it. Without this migration "knowledge" is mere pragmata, registering what the other is to us.

The lover goes out of himself, he is "not himself." Here lies the association of love with madness. The lover is suddenly indifferent to ordinary prudential concerns, he is deaf to "commonsense." But this is precisely love's virtue according to which Plato terms its madness "the greatest of heaven's blessings." For Plato is no friend of commonsense, but views it as shared prejudice about, not reality, but shadows in a cave. Accordingly to "release the soul from the yoke of custom and convention" is the divine function of love.

Against the worldly advice that love is blind Plato insists that blindness is the consequence of the absence of love.

Socrates: Know then, fair youth, that the former discourse was the word of Phaedrus, the son of Vain Man, who dwells in the city of Myrrhina (Myrrhinusius). And this which I am about to utter is the recantation of Stesichorus the son of Godly Man (Euphemus), who comes from the town of Desire (Himera), and is to the following effect: 'I told a lie when I said' that the beloved ought to accept the nonlover when he might have the lover, because the one is sane, and the other mad. It might be so if madness were simply an evil; but there is also a madness which is a divine gift, and the source of the chiefest blessings granted to men. For prophecy is a madness, and the prophetess at Delphi and the priestesses at Dodona when out of their senses have conferred great benefits on Hellas, both in public and private life, but when in their senses few or none. And I might also tell you how the Sibyl and other inspired persons have given to many

From the *Phaedrus. The Dialogues of Plato*, trans. B. Jowett, 3rd ed. (Oxford University Press, 1892), Vol. 1, pp. 449-451, 453-456, 458-460. Reprinted by permission of Oxford University Press.

an one many an intimation of the future which has saved them from falling. But it would be tedious to speak of what every one knows.

There will be more reason in appealing to the ancient inventors of names, who would never have connected prophecy (μαντική), which foretells the future and is the noblest of arts, with madness (μανική), or called them both by the same name, if they had deemed madness to be a disgrace or dishonour;—they must have thought that there was an inspired madness which was a noble thing; for the two words, μαντική and μανική, are really the same, and the letter τ is only a modern and tasteless insertion. And this is confirmed by the name which was given by them to the rational investigation of futurity, whether made by the help of birds or of other signs—this, for as much as it is an art which supplies from the reasoning faculty mind (νοῦς) and information (ἱστορία) to human thought (οἴησις), they originally termed οἰονοιοτική, but the word has been lately altered and made sonorous by the modern introduction of the letter Omega (οἰονοιοτική and οἰωνστική), and in proportion as prophecy (μαντική) is more perfect and august than augury, both in name and fact, in the same proportion, as the ancients testify, is madness superior to a sane mind (σωφροσύνη), for the one is only of human, but the other of divine origin. Again, where plagues and mightiest woes have bred in certain families, owing to some ancient blood-guiltiness, there madness has entered with holy prayers and rites, and by inspired utterances found a way of deliverance for those who are in need; and he who has part in this gift, and is truly possessed and duly out of his mind, is by the use of purifications and mysteries made whole and exempt from evil, future as well as present, and has a release from the calamity which was afflicting him. The third kind is the madness of those who are possessed by the Muses; which taking hold of a delicate and virgin soul, and there inspiring frenzy, awakens lyrical and all other numbers; with these adorning the myriad actions of ancient heroes for the instruction of posterity. But he who, having no touch of the Muses' madness in his soul, comes to the door and thinks that he will get into the temple by the help of art—he, I say, and his poetry are not admitted; the sane man disappears and is nowhere when he enters into rivalry with the madman.

I might tell of many other noble deeds which have sprung from inspired madness. And therefore, let no one frighten or flutter us by saying that the temperate friend is to be chosen rather than the inspired, but let him further show that love is not sent by the gods for any good to lover or beloved; if he can do so we will allow him to carry off the palm. And we, on our part, will prove in answer to him that the madness of love is the greatest of heaven's blessings, and the proof shall be one which the wise will receive, and the witling disbelieve. . . .

But of the heaven which is above the heavens, what earthly poet ever did or ever will sing worthily? It is such as I will describe; for I must dare to speak the truth, when truth is my theme. There abides the very being with which true knowledge is concerned; the colourless, formless, intangible essence, visible only to mind, the pilot of the soul. The divine intelligence, being nurtured upon mind and pure knowledge, and the intelligence of every soul which is capable of receiving the food proper to it, rejoices at beholding reality, and once more gazing upon truth, is replenished and made glad, until the revolution of the worlds brings her round again to the same place. In the revolution she beholds justice, and temperance, and knowledge absolute, not in the form of generation or of relation, which men call existence, but knowledge absolute in existence absolute; and beholding the other true existences in like manner, and feasting upon them, she passes down into the interior of the heavens and returns home; and there the charioteer putting up his horses at the stall, gives them ambrosia to eat and nectar to drink.

Such is the life of the gods; but of other souls, that which follows God best and is likest to him lifts the head of the charioteer into the outer world, and is carried round in the revolution, troubled indeed by the steeds, and with difficulty beholding true being; while another only rises and falls, and sees, and again fails to see by reason of the unruliness of the steeds. The rest of the souls are also longing after the upper world and they all follow, but not being strong enough they are carried round below the surface, plunging, treading on one another, each striving to be first; and there is confusion and perspiration and the extremity of effort; and many of them are lamed or have their wings broken through the ill-driving of the charioteers; and all of them after a fruitless toil, not having attained to the mysteries of true being, go away, and feed upon opinion. The reason why the souls exhibit this exceeding eagerness to behold the plain of truth is that pasturage is found there, which is suited to the highest part of the soul; and the wing on which the soul soars is nourished with this. And there is a law of Destiny, that the soul which attains any vision of truth in company with a god is preserved from harm until the next period, and if attaining always is always unharmed. But when she is unable to follow, and fails to behold the truth, and through some ill-hap sinks beneath the double load of forgetfulness and vice, and her wings fall from her and she drops to the ground, then the law ordains that this soul shall at her first birth pass, not into any other animal, but only into man; and the soul which has seen most of truth shall come to the birth as a philosopher, or artist, or some musical and loving nature; that which has seen truth in the second degree shall be some righteous king or warrior chief; the soul which is of the third class shall be a politician, or economist, or trader; the fourth shall be a lover of gymnastic toils, or a physician; the fifth shall lead the life of a prophet or hierophant; to the sixth the character of a poet or some other imitative artists will be assigned; to the seventh the life of an artisan or husbandman; to the eighth that of a sophist or demagogue; to the ninth that of a tyrant;—all these are states of probation, in which he who does righteously improves, and he who does unrighteously, deteriorates his lot.

Ten thousand years must elapse before the soul of each one can return to the place from whence she came, for she cannot grow her wings in less; only the soul of a philosopher, guileless and true, or the soul of a lover, who is not devoid of philosophy, may acquire wings in the third of the recurring periods of a thousand year; he is distinguished from the ordinary good man who gains wings in three thousand years:—and they who choose this life three times in succession have wings given them, and go away at the end of three thousand years. But the others[1] receive judgment when they have completed their first life, and after the judgment they go, some of them to the houses of correction which are under the earth, and are punished; others to some place in heaven whither they are lightly borne by justice, and there they live in a manner worthy of the life which they led here when in the form of men. And at the end of the first thousand years the good souls and also the evil souls both come to draw lots and choose their second life, and they may take any which they please. The soul of a man may pass into the life of a beast, or from the beast return again into the man. But the soul which has never seen the truth will not pass into the human form. For a man must have intelligence of universals, and be able to proceed from the many particulars of sense to one conception of reason;—this is the recollection of those things which our soul once saw while following God—when regardless of that which we now call being she raised her head up towards the true being. And therefore the mind of the philosopher alone has wings; and this is just, for he is always, according to the measure of his abilities, clinging in recollection to those things in which God abides, and in beholding which He is what He is. And he who employs aright these memories is ever being initiated into perfect mysteries and alone becomes truly perfect. But, as he forgets earthly interests and is rapt in the divine, the vulgar deem him mad, and rebuke him; they do not see that he is inspired.

Thus far I have been speaking of the fourth and last kind of madness, which is imputed to him who, when he sees the beauty of earth, is transported with the recollection of the true beauty; he would like to fly away, but he cannot; he is like a bird fluttering and looking upward and careless of the world below; and he is therefore thought to be mad. And I have shown this of all inspirations to be the noblest and highest and the offspring of the highest to him who has or shares in it, and that he who loves the beautiful is called a lover because he partakes of it. For, as has been already said, every soul of man has in the way of nature beheld true being; this was the condition of her passing into the form of man.

[1]The philosopher alone is not subject to judgment (κρίσις) for he has never lost the vision of truth.

But all souls do not easily recall the things of the other world; they may have been unfortunate in their earthly lot, and, having had their hearts turned to unrighteousness through some corrupting influence, they may have lost the memory of the holy things which once they saw. Few only retain an adequate remembrance of them; and they, when they behold here any image of that other world, are rapt in amazement; but they are ignorant of what this rapture means, because they do not clearly perceive. . . .

The soul of the lover will never forsake his beautiful one, whom he esteems above all; he has forgotten mother and brethren and companions, and he thinks nothing of the neglect and loss of his property; the rules and proprieties of life, on which he formerly prided himself, he now despises, and is ready to sleep like a servant, wherever he is allowed, as near as he can to his desired one, who is the object of his worship, and the physician who can alone assuage the greatness of his pain. And this state, my dear imaginary youth to whom I am talking, is by men called love, and among the gods has a name at which you, in your simplicity, may be inclined to mock; there are two lines in the apocryphal writings of Homer in which the name occurs. One of them is rather outrageous, and not altogether metrical. They are as follows:—

> 'Mortals call him fluttering love,
> But the immortals call him winged one,
> Because the growing of wings is a necessity to him.'

You may believe this, but not unless you like. At any rate the loves of lovers and their causes are such as I have described.

Now the lover who is taken to be the attendant of Zeus is better able to bear the winged god, and can endure a heavier burden; but the attendants and companions of Ares, when under the influence of love, if they fancy that they have been at all wronged, are ready to kill and put an end to themselves and their beloved. And he who follows in the train of any other god, while he is unspoiled and the impression lasts, honours and imitates him, as far as he is able; and after the manner of his God he behaves in his intercourse with his beloved and with the rest of the world during the first period of his earthly existence. Every one chooses his love from the ranks of beauty according to his character, and this he makes his god, and fashions and adorns as a sort of image which he is to fall down and worship. The followers of Zeus desire that their beloved should have a soul like him; and therefore they seek out some one of a philosophical and imperial nature, and when they have found him and loved him, they do all they can to confirm such a nature in him, and if they have no experience of such a disposition hitherto, they learn of any one who can teach them, and themselves follow in the same way. And they have the less difficulty in finding the nature of their own god in themselves, because they have been compelled to gaze intensely on him; their recollection clings to him, and they become possessed of him, and receive from him their character and disposition, so far as man can participate in God. The qualities of their god they attribute to the beloved, wherefore they love him all the more, and if, like the Bacchic Nymphs, they draw inspiration from Zeus, they pour out their own fountain upon him, wanting to make him as like as possible to their own god. But those who are the followers of Herè seek a royal love, and when they have found him they do just the same with him; and in like manner the followers of Apollo, and of every other god walking in the ways of their god, seek a love who is to be made like him whom they serve, and when they have found him, they themselves imitate their god, and persuade their love to do the same, and educate him into the manner and nature of the god as far as they each can; for no feelings of envy or jealousy are entertained by them towards their beloved, but they do their utmost to create in him the greatest likeness of themselves and of the god whom they honour. Thus fair and blissful to the beloved is the desire of the inspired lover, and the initiation of which I speak into the mysteries of true love, if he be captured by the lover and their purpose is effected.

 *SELF-LOVE*

Aristotle

"Become what you are" is the second great humanist imperative. It follows "Know Thyself" out of the recognition that the individual is free to affirm or deny himself. He may fear, despise, or hate himself, and long to be relieved of himself in favor of a life the responsibility for which lies elsewhere. Against this humanism demands self-affirmation—love of the unique and innate ideal within each person which constitutes the person's truest self and his task.

Aristotle discusses those who "shun" themselves, observing that he who is not "amicably disposed" to himself cannot be friend to others but spreads the diseases of hatred and dissention wherever he goes. Here is the locus classicus *of humanism's diagnosis of human evil: the source of the hatred of others is self-hatred; the source of envy and jealousy is lack of self-esteem; the ground of ignorance of life and the world is absence of self-knowledge.*

It is to this core that all of the healing effort of Greek pedagogy, Renaissance humanism, contemporary existential and humanistic psychotherapy, is directed.

In the second part of the selection Aristotle seeks to distinguish self-love in the mode of Eros from the vanity and egoism with which it is sometimes confused.

Friendly relations with one's neighbours, and the marks by which friendships are defined, seem to have proceeded from a man's relations to himself. For (1) we define a friend as one who wishes and does what is good, or seems so, for the sake of his friend, or (2) as one who wishes his friend to exist and live, for his sake; which mothers do to their children, and friends do who have come into conflict. And (3) others define him as one who lives with and (4) has the same tastes as another, or (5) one who grieves and rejoices with his friend; and this too is found in mothers most of all. It is by some one of these characteristics that friendship too is defined.

Now each of these is true of the good man's relation to himself (and of all other men in so far as they think themselves good; virtue and the good

Nichomachean Ethics, Book 9, Chaps. 4 and 8, trans. W. D. Ross, from *The Oxford Translation of Aristotle*, Ed. W. D. Ross, vol. 9 (1925). Reprinted by permission of the Clarendon Press, Oxford and Random House, Inc. The text used here is from *The Basic Works of Aristotle*, ed. Richard McKeon (New York: Random House, 1941), pp. 1081–1083 and 1086–1088.

man seem, as has been said, to be the measure of every class of things). For his opinions are harmonious, and he desires the same things with all his soul; and therefore he wishes for himself what is good and what seems so, and does it (for it is characteristic of the good man to work out the good), and does so for his own sake (for he does it for the sake of the intellectual element in him, which is thought to be the man himself); and he wishes himself to live and be preserved, and especially the element by virtue of which he thinks. For existence is good to the virtuous man, and each man wishes himself what is good, while no one chooses to possess the whole world if he has first to become some one else (for that matter, even now God possesses the good[1]); he wishes for this only on condition of being whatever he is; and the element that thinks would seem to be the individual man, or to be so more than any other element in him. And such a man wishes to live with himself; for he does so with pleasure, since the memories of his past acts are delightful and his hopes for the future are good, and therefore pleasant. His mind is well stored too with subjects of contemplation. And he grieves and rejoices, more than any other, with himself; for the same thing is always painful, and the same thing always pleasant, and not one thing at one time and another at another; he has, so to speak, nothing to repent of.

Therefore, since each of these characteristics belongs to the good man in relation to himself, and he is related to his friend as to himself (for his friend is another self), friendship too is thought to be one of these attributes, and those who have these attributes to be friends. Whether there is or is not friendship between a man and himself is a question we may dismiss for the present; there would seem to be friendship in so far as he is two or more, to judge from the aforementioned attributes of friendship, and from the fact that the extreme of friendship is likened to one's love for oneself.

But the attributes named seem to belong even to the majority of men, poor creatures though they may be. Are we to say then that in so far as they are satisfied with themselves and think they are good, they share in these attributes? Certainly no one who is thoroughly bad and impious has these attributes, or even seems to do so. They hardly belong even to inferior people; for they are at variance with themselves, and have appetites for some things and rational desires for others. This is true, for instance, of incontinent people; for they choose, instead of the things they themselves think good, things that are pleasant but hurtful; while others again, through cowardice and laziness, shrink from doing what they think best for themselves. And those who have done many terrible deeds and are hated for their wickedness even shrink from life and destroy themselves. And wicked men

[1] *sc.* but as no one gains by God's now having the good, he would not gain if a new person which was no longer himself were to possess it.

seek for people with whom to spend their days, and shun themselves; for they remember many a grievous deed, and anticipate others like them, when they are by themselves, but when they are with others they forget. And having nothing lovable in them they have no feeling of love to themselves. Therefore also such men do not rejoice or grieve with themselves; for their soul is rent by faction, and one element in it by reason of its wickedness grieves when it abstains from certain acts, while the other part is pleased, and one draws them this way and the other that, as if they were pulling them in pieces. If a man cannot at the same time be pained and pleased, at all events after a short time he is pained *because* he was pleased, and he could have wished that these things had not been pleasant to him; for bad men are laden with repentance.

Therefore the bad man does not seem to be amicably disposed even to himself, because there is nothing in him to love; so that if to be thus is the height of wretchedness, we should strain every nerve to avoid wickedness and should endeavour to be good; for so and only so can one be either friendly to oneself or a friend to another. . . .

The question is also debated, whether a man should love himself most, or some one else. People criticize those who love themselves most, and call them self-lovers, using this as an epithet of disgrace, and a bad man seems to do everything for his own sake, and the more so the more wicked he is— and so men reproach him, for instance, with doing nothing of his own accord—while the good man acts for honour's sake, and the more so the better he is, and acts for his friend's sake, and sacrifices his own interest.

But the facts clash with these arguments, and this is not surprising. For men say that one ought to love best one's best friend, and a man's best friend is one who wishes well to the object of his wish for his sake, even if no one is to know of it; and these attributes are found most of all in a man's attitude towards himself, and so are all the other attributes by which a friend is defined; for, as we have said, it is from this relation that all the characteristics of friendship have extended to our neighbours. All the proverbs, too, agree with this, e.g. 'a single soul', and 'what friends have is common property', and 'friendship is equality', and 'charity begins at home'; for all these marks will be found most in a man's relation to himself; he is his own best friend and therefore ought to love himself best. It is therefore a reasonable question, which of the two views we should follow; for both are plausible.

Perhaps we ought to mark off such arguments from each other and determine how far and in what respects each view is right. Now if we grasp the sense in which each school uses the phrase 'lover of self,' the truth may become evident. Those who use the term as one of reproach ascribe self-love to people who assign to themselves the greater share of wealth, honours, and bodily pleasures; for these are what most people desire, and busy themselves about as though they were the best of all things, which is the reason, too, why they become objects of competition. So those who are grasping with regard to these things gratify their appetites and in general their feelings and the irrational element of the soul; and most men are of this nature (which is the reason why the epithet has come to be used as it is—it takes its meaning from the prevailing type of self-love, which is a bad one); it is just, therefore, that men who are lovers of self in this way are reproached for being so. That it is those who give themselves the preference in regard to objects of this sort that most people usually call lovers of self is plain; for if a man were always anxious that he himself, above all things, should act justly, temperately, or in accordance with any other of the virtues, and in general were always to try to secure for himself the honourable course, no one will call such a man a lover of self or blame him.

But such a man would seem more than the other a lover of self; at all events he assigns to himself the things that are noblest and best, and gratifies the most authoritative element in himself and in all things obeys this; and just as a city or any other systematic whole is most properly identified with the most authoritative element in it, so is a man; and therefore the man who loves this and gratifies it is most of all a lover of self. Besides, a man is said to have or not to have self-control according as his reason has or has not the control, on the assumption that this is the man himself; and the things men have done on a rational principle are thought most properly their own acts and voluntary acts. That this is the man himself, then, or is so more than anything else, is plain, and also that the good man loves most this part of him. Whence it follows that he is most truly a lover of self, of another type than that which is a matter of reproach, and as different from that as living according to a rational principle is from living as passion dictates, and desiring what is noble from desiring what seems advantageous. Those, then, who busy themselves in an exceptional degree with noble actions all men approve and praise; and if *all* were to strive towards what is noble and strain every nerve to do the noblest deeds, everything would be as it should be for the common weal, and every one would secure for himself the goods that are greatest, since virtue is the greatest of goods.

Therefore the good man should be a lover of self (for he will both himself profit by doing noble acts, and will benefit his fellows), but the wicked man should not; for he will hurt both himself and his neighbours, following as he does evil passions. For the wicked man, what he does clashes with what he ought to do, but what the good man ought to do he does; for reason in each of its possessors chooses what is best for itself, and the good man obeys his reason. It is true of the good man too that he does many acts for the sake of his friends and his country, and if necessary dies for them; for he will throw away both wealth and honours and in general the goods that are objects of competition, gaining for himself nobility; since he would prefer a short period of intense pleasure to a long one of mild enjoyment, a twelvemonth of noble life to many years of humdrum existence, and one great and noble action to many trivial ones. Now those who die for others doubtless attain this result; it is therefore a great prize that they choose for themselves. They will throw away wealth too on condition that their friends will gain more; for while a man's friend gains wealth he himself achieves nobility; he is therefore assigning the greater good to himself. The same too is true of honour and office; all these things he will sacrifice to his friend; for this is noble and laudable for himself. Rightly then is he thought to be good, since he chooses nobility before all else. But he may even give up actions to his friend; it may be nobler to become the cause of his friend's acting than to act himself. In all the actions, therefore, that men are praised for, the good man is seen to assign to himself the greater share in what is noble. In this sense, then, as has been said, a man should be a lover of self; but in the sense in which most men are so, he ought not.

MAN'S VOCATION

José Ortega y Gasset

Ortega's little essay is deceptive in a number of ways. It is written in galloping style, but it is the product of long and careful thought. And its apparent subject is Goethe (it was written for the centenary of Goethe's death), while its true theme is Eros. It is a mine of insights into the processes of self-discovery and self-realization which are central to the Eros tradition. Under Ortega's hastening pen these insights wink on and off like fireflies, hence it will be helpful to identify some of the features of "vocation" at the outset.

"Vocation" is Ortega's synonym for the Greek "destiny." It is the individual's true direction in life, the path lying between his actuality and the ideal possibility within him which it is his task to become. Vocation (or destiny) is "precisely that which is not chosen." Ortega means by this that each person is given his destiny at birth, as the latent potential for the development of a distinctive personality and life-style. But the task of self-discovery is fraught with difficulties, for when the individual first turns in search of himself he must break through the child-identities which have been fashioned for him by parents and community. In search of this "programmatic personage" which he is, Ortega advises that the method of introspection is inadequate. For what he seeks "is discernible only a posteriori, in its collision with what befalls it." Destiny is lived outward, into an environment, and requires environmental resistances in order to manifest itself. The meaning of this is that exploration among alternative situations is necessary to self-discovery. Adolescence, then, should provide opportunity for such explorations, freeing the young person from the confines of childhood and at the same time postponing the need for decision.

Each person's vocation is utterly unique, representing a value which will not be realized other than through him. The process of self-realization is the emergence of individuality out of generality. Each of us begins as "herd" or "mass." Our early thoughts and feelings are by no means distinctively ours, having been imbibed from our surroundings. "Commonsense" and common feelings are "everyone's," which is to say no one's in particular. They are anonymous, and to the degree to which we partake of

From "In Search of Goethe from Within," by José Ortega y Gasset, trans. Willard R. Trask, copyright December, 1949, by *Partisan Review*. In José Ortega y Gasset, *The Dehumanization of Art and Other Essays on Art, Culture, and Literature* (Princeton University Press, 1968), pp. 133–135, 136–137, 140–145, 152–155, 159–160, and 168–170. Reprinted by permission of *Partisan Review*.

them we ourselves are anonymous. To the end, each of us will retain aspects of "mass" within him. But to the degree to which we pursue the course of our destiny, our beliefs and feelings will gain the special flavor which marks our distinction from others. Thus at the projected end of self-realization we find, not persons who have sought the same ideal and have merged into identity with one another, but a community of interacting uniquenesses, each of which contributes its special value to the whole.

"A man can have but one authentic life." By this Ortega calls attention to the exclusiveness of personal destiny. To become what my destiny calls me to be is at the same time not to become everything else. The youth is "everything potentially" because he is "not yet anything determinate and irrevocable." Here Ortega points out that a multiplicity of talents can disorient an individual and impede his decision for himself. To truly become a dancer a woman may be forced to abandon the idea of college and perhaps also marriage and motherhood. More important, if she retains to herself both marriage and motherhood, she cannot do so in the way in which these commitments are met by the woman whose vocation they constitute. She is wife and mother as a dancer. Today many women feel that this choice is unfairly imposed upon them by cultural convention and male domination. Ortega insists that such hard choices are the lot of men and women equally, imposed upon us by the requirement for determinacy. To remain "perpetually available," to keep all door open, is to preclude determinacy. The result is the life-style of the dilettante—a bit of this, that, and the other, but in the end nothing distinguishable.

The reader who gives thought to the features of "vocation" as here offered by Ortega will be helped to uncover the deeper meaning of the self-love (self-realization) which takes priority under Eros.

Life is an operation which is done in a forward direction. One lives *toward* the future, because to live consists inexorably in *doing*, in each individual life *making* itself. To call this "doing and making," "action," is only to becloud the terrible reality. "Action" is only the beginning of doing. It is only the moment when one decides what to do, when one makes up one's mind. *Im Anfang war die Tat*[1] is, therefore, a good saying. But life is not only beginning. Beginning is already *now*. And life is continuation, is survival into the moment which will arrive after *now*. Life, therefore, suffers under an inevitable imperative of realization. This necessity for actual realization in the world, beyond our simple subjectivity and intention, is what is expressed by "doing." It obliges us to seek means to survive, to execute the future—whereupon we discover the past as an arsenal of means, receipts, norms. The man who has not lost faith in the past is not frightened by the future, because he is sure that in the past he will

[1]"In the beginning was the act."

find the tactic, the method, the course, by which he can sustain himself in the problematic tomorrow. The future is the horizon of problems, the past is the *terra firma* of methods, of the roads which we believe we have under our feet. Consider, my dear friend, the terrible situation of the man to whom the past, the stable, suddenly becomes problematical, suddenly becomes an abyss. Previously, danger appeared to lie only before him, in the hazardous future; now he finds it also behind his back and under his feet.

Are we not undergoing something of the sort ourselves? We believed that we were the heirs of a magnificent past, and that we could live on the income of it. We find the future bearing down on us rather harder than it bore down on previous generations, we look back, according to our wont, for the traditional weapons; but when we take them up, we find that they are rubber daggers, inadequate gestures, theatrical "props" which shatter on the hard bronze of our future, of our problems. And suddenly we feel disinherited, traditionless, destitute, as if we were recent emigrants into life, without predecessors. "Patrician" was the Roman term for the man who could make a will and who left an inheritance. The rest were proletarians—descendants, but not heirs. Our heritage consisted in our methods—that is, in the classics. But the European crisis, which is the world crisis, may be diagnosed as a crisis of all classicism. We feel that the traditional ways are useless to solve our problems. People can go on writing books about the classics indefinitely. The easiest thing to do about anything is to write a book about it. The hard thing is to *live on* it. Can we live on our classics today? Is not Europe suffering from a strange proletarization? . . .

Life is, in itself and forever, shipwreck. To be shipwrecked is not to drown. The poor human being, feeling himself sinking into the abyss, moves his arms to keep afloat. This movement of the arms which is his reaction against his own destruction, is culture—a swimming stroke.— When culture is no more than this, it fulfills its function and the human being rises above his own abyss. But ten centuries of cultural continuity brings with it—among many advantages—the great disadvantage that man believes himself safe, loses the feeling of shipwreck, and his culture proceeds to burden itself with parasitic and lymphatic matter. Some discontinuity must therefore intervene, in order that man may renew his feeling of peril, the substance of his life. All his life-saving equipment must fail, he must find nothing to cling to. Then his arms will once again move redeemingly.

Consciousness of shipwreck, being the truth of life, constitutes salvation. Hence I no longer believe in any ideas except the ideas of shipwrecked men. We must call the classics before a court of shipwrecked men to answer certain peremptory questions with reference to real life. . . .

If you ask your own self, strictly and peremptorily, Who am I?—not,

What am I? but, Who is that *I* of whom I perpetually talk in my daily life—you will become aware of the incredible manner in which philosophy has always gone astray by giving the name of "I" to the most unlikely things but never to the thing that you call "I" in your daily life. That I which is you, my dear friend, does not consist in your body, nor yet in your soul, your consciousness, or your character. You found yourself with a body, a soul, a character, as you found yourself with the capital which your parents left you, with the country in which you were born, and with the human society in which you move. Just as you are not your liver, be it sound or diseased, neither are you your memory, be it good or bad, nor your will, be it strong or weak, nor your intelligence, be it acute or dull. The I which you are, found itself with these physical or psychical *things* when it found itself alive. You are the person who has to live *with* them, *by means of* them, and perhaps you spend your life protesting against the soul with which you were endowed—of its lack of will, for example—as you protest against your bad stomach or of the cold climate of your country. The soul, then, remains as much *outside* the *I* which you are, as the landscape remains outside your body. Let us say, if you choose, that among the things with which you found yourself, your soul is the closest to you, but it is not you yourself. We must learn to free ourselves from the traditional idea which would have reality always consist in some *thing*, be it physical or mental. You are no *thing*, you are simply the person who has to live *with* things, *among* things, the person who has to live, not *any* life but a *particular* life. There is no abstract living. Life means the inexorable necessity of realizing the design for an existence which each one of us is. This design in which the I consists, is not an idea or plan ideated by the person involved, and freely chosen. It is anterior to (in the sense of independent from) all the ideas which his intellect forms, to all the decisions of his will. Our will is free *to realize or not to realize* this vital design which we ultimately are, but it cannot correct it, change it, abbreviate it, or substitute anything for it. We are indelibly that single programmatic personage who must be realized. The outside world or our own character makes that realization easier or more difficult. Life is essentially a drama, because it is a desperate struggle—with things and even with our character—to succeed in being in fact that which we are in design.

This consideration permits us to give a biography a different structure from the usual one. Until now, the biographer at his most perspicacious has been a psychologist. He has had the gift of entering *into* a man and discovering all the clockwork which forms the character and, in general, the soul of his subject. Far be it from me to disdain these investigations. Biography requires psychology as it requires physiology. But all that is pure information.

We must get over the error which makes us think that a man's life takes place inside himself and that, consequently, it can be reduced to pure psychology. Would that our lives did take place inside ourselves! Then life would be the easiest thing imaginable: it would be to float in its own element. But life is as far as possible from a subjective phenomenon. It is the most objective of all realities. It is a man's *I* finding itself submerged in precisely what is not himself, in the pure *other* which is his environment. To live is to be outside oneself, to realize oneself.—The vital program which each one of us irremediably is, overpowers environment to lodge itself there. This unity of dramatic dynamism between the two elements, the I and the world—is life. Hence it forms a circumference within which are the person, the world, and . . . the biographer. . . .

Nothing can so properly be called *I* as that programmatic personage, because upon its peculiarity depends the value which all *our* things—our body, our soul, our character, our circumstances—finally assume in our life. They are ours through their favorable or unfavorable relation to the personage who has to be realized. For this reason, it cannot be said that two different men find themselves in the same situation. The disposition of things around them, which abstractly would seem to be identical, responds differently to the different inner destiny which is each of them. I am a certain absolutely individual pressure upon the world: the world is the no less definite and individual resistance to that pressure.

A man—that is, his soul, his gifts, his character, his body—is the sum of organs *by* which his life is lived; he is therefore equivalent to an actor bidden to represent the personage which is his real I. And here appears the most surprising thing in the drama of life: a man possesses a wide margin of freedom with respect to his I or destiny. He can refuse to realize it, he can be untrue to himself. Then his life lacks authenticity. If "vocation" is not taken to mean what it commonly does—merely a generic form of professional occupation, of the civil *curriculum*—but to mean an integral and individual program of existence, the simplest thing would be to say that our I is our vocation. Thus we can be true to our vocation to a greater or lesser degree, and consequently have a life that is authentic to a greater or lesser degree.

If the structure of human life is viewed in this light, the most important problems for a biography will be the two following, which have not as yet been much considered by biographers. The first consists in determining what the subject's vital vocation was, though it is entirely possible that he was never aware of it. Every life is, more or less, a ruin among whose debris we have to discover what the person ought to have been. This obliges us to construct for ourselves—as the physicist constructs his "models"—an imaginary life of the individual, the graph of his successful life, upon which we can then distribute the jags (they are sometimes enormous) which external destiny inflicted. We all feel our real life to be a deformation—sometimes greater, sometimes less—of our possible life. The second problem is to weigh the subject's fidelity to this unique destiny of his, to his possible life. This permits us to determine the degree of authenticity of his actual life.

The matter of the greatest interest is not the man's struggle with the world, with his external destiny, but his struggle with his vocation. How does he behave when faced with his inexorable vocation? Does he subscribe to it basically; or, on the contrary, is he a deserter from it, does he fill his existence with substitutes for what would have been his authentic life? Perhaps the most tragic thing about the human situation is that a man may try to supplant himself, that is, to falsify his life.—Do we know of any other reality which can be precisely what it is not, the negation of itself, the void of itself ? . . .

A life viewed in this way, from its inwardness, has no "form." Nothing seen from within has form. Form is always the external appearance which a reality offers to the eye when the eye contemplates it from outside, making it a mere object. When something is merely an object, it is merely an appearance for another and not a reality for itself. Life cannot be a mere object, because it consists precisely in its execution, in being actually lived, and hence being never concluded, never definitive. It does not allow itself to be contemplated from without: the eye must transport itself there and *make reality itself its point of view.* . . .

Man recognizes his I, his unique vocation, only through the liking or aversion aroused in him by each separate situation. Unhappiness, like the needle of a registering apparatus, tells him when his actual life realizes his vital program, his entelechy, and when it departs from it. So Goethe to Eckermann in 1829: "Man, with all his preoccupations and efforts, is delivered over to the outward, to the world around him, and must try to know it and make it serviceable to him to the extent required by his ends. But concerning himself he knows only when he is satisfied and when he suffers, and only his sufferings and his satisfactions instruct him concerning himself, teach him what to seek and what to avoid. For the rest, man is a confused creature; he knows not whence he comes or whither he goes, he knows little of the world, and above all, he knows little of himself."

Only his sufferings and his satisfactions instruct him concerning himself. Who is this "himself" which is only discernible *a posteriori*, in its collision with what befalls it? Obviously it is our life-design, which, in the case of suffering, does not coincide with our actual life: the man is torn apart, is cut in two—the man who had to be and the man he came to be. Such a dislocation manifests itself in the form of grief, anxiety, ennui, depression, emptiness; coincidence, on the contrary, produces the prodigious phenomenon of happiness. . . .

I am not going to abuse your patience by developing the theory of vocation for you—it implies a whole philosophy. I should only like to call to your attention the fact that a vocation, although it is always individual, is obviously composed of numerous generic ingredients. However much of an individual you may be, my dear friend, you have to be a man, to be a German or a Frenchman, to be of one period or another, and each one of these designations brings in its train a whole repertory of definite destinies. However, all this is not properly destiny until it has been individually modulated. Destiny is never abstract and generic, although not all destinies have the same degree of concretion. One man is born into the world to fall in love with a single and particular woman, and, consequently, it is not likely that he will find her. Fortunately, most men have a less differentiated amatory destiny and can actualize their sentiments with vast legions of homogeneous feminity—as who should say, one with blondes, another with brunettes. When we speak of life, every word must be completed by the appropriate index of individuation. This deplorable necessity is indeed a part of man's destiny as man: to live *in particular* he has to speak *in general*. . . .

Certainly, it would be a fundamental error to believe that a man's vocation coincides with his most indisputable gifts. Schlegel said: "Where there is pleasure in a thing, there is a talent for it." What he so absolutely affirms is highly questionable. The same is true if the proposition is inverted. No doubt the exercise of an outstanding capacity commonly evokes delight automatically. But this pleasure, this automatic delight, is not the happiness of a destiny fulfilling itself. Sometimes a man's vocation does not run in the direction of his gifts, sometimes it runs contrary to them. There are cases—such as Goethe's—in which the multiplicity of gifts troubles and disorients the vocation, or at least the man who is its axis. . . .

The fact is that *there is no species aeternitatis*. And not fortuitously. What there *is*, is the real, *what composes destiny*. And the real is never *species*, *aspect*, *spectacle*, an object of contemplation. All that is precisely the unreal. "It is our idea, not our being. Europe needs to cure itself of its "Idealism"—which is also the only way to overcome all materialism, positivism, utopism. Ideas are always too close to our whim, are obedient to it—they are always revocable. We have, no doubt, increasingly to live *with* ideas—but we must stop living *from* our ideas and learn to live *from* our inexorable, irrevocable destiny. Our destiny must determine our ideas, and not vice versa. Primitive man was lost in the world of things, there in the forest; we are lost in a world of ideas which show us existence as a cupboard full of equivalent possibilities, of things comparatively indifferent, of *Ziemlichgleichgültigkeiten*. (Our ideas—that is, culture. The present crisis is less a crisis of culture than of the position we have given to culture. We have set it before and above life, when it ought to be behind and below life—because it is a reaction to life. We must now stop putting the cart before the horse.)

Life consists in giving up the state of availability. Mere availability is the characteristic of youth faced with maturity. The youth, because he is not yet anything determinate and irrevocable, is everything potentially. Herein lies his charm and his insolence. Feeling that he is everything potentially he *supposes* that he is everything actually. The youth does not need to live on himself: he lives all other lives potentially—he is simultaneously Homer and Alexander, Newton, Kant, Napoleon, Don Juan. He has *inherited* all these lives. The youth is always a *patrician*, always the "young master." The growing insecurity of his existence proceeds to eliminate possibilities, matures him. But try to picture to yourself a man whose youth surrounds him with conditions of abnormal security. What will happen? Probably he will never cease to be a youth, his tendency to remain "available" will be flattered and encouraged and finally fixed. . . .

Youth, usually, is the first time that we feel the pressure of our surroundings. Serious economic difficulties begin, the struggle with the rest of mankind begins. The asperity, the bitterness, the hostility of our mundane environment appear. This first attack either forever annihilates our heroic resolve to be what we secretly are and gives birth to the Philistine in us; or, on the other hand, in the collision with the *counter-I* which the universe is, our I is revealed to itself, resolves to be, to impose itself, to stamp its image on external destiny. But if at this period, instead of coming against the world's resistance for the first time, we find it giving way before us, roused to no waves by our passage, fulfilling our desires with magic docility, our I will fall voluptuously asleep; instead of being revealed to itself, it remains vague. Nothing so saps the profound resources of a life as finding life too easy.

EUDAIMONIA

Abraham H. Maslow

As the torments of the hero upon the tragic stage indicate, the Greeks did not propose that living in truth to oneself promises either worldly success or happiness. No less than we, they knew that others are pleased by an individual's fulfillment of their expectations of him, rather than his own. Yet the Greeks perceived a special inner reward which is reserved for the man or woman who is "becoming what he is." They named it eudaimonia.

Eudaimonia is commonly translated as "happiness," but this substitutes a different meaning. We think of happiness as an end in itself and the object of every man's search. But eudaimonia is not an end to be aimed at, but rather a sign. Literally it means the condition of living at peace with one's daimon—*the true self. Fundamentally it means living the life which is your own, fulfilling the ideal possibility within which is uniquely yours. It is the feeling of being at one with oneself. Conversely* dysdaimonia *is the feeling of being divided against oneself, in Aristotle's phrase "rent by faction."*

Feelings of eudaimonia or dysdaimonia do not signify resting points or end results, but processes. They attend the process of growth, indicating a right or wrong direction. Whether an individual has pursued his true course to the very horizon or has just yesterday set foot upon the path— eudaimonia attends his steps.

"Happiness" is closely associated with pleasure, being thought to constitute "pleasure in the long run." Pleasure (and happiness) attend the gratification of desire. But the theme of eudaimonia dives beneath this level to question the desire. Often we desire things which are not meant for us, which are dissonant to our nature. I hunger for the celebrity of the politician, let us say, but the political life would be antithetical to my temperament. Eudaimonism does not approve all desires (nor, therefore, all "happiness"), but calls upon the test of self-knowledge. Here is the great Greek counsel of sophrosyne *(moderation). It does not mean a tepid, middling course in all things; it admonishes us to keep our desires consonant with what we are.*

As prologue to Maslow's analysis this much can be said of eudaimonia: it is the feeling of being where one wants to be, doing what one wants to do. No sooner is this before us than signs of dysdaimonia swarm. The man who is apologetic about his job (he is waiting for something better, he is en-

From *The Journal of Humanistic Psychology*, Vol. VII, No. 2, Fall, 1967, pp. 93–102. Reprinted by permission of Brandeis University. Bibliographic references from the original have been retained here.

tertaining many offers, etc., etc.), the woman who squirms about her husband ("Harry caught me on the rebound," "I was so young and inexperienced,"), the person who disparages his house or town or state to let us know that he was meant for better places—these people radiate the signs of dysdaimonia.

Despite the antiquity of the term and its long usage in philosophical discourse, almost no serious study of eudaimonia and its conditions has been undertaken, and it remains a fertile and virgin tract. Just lately, at long last, a bit of serious interest has arisen within phenomenology and existential and humanistic psychology. In virtue of his long-term study of "self-actualizing" persons, Professor Maslow is foremost within the last-named group.

I

Self-actualizing individuals (more matured, more fully-human), by definition, already suitably gratified in their basic needs, are now motivated in other higher ways, to be called "metamotivations."

By definition, self-actualizing people are gratified in all their basic needs (of belongingness, affection, respect, and self-esteem). This is to say that they have a feeling of belongingness and rootedness, they are satisfied in their love needs, have friends and feel loved and loveworthy, they have status and place in life and respect from other people, and they have a reasonable feeling of worth and self-respect. If we phrase this negatively—in terms of the frustration of these basic needs and in terms of pathology—then this is to say that self-actualizing people do not (for any length of time) feel anxiety-ridden, insecure, unsafe, do not feel alone, ostracized, rootless, or isolated, do not feel unlovable, rejected, or unwanted, do not feel despised and looked down upon, and do not feel deeply unworthy, nor do they have crippling feelings of inferiority or worthlessness (Maslow, 1954, Chap. 12).

Of course this can be phrased in other ways and this I have done. For instance, since the basic needs had been assumed to be the only motivations for human beings, it was possible, and in certain contexts also useful, to say of self-actualizing people that they were "unmotivated" (Maslow, 1954, Chap. 15). This was to align these people with the Eastern philosophical view of health as the transcendence of striving or desiring or wanting. (And something of the sort was also true of the Roman stoic view.)

It was also possible to describe self-actualizing people as expressing rather than coping, and to stress that they were spontaneous, and natural, that they were more easily themselves than other people. This phrasing had the additional usefulness of being compatible with the view of neurosis as an understandable coping mechanism and as a reasonable (though stupid and fearful) effort to satisfy the needs of a deeper-lying, more intrinsic, more biological self (Maslow, 1965, pp. 33–47; 1967).

Each of these phrasings has its own operational usefulness in particular research contexts, But it is also true that for certain purposes it is best to ask the questions, "What motivates the self-actualizing person? What are the psychodynamics in self-actualization? What makes him move and act and struggle? What drives (or pulls) such a person on? What attracts him? For what does he hope? What makes him angry, or dedicated, or self-sacrificing? What does he feel loyal to? Devoted to? What does he value, aspire to, and yearn for? What would he die (or live) for?"

Clearly we must make an immediate distinction between the ordinary motives of people below the level of self-actualization—that is, people motivated by the basic needs—and the motivations of people who are sufficiently gratified in all their basic needs and therefore are no longer motivated by them primarily, but rather by "higher" motivations. It is therefore convenient to call these higher motives and needs of self-actualizing persons by the name "metaneeds" and also to differentiate the category of motivation from the category of "metamotivation."

(It is now more clear to me that gratification of the basic needs is not a sufficient condition for metamotivation, although it may be a necessary precondition. I have individual subjects in whom apparent basic-need-gratification is compatible with "existential neurosis," meaninglessness, valuelessness, or the like. Metamotivation now seems *not* to ensue automatically after basic-need-gratification. One must speak also of the additional variable of "defenses against metamotivation" [Maslow, 1967]. This implies that, for the strategy of communication and of theory-building, it may turn out to be useful to add to the definition of the self-actualizing person, not only [a] that he be sufficiently free of illness, [b] that he be sufficiently gratified in his basic needs, and [c] that he be positively using his capacities, but also [d] that he be motivated by some values which he strives for or gropes for and to which he is loyal.)

II

All such people are devoted to some task, call, vocation, beloved work ("outside themselves").

In examining self-actualizing people directly, I find that in all cases, at least in our culture, they are dedicated people, devoted to some task "outside themselves," some vocation, or duty, or beloved job. Generally the devotion and dedication is so marked that one can fairly use the old words vocation, calling, or mission to describe their passionate, selfless, and profound feeling for their "work." We could even use the words destiny or fate. I have sometimes gone so far as to speak of oblation in the religious sense, in the sense of offering oneself or dedicating oneself upon some altar for some particular task, some cause outside oneself and bigger than oneself, something not merely selfish, something impersonal.

I think it is possible to go pretty far with the notion of destiny or fate.

This is a way of putting into inadequate words the feeling that one gets when one listens to self-actualizing people (and some others) talking about their work or task (Maslow, 1965). One gets the feeling of a beloved job, and furthermore, of something for which the person is a "natural," something that he is suited for, something that is right for him, even something that he was born for. It is easy to sense something like a pre-established harmony or, perhaps one could say, a good match like the perfect love affair or friendship, in which it seems that people belong to each other and were meant for each other. In the best instances, the person and his job fit together and belong together perfectly like a key and a lock, or perhaps resonate together like a sung note which sets into sympathetic resonance a particular string in the piano keyboard.

It should be said that the above seems to hold true for my female subjects even though in a different sense. I have at least one woman subject who devoted herself entirely to the task of being the mother, the wife, the housewife and the clan matriarch. Her vocation, one could very reasonably call it, was to bring up her children, to make her husband happy, and to hold together a large number of relatives in a network of personal relations. This she did very well and, as nearly as I could make out, this she enjoyed. She loved her lot completely and totally, never yearning for anything else so far as I could tell, and using all her capacities well in the process. Other women subjects have had various combinations of home life and professional work outside the home which could produce this same sense of dedication to something perceived simultaneously, both as beloved and also as important and worthwhile doing. In some women, I have also been tempted to think of "having a baby" as fullest self-actualization all by itself, at least for a time. However, I should say that I feel less confident in speaking of self-actualization in women.

III

In the ideal instance, inner requiredness coincides with external requiredness, "I want to" with "I must."

I often get the feeling in this kind of situation that I can tease apart two kinds of determinants of this transaction (or alloying, fusion, or chemical reaction) which has created a unity out of a duality, and that these two sets of determinants can and sometimes do vary independently. One can be spoken of as the responses within the person, e.g., "I love babies (or painting, or research, or political power) more than anything in the world. I am fascinated with it. . . . I am inexorably drawn to . . . I need to . . ." This we may call "inner requiredness" and it is felt as a kind of self-indulgence rather than as a duty. It is different from and separable from "external requiredness," which is rather felt as a response to what the environment, the situation, the problem, the external world calls for or requires of the person, as a fire "calls for" putting out, or as a helpless baby demands that one take care of it, or as some obvious injustice calls for righting (Maslow, 1963). Here one feels more the element of duty, or obligation, or responsibility, of being compelled helplessly to respond no matter what one was planning to do, or wished to do. It is more "I must, I have to, I am compelled" than "I want to."

In the ideal instance, which fortunately also happens in fact in many of my instances, "I want to" coincides with "I must." There is a good matching of inner with outer requiredness. And the observer is then overawed by the degree of compellingness, of inexorability, of preordained destiny, necessity and harmony that he perceives. Furthermore, the observer (as well as the person involved) feels not only that "it has to be" but also that "it ought to be, it is right, it is suitable, appropriate, fitting, and proper." I have often felt a gestalt-like quality about this kind of belonging together, the formation of a "one" out of "two."

I hesitate to call this simply "purposefulness" because that may imply that it happens only out of will, purpose, decision, or calculation, and doesn't give enough weight to the subjective feeling of being swept along, of willing and eager surrender, or yielding to fate and happily embracing it at the same time. Ideally, one also *discovers* one's fate; it is not only made or constructed or decided upon. It is recognized as if one had been unwittingly waiting for it. Perhaps the better phrase would be "Spinozistic" or "Taoistic" choice or decision or purpose—or even will.

The best way to communicate these feelings to someone who doesn't intuitively, directly understand them is to use as a model "falling in love." This is clearly different from doing one's duty, or doing what is sensible or logical. And clearly also "will," if mentioned at all, is used in a very special sense. And when two people love each other fully, then each one knows what it feels like to be magnet and what it feels like to be iron filings, and what it feels like to be both simultaneously.

IV

This ideal situation generates feelings of good fortune and also of ambivalence and unworthiness.

This model also helps to convey what is difficult to communicate in words, that is, their sense of good fortune, of luck, of gratuitous grace, of awe that this miracle should have occurred, of wonder that they should have been chosen, and of the peculiar mixture of pride fused with humility, of arrogance shot through with the pity-for-the-less-fortunate that one finds in lovers.

Of course the possibility of good fortune and success also can set into motion all sorts of neurotic fears, feelings of unworthiness, counter-values, Jonah-syndrome dynamics (Maslow, 1967), etc. These defenses against our highest possibilities must be overcome before the highest values can be wholeheartedly embraced.

V

At this level the dichotomizing of work and play is transcended; wages, hobbies, vacations, etc., must be defined at a higher level.

And then, of course, it can be said of such a person with real meaningfulness that he is being his own kind of person, or being himself, or actualizing his real self. An abstract statement, an extrapolation out from this kind of observation toward the ultimate and perfect ideal would run something like this: This person is the best one in the whole world for this particular job, and this particular job is the best job in the whole world for this particular person and his talents, capacities, and tastes. He was meant for it, and it was meant for him.

Of course, as soon as we accept this and get the feel of it, then we move over into another realm of discourse, i.e., the realm of being (Maslow, 1962a; Maslow, 1962b), of transcendence. Now we can speak meaningfully only in the language of being ("The B-language," communication at the mystical level, etc.). For instance, it is quite obvious with such people that the ordinary or conventional dichotomy between work and play is transcended totally (Marcuse, 1955; Maslow, 1965). That is, there is certainly no distinction between work and play in such a person in such a situation. His work is his play and his play is his work. If a person loves his work and enjoys it more than any other activity in the whole world and is eager to get to it, to get back to it after any interruption, then how can we speak about "labor" in the sense of something one is forced to do against one's wishes?

What sense, for instance, is left to the concept "vacation"? For such individuals it is often observed that during their vactions, that is, during the periods in which they are totally free to choose whatever they wish to do and in which they have no external obligations to anyone else, that it is precisely in such periods that they devote themselves happily and totally to their "work." Or, what does it mean "to have some fun," to seek amusement? What is now the meaning of the word "entertainment"? How does such a person "rest"? What are his "duties," responsibilities, obligations? What is his "hobby"?

What meaning does money or pay or salary have in such a situation? Obviously the most beautiful fate, the most wonderful good fortune that can happen to any human being, is to be paid for doing that which he passionately loves to do. This is exactly the situation, or almost the situation, with many (most?) of my subjects. Of course money is welcome, and in certain amounts is needed. But it is certainly not the finality, the end, the ultimate goal (that is, in the affluent society, and for the fortunate man).

The salary check such a man gets is only a small part of his "pay." Self-actualizing work or B-work (work at the level of being), being its own intrinsic reward, transforms the money or pay-check into a by-product, an epiphenomenon. This is, of course, very different from the situation of the large majority of human beings who do something they do not want to do in order to get money, which they then use to get what they really want. The role of money in the realm of being is certainly different from the role of money in the realm of deficiencies and of basic needs.

Indeed, it is theoretically possible to conceive of people with a mission, or with some great duty, not being paid *at all* with money, but of preferring not to be bothered with it, as in some religious orders. That is, they would be paid in higher need and metaneed gratifications. My guess is that in a Eupsychia (Maslow, 1961, 1965), the leaders, the ones given power, the bosses, etc., had better be paid less money and own less objects than others in order to guard them from envy, jealousy, resentment, the "evil eye." In such a society, where arbitrary and stupid social injustices are minimized, and which therefore permits the full impact of biological inequality and "injustice" to be felt without any possibility of blaming or alibi, the biologically privileged superiors may have to be protected from the fury of resentment against their unmerited, biological good luck. "Biological injustice" is probably more productive of resentment than is social injustice, for which there is always an alibi.

It will help to make my point that these are scientific questions, and can be investigated in scientific ways, if I point out that they already have been investigated in monkeys and apes to a degree. The most obvious example, of course, is the rich research literature on monkey curiosity and other precursors of the human yearning for and satisfaction with the truth (Maslow, 1962a). But it will be just as easy in principle to explore the esthetic choices of these and other animals under conditions of fear, and of lack of fear by healthy specimens or by unhealthy ones, under good choice conditions or bad ones, etc. So also for such other B-values as order, unity, justice, lawfulness, completion; it should be possible to explore these in animals, children, etc.

Of course, "highest" means also weakest, most expendable, least urgent, least conscious, most easily repressed (Maslow, 1954, Chap. 8). The basic needs, being prepotent, push to the head of the line, so to speak, being more necessary for life itself, and for sheer physical health and survival. And yet metamotivation *does* exist in the natural world and in ordinary human beings. Supernatural intervention is not needed in this theory, nor is it necessary to invent the B-values arbitrarily, or *a priori*, nor are they merely logical products or the products by fiat of an act of will. They can be uncovered or discovered by anyone who is willing and able to repeat these operations. That is, these propositions are verifiable or falsifiable, and they are repeatable. They can be operationally stated.

Many of them can be made public or demonstrable, that is, perceived simultaneously by two or more investigators.

If, then the higher life of values is open to scientific investigation and clearly lies within the jurisdiction of (humanistically defined) science (Polanyi, 1958; Maslow, 1966), we may reasonably affirm the likelihood of progress in this realm. The advancement of knowledge of the higher life of values should make possible not only greater understanding, but also should open up new possibilities of self-improvement, of improvement of the human species and of all its social institutions (Maslow, 1965). Of course, it goes without saying that we need not shiver at the thought of "the strategy of compassion" or of "spiritual technologies": obviously, they would have to be extremely different in kind from the "lower" strategies and technologies we now know.

VI

Such vocation-loving individuals tend to identify (introject, incorporate) with their "work" and to make it into a defining-characteristic of the self. It becomes part of the self.

If one asks such a person, i.e., self-actualizing, work-loving, "Who are you?" or "What are you?" he often tends to answer in terms of his "call," e.g., "I am a lawyer." "I am a mother." "I am a psychiatrist." "I am an artist," etc. That is, he tells you that he identifies his call with his identity, his self. It tends to be a label for the whole of him, i.e., it becomes a defining characteristic of the person.

Or, if one asks him, "Supposing you were not a scientist (or a teacher, or a pilot), then what would you be?" Or, "Supposing you were not a psychologist, then what?" It is my impression that his response is apt to be one of puzzlement, thoughtfulness, being taken aback, i.e., not having a ready answer. Or the response can be one of amusement, i.e., it is funny. In effect, the answer is, "If I were not a mother (anthropologist, industrialist), then I wouldn't be *me*. I would be someone else. And I can't imagine being someone else."

This kind of response parallels the confused response to the question, "Supposing you were a woman rather than a man?"

A tentative conclusion is then that in self-actualizing subjects, their beloved calling tends to be perceived as a defining characteristic of the self, to be identified with, incorporated, introjected. It becomes an inextricable aspect of one's being.

(I do not have experience with deliberately asking this same question of less fulfilled people. My impression is that the above generalization is less true for some people [for whom it is an extrinsic job] and that in other individuals the job or profession can become functionally autonomous, i.e., the person is *only* a lawyer and not a person apart from this.)

VII

The tasks to which they are dedicated seem to be interpretable as embodiments or incarnations of intrinsic values (rather than as a means to ends outside the work itself, and rather than as functionally autonomous). The tasks are loved (and introjected) BECAUSE *they embody these values. That is, ultimately it is the values that are loved rather than the job as such.*

If one asks these people why they love their work (or, more specifically, which are the moments of higher satisfaction in their work, which moments of reward make all the necessary chores worthwhile and acceptable, which are the peak moments or peak-experiences), one gets many specific and *ad hoc* answers of the type listed and summarized in Table 1.

TABLE 1

MOTIVATIONS AND GRATIFICATIONS OF SELF-ACTUALIZING PEOPLE, OBTAINED THROUGH THEIR WORK AS WELL AS IN OTHER WAYS. (THESE ARE IN ADDITION TO BASIC NEED GRATIFICATIONS)

Delight in bringing about justice.
Delight in stopping cruelty and exploitation.
Fighting lies and untruths.
They love virtue to be rewarded.
They seem to like happy endings, good completions.
They hate sin and evil to be rewarded, and they hate people to get away with it.
They are good punishers of evil.
They try to set things right, to clean up bad situations.
They enjoy doing good.
They like to reward and praise promise, talent, virtue, etc.
They avoid publicity, fame, glory, honors, popularity, celebrity, or at least do not seek it. It seems to be not awfully important one way or another.
They do not *need* to be loved by everyone.
They generally pick out their own causes, which are apt to be few in number, rather than responding to advertising or to campaigns or to other people's exhortations.
They tend to enjoy peace, calm, quiet, pleasantness, etc., and they tend *not* to like turmoil, fighting, war, etc. (they are *not* general-fighters on every front), and they can enjoy themselves in the middle of a "war."
They also seem practical and shrewd and realistic about it, more often than impractical. They like to be effective and dislike being ineffectual.
Their fighting is not an excuse for hostility, paranoia, grandiosity, authority, rebellion, etc., but is for the sake of setting things right. It is problem-centered.
They manage somehow simultaneously to love the world as it is and to try to improve it.
In all cases there was some hope that people and nature and society could be improved.
In all cases it was as if they could see both good and evil realistically.
They respond to the challenge in a job.
A chance to improve the situation or the operation is a big reward. They enjoy improving things.
Observations generally indicate great pleasure in their children and in helping them grow into good adults.

They do not need or seek for or even enjoy very much flattery, applause, popularity, status, prestige, money, honors, etc.

Expressions of gratitude, or at least of awareness of their good fortune, are common.

They have a sense of *noblesse oblige*. It is the duty of the superior, of the one who sees and knows, to be patient and tolerant, as with children.

They tend to be attracted by mystery, unsolved problems, by the unknown and the challenging, rather than to be frightened by them.

They enjoy bringing about law and order in the chaotic situation, or in the messy or confused situation, or in the dirty and unclean situation.

They hate (and fight) corruption, cruelty, malice, dishonesty, pompousness, phoniness, and faking.

They try to free themselves from illusions, to look at the facts courageously, to take away the blindfold.

They feel it is a pity for talent to be wasted.

They do not do mean things, and they respond with anger when other people do mean things.

They tend to feel that every person should have an opportunity to develop to his highest potential, to have a fair chance, to have equal opportunity.

They like doing things well, "doing a good job," "to do well what needs doing." Many such phrases add up to "bringing about good workmanship."

One advantage of being a boss is the right to give away the corporation's money, to choose which good causes to help. They enjoy giving their own money away to causes they consider important, good, worthwhile, etc. Pleasure in philanthropy.

They enjoy watching and helping the self-actualizing of others, especially of the young.

They enjoy watching happiness and helping to bring it about.

They get great pleasure from knowing admirable people (courageous, honest, effective, "straight," "big," creative, saintly, etc.). "My work brings me in contact with many fine people."

They enjoy taking on responsibilities (that they can handle well), and certainly don't fear or evade their responsibilities. They respond to responsibility.

They uniformly consider their work to be worthwhile, important, even essential.

They enjoy greater efficiency, making an operation more neat, compact, simpler, faster, less expensive, turning out a better product, doing with less parts, a smaller number of operations, less clumsiness, less effort, more foolproof, safer, more "elegant," less laborious.

In addition, of course, one gets many "end-answers" of the type—"I just love my baby, that's all. Why do I love him? I just do"; or "I just get a big kick out of improving the efficiency of my plant. Why? I just get a big bang out of it." Peak-experiences, intrinsic pleasures, worthwhile achievements, whatever their degree, need no further justification or validation. They are intrinsic reinforcers.

It is possible to classify these moments of reward, and to boil them down into a smaller number of categories. As I tried to do this, it quickly became apparent that the best and most "natural" categories of classification were mostly or entirely abstract "values" of an ultimate and irreducible kind, such values as truth, beauty, newness, uniqueness, justice, compactness, simplicity, goodness, neatness, efficiency, love, honesty, innocence, improvement, orderliness, elegance, growth, cleanliness, authenticity, serenity, peacefulness, and the like.

For these people the profession seems to be *not* functionally autonomous, but rather to be a carrier of, an instrument of, or an incarnation of ultimate values. For them the profession of, e.g., law is a means to the end of justice, and not an end in itself. Perhaps I can communicate my feeling for the subtle difference in this way: for one man the law is loved because it *is* justice, while another man, the pure value-free technologist, might love the law simply as an intrinsically lovable set of rules, precedents, procedures without regard to the ends or products of their use. He may be said to love the vehicle itself without reference to its ends, as one loves a game which has no end other than to be a game, e.g., chess.

I have had to learn to differentiate several kinds of identification with a "cause" or a profession or a calling. A profession can be a means to covert and repressed ends as easily as it can be an end in itself. Or, better said, it can be motivated by deficiency-needs or even neurotic needs as well as by metaneeds. It can be multiply-determined or over-determined by all or any of those needs and metaneeds in any patterning. From the simple statement, "I am a lawyer and I love my work," one cannot assume very much.

It is my strong impression that the closer to self-actualizing, to full-humanness, etc., the person is, the more likely I am to find that his "work" is metamotivated rather than basic-need-motivated. For more highly evolved persons, "the law" is apt to be more a way of seeking justice, truth, goodness, etc., rather than financial security, admiration, status, prestige, dominance, masculinity, etc. When I ask the questions: Which aspects of your work do you enjoy most? What gives you your greatest pleasures? When do you get a kick out of your work? etc., such people are more apt to answer in terms of intrinsic values, of transpersonal, beyond-the-selfish, altruistic satisfactions, e.g., seeing justice done, doing a more perfect job, advancing the truth, rewarding virtue and punishing evil, etc.

PHILANTHROPY

George Santayana

In the form of a dialogue in afterlife between the pagan Socrates and a Christian "stranger," Santayana asks what it is which is loveable in man. Is it childhood?—but the pleasure to be taken in the play of children is momentary and soon followed by boredom. Youth, then?—but the youth is insufferably arrogant as the result of his ignorance. Middle age?—but no, for then the little that has been learned produces ridiculous dogmatism. Old age?—but old men pontificate endlessly about matters the world has passed by. Well, then, surely woman? "Alas, shade of Xanthippe (Socrates's wife); woman is the "eternal impediment."

This despairing catalogue of infirmities prompts Socrates to the question: Is the real obstacle to philanthropy man himself?

The catalogue has demonstrated that actual man, man as he appears before our eyes, is unloveable. But something is as yet missing, and it constitutes what is most real in man. It is his daimon—*that which he aspires to become. It represents the unactualized (and perhaps unactualizable) perfection of humanity, yet it is at work in man now insofar as any human being aspires toward it. It is this possibility which is intrinsically loveable and which supports philanthropy.*

In the second portion Socrates compares himself with Jesus as Christ and calls attention to the fact that his own philanthropy rests upon a knowledge of man by one who was a man himself, while the Christian savior only played at being a man, having other options and being in his nature a god. Socrates examines Christian love and finds that as charity, pity, and consolation, it is the feeling appropriate to gods who look down from the heights upon troubled creatures below. He asks whether this condescension is really philanthropy, or whether instead it serves to fasten men to their infirmities as hatred seeks to do.

Widely regarded as one of America's greatest philosophers, Santayana was only dubiously American. He was born in Madrid in 1863 and he died in Rome in 1952. He was educated at Boston Latin School and Harvard but took the first opportunity to leave his teaching post at Harvard for European "retirement" and writing. A lifelong Roman Catholic, he saw religion as a poetry of ideals, not as description of fact, and he appeared to see in the Church, at its best, a glimpse of one viable moral ideal among many. But his philosophical roots were deeply Greek and pagan, and in "The Philanthropist" the viability of the Christian ideal is brought into question.

You say, do you not, that I am no philanthropist, because a philanthropist should love men as they are, whereas I, falsely calling myself a lover of men, love only my notion of what men should be?

The Stranger. Yes, some such feeling was in my mind.

Socrates. Now would you say that the love which a man has for himself is genuine or feigned and hypocritical?

The Stranger. Unmistakably genuine.

Socrates. And does he love himself as he actually is or rather as he would wish to be?

The Stranger. That is a hard question.

Socrates. Suppose I have two friends, one who knows and loves me exactly as I am, describing me with gusto as an old, pot-bellied, bald, mechanical rogue, useless and tiresome, and another friend (perhaps you yourself) who knows and loves me as I should like to have been, calling me the daylight conscience of Athens or a discerner and companion of all that is beautiful: which of these two friends do you think I should regard as truly sympathetic and as sharing with me the genuine love which I have for myself?

The Stranger. In this case certainly the flatterer would be the better critic and would describe the deeper truth.

Socrates. Is not, then, the true philanthropist a flatterer of mankind, not, of course, like a politician for his own advancement, but as the self-love of mankind is itself a flatterer, seeing their better side and their missed possibilities, and loving them as they would wish to be rather than as they are?

The Stranger. I suppose that our wishes and ideals are a part of our present selves, and that a true lover of men would not love them apart from that idealism in them which keeps them alive and human.

Socrates. If a boy has been reading the *Odyssey* and wishes to be wrecked on a desert island and to become king over it, that day-dream is a part of the boy; and if you truly love the boy, you must love that daydream in him. Is that your meaning?

The Stranger. I should not wish him, at his age, to be without something of the sort; and I certainly should like a boy the better for being fond of the *Odyssey*.

Socrates. And if the boy attempted to set sail alone in a small boat, hoping to be actually wrecked, would you wish the same thing for him in consequence of your affection?

The Stranger. Of course, he must be prevented.

Socrates. How, then, does the argument stand? Men, you say, love themselves as they wish to be, but the philanthropist loves them as they are and is ready, in some cases, to prevent them by force from realizing their desires; and yet he wishes them, at least if they are boys, to cultivate those desires without realizing them? Is that the position?

The Stranger. So it would seem.

Socrates. Perhaps our supposition was unnatural, because boys, even when fond of the *Odyssey* and of gloating over imaginary adventures, are in fact little cowards, and would be terrified at finding themselves adrift, I will not say at sea, but in a duck-pond. Let us suppose that our young hero was rendered so exceptionally brave not simply by reading the *Odyssey*, but by falling into a fever after reading it, and becoming delirious; and let us suppose that in his lucid intervals he did not wish to be wrecked, but to get well. Now if you were a true friend to that boy would you share his wish in this instance, actually assisting him, to the best of your knowledge and power, to recover his health as soon as possible, or would you still, as in the other instance, love him and wish him to remain just as he was, intermittently feverish and entertaining at intervals the warm ideals proper to a fever, without, of course, ever reducing them to act?

The Stranger. You are bringing ridicule upon me, but not conviction.

Socrates. All the ridicule I may bring upon you will not hurt you, if you bring no ridicule upon yourself. But let us coldly consider the facts. Suppose some one is found so entirely devoted to your interests that he never exercises his own judgement but labours to carry out instantly your every wish: would you think him the best of friends?

The Stranger. I should think him a good servant. A friend may do an occasional service, and a servant, in his feelings, may be sometimes a friend; but service is not true friendship. A good servant follows my directions, a bad one studies my character in order to profit by my foibles, as a demagogue studies public opinion. A friend would rather communicate to me his own pleasures and insights.

Socrates. Partners in vice are not true friends?

The Stranger. No, they are accomplices. All your boon-companions, adulterous lovers, fellow-conspirators, bandits, and partisans may imagine that they are friends pursuing a common interest, but in reality each obeys a private impulse and cares only for his own dream. The others are but his chance instruments in debauch. Presently they will fall out over the spoils or take to railing at one another for failure or treachery.

Socrates. But what of those who, as the phrase is, are in love?

The Stranger. Each of them, too, is moved by a private mysterious passion. At first they are in a flutter, or love-sick and full of dreams; later they pursue each other with sensitive claims, exactions, and jealousies. Sometimes, for a while, they are wildly happy; then they begin to feel imprisoned, and perhaps grow bitter and quarrelsome, even to the point of violence and murder.

Socrates. Is there not often a lifelong and tender affection between husband and wife, parents and children, brothers and sisters?

The Stranger. There is: sometimes sugary, sometimes seasoned with a little sarcasm.

Socrates. At least young children, red-cheeked and vigorous, running and romping about with shrill cries, must be a perfect delight to you?

The Stranger. Yes, for half an hour.

Socrates. You find more peace, no doubt, among wrinkled white-bearded elders sitting in the sun or tottering on knotted staves, well pleased with themselves and their old saws?

The Stranger. They, too, are picturesque, but at their best in the background. Otherwise such old men are a danger to philanthropy.

Socrates. I see that your preference, like mine, is decidedly for the plastic and generous temper of young men, who embody human health and freedom to perfection.

The Stranger. Yes, but our preference in this matter is three-quarters illusion. In reality, what is a youth but a tadpole? And what can be more odious than their conceit when they have some cleverness and transgress their sphere?

Socrates. What? Are you entirely weaned from the love of images? Do you now prize nothing in man save his active virtues, such as can be exercised in their fullness only in middle life?

The Stranger. Active virtues? Say rather active vices. Men in middle life are for the most part immersed in affairs to which they give too much importance, having sold their souls to some sardonic passion and become dangerous and repulsive beasts.

Socrates. What, then, is your conclusion? That the one great obstacle to philanthropy is man?

The Stranger. You forget woman.

Socrates. Alas, shade of Xanthippe, it is not easy to forget her. Woman is the eternal impediment.

The Stranger. Being incomplete she wishes man to be so, and her ascendancy is a wile of nature that keeps the race jogging along in spite of all the philosophers. Nowadays the manly heart is entirely dominated by the sentiments she inspires or by those she approves. Nor does he think this woman-worship degrading; integrity is out of date; and in woman he seems to find concentrated all the beauty and fineness, all the ardour and religion, that still remain in the world.

Socrates. Can it be so bad as that? You are indulging, I know, your spleen or your fancy; yet after painting such a picture of mankind, can you still maintain that true philanthropy must be love of men and women as they are? If you care for them at all, must it not be your constant endeavour entirely to transform them?

The Stranger. I begin to see your drift and the refutation which you intend me to supply to my own opinion. Let me then expedite my fate, and confess at once that the philanthropist should strive to secure the *true* good of mankind, a good predetermined for them by their nature and faculties without their knowledge, and by no means realized in their actual condition nor expressed in their loose wishes, nor always furthered by their political maxims and superstitious morality. This was what I had in mind, though I expressed myself badly, when I said that the true philanthropist loves men as they are: for their true nature is not adequately manifested in their condition at any moment, or in their words and thoughts vapidly flowing, or even in their prevalent habits. Their real nature is what they would discover themselves to be if they possessed self-knowledge or, as the Indian scripture has it, if they became what they are. This admission, Socrates, does not remove the objection which I have to meddlesome censors calling themselves philanthropists, but abounding only in their own conceit, and wedded to their nostrums. Let them help me, as you so generously help me, to know myself; but let them not browbeat me in the name of virtue, seeking to palm off their prejudices upon me as moral first principles, which would turn my whole life, if I followed them, into a slow and miserable suicide.

Socrates. You go faster and farther than is safe. But let us agree that the philanthropist is a diviner. The scars and deformities of men do not beguile him: would they be deformities or scars if there were not whole and beautiful humanity beneath which they could disfigure? The lover's eye when most open is most full of dreams; it pierces through the incrustations of fortune, or does not perceive them, and sees only the naked image of the god beneath. . . .

The Stranger. You are the friend of youth, of the soul flushed with brave hopes, and you teach us to disentangle and understand our loves, and so to train ourselves in art and government that life in our cities may be both free and beautiful. You are the prophet of success. But how much success is there or has there ever been on earth? Who shall be the prophet of old age, of sorrow, or servitude? What god shall help us where we have failed?

Socrates. Can even a god help you there?

The Stranger. That is the mystery.

Socrates. Then let us pass it by. The initiated, who alone understand mysteries, have sworn not to reveal them.

The Stranger. In the religion which the Greeks adopted after your time, mysteries are public; in the midst of them is sung a hymn: "Publish, O tongue, the mystery," and though I am but a lame mystic and hardly initiated, I should undertake to publish it, if you did not forbid.

Socrates. Publish it by all means.

The Stranger. The sum of it is this: that we must leave glory to God and be content with failure for ourselves.

Socrates. Is your God, then, an enemy to man, that he finds his glory in the ruin of his creatures?

The Stranger. Their ruin is a part of their mode of existence, as the silence which follows upon speech is part of its eloquence. The founder of our spiritual city saw in God, whom he called his Father, a great lover of life, as you, too, once called him: but not a lover of human life only, or of any life only in its perfection. His hand had scattered bountifully throughout the chaos of matter the seeds of all sorts of perfections, setting the love and the need of a special perfection in each creature's heart; but the path of any incarnate spirit, buried as it must be in matter and beset by accidents, is necessarily long and perilous; and few there are who ever reach the goal. Yet the perfections of all those who fall by the way and never attain perfection are none the less present for ever to the mind of God, and a part of his glory: and such of us as have no glory here may be content with our glory there. As to our life on earth, whether it ever touch perfection, as yours seemed to do for a moment in Greece, or be utterly distracted, as ours has been since, it must in any case presently perish: the torrent is too mighty for any swimmer. You may laugh at me, if you will, and call me a theologian; yet we must somehow speak of nature and the gods, and how shall we ever speak of them except in parables? Did you not yourself repeat a tale about the birth of Love, that he was the child of Plenty and Want? Let me then enlarge upon your apologue and say that the satisfaction which God finds eternally in the idea of human perfection, and in all other good ideas, is not properly called love, because there is no want and no sorrow in it; it is but a part of his joy in the fullness of his own being. The true seat of love is matter, when its inner yearning and absolute want are, by chance, directed towards the idea of humanity, or towards any other divine idea. Now there have been prophets in India and even in Greece who have soared altogether above this painful love and have studied to become impassible and utterly blissful, even like God; but the Prophet of Nazareth, who said he was the Son of God but also the son of man, taught and practised the love of man superhumanly, in a spirit that has never animated any other prophet; so that his philanthropy bears a special name and is called charity.

Socrates. Anything you may tell me about your Prophet will not be without interest for me, because I have already heard sundry comparisons and couplings of his name with mine, and perhaps if his maxims were repeated to me by some rational person (which was never yet the case), they might teach me to correct or extend my own suppositions. What, for instance, is this charity of his, of which you speak so darkly?

The Stranger. Definition is not my art; yet perhaps if you will define philanthropy I may be able to add some qualification to mark the difference which I vaguely feel to exist between philanthropy and charity.

Socrates. Have we not defined philanthropy already? Is it not love of that beauty and goodness in man which if realized would make his happiness? In what, pray, is your charity more or less than that?

The Stranger. I will venture to improvise an answer, although I may soon have cause to retract it. Charity is less than philanthropy in that it expects the defeat of man's natural desires and accepts that defeat; and it is more than philanthropy in that, in the face of defeat, it brings consolation.

Socrates. But what, may I ask, are natural desires?

The Stranger. I don't mean mere whims or follies, whether in children or nations, which may be naturally inevitable but which a good regimen would weed out or allow to blow over. I mean profound aspirations, seated in our unregenerate nature, which fate nevertheless forbids us to realize, such as the desire to understand everything (which you, Socrates, have wisely renounced) or to be beautiful, or the first or free or immortal. The spirit in most of us has but a poor prospect. From the beginning we are compelled to put up with our parents, our country, our times, and the relentless approach of old age and death; and on the way we are lucky if we escape disease, deformity, crossed hopes, or desperate poverty. You may paint a picture of the Golden Age or of an ideal republic in which these evils are softened, or are forgotten; but meantime we must endure them, and live and die in a far exile from our natural good. Charity is the friendship of one exile for another.

Socrates. You must excuse my dull wits, but I have not yet gathered from your eloquence whether the natural good from which you are banished is the happiness proper to man at home, or is perhaps the life of the gods in Olympus, to which you think yourself entitled and fitted by nature. Is a part of what troubles you, for instance, the fatality of having hands instead of wings? And might a bird, on the same principle, deeply suffer for the lack of hands, and require the ministrations of charity to reconcile him to being covered with feathers?

The Stranger. I confess that the life of birds, too, seems rather pitiful, and that even feasting for ever on nectar and ambrosia might be a dull business and cloying. Must not any incarnate spirit renounce beforehand almost everything that a free spirit might have desired?

Socrates. If there is an immortal spirit in every creature which chafes at its limitations, does it not also, at death, escape those limitations, and does it not live many another life in many another creature? Let us leave the fortunes of spirit to the hidden justice which probably rules the world and whose decrees, at any rate, we cannot alter. But in so far as spirit is incarnate in man and addressed to human happiness, it is not hampered by the conditions of this human life but is supported by them. Man presupposes nature. Nature sets before him his proper virtue, as a child, as a soldier, as a father, as a cultivator of divine grace; and he is happy if that grace descends upon him in all the offices of his humanity and renders him as nearly perfect as, amid the accidents of fortune, it is possible for a man to be. A man content to fail in his proper virtue would show himself a scorner of humanity and a misanthrope. If your Prophet, as I seem to have heard, despised in men all their proper virtue, their beauty, valour, enterprise, and science, and loved them only for being halt, blind, poor, and diseased in both mind and body, I do not understand in what respect I can be compared with him, or how his charity has any touch of philanthropy in it.

The Stranger. I think that our Prophet, if he had been man only, would have shared your philanthropy to the full, and that initially his heart would have longed with an even greater intensity than yours for all the beauty and splendour of existence. He was no coward, he was no eunuch; but he was not sent (as he was wont to say) to speak for himself, to give voice to his own nature; he was sent to speak in God's name, and to teach mankind to judge themselves as God judged them. Now God, being their creator, could not hate the soul which he had kindled in their dust; and a man filled with the divine spirit could not bemoan the creation, or condemn the warmth and beauty which, at the word of God, had turned that dust into flesh. Yet as the Father was not the creator of man alone, so the Son could not confine his sympathy to the human soul, but extended it to every creature, and also to that tragic economy by which the fortunes of each are determined according to the divine will. Thus in love for created things, when it is divinely inspired, there is perforce an element of impartiality, a conditioned allegiance, and a tenderness swallowed up in resignation, the love of God always dominating the love of man and being at bottom the only ground for it. For why should a religious mind foster the human will or share its aspirations at all, except because God has breathed that human will into some parcels of matter, being pleased that they should live after that human fashion? Hence the celestial colour of charity, which has passed through the presence and through the love of God as through an infinite fire, before reaching either the beauty or the suffering of any creature. Our Prophet did not look upon the world with the eyes of a mortal; he was deeply disenchanted with all the glories of which human life is capable. He ignored, with a compassionate indulgence, all liberal arts, sciences and ambitions: not one hint of comforts or sports or manly adventure, not one thought of political institutions to be built up laboriously or defended rationally or handed down as a heritage. The end of the world was at hand, as, indeed, it is for each of us in turn; and charity, knowing that events are in other hands, sees in mankind nothing but a swarm of moths fluttering round the flame, each with its separate sorrow and its dazzled spirit, needing to be saved. His maxims were not those of a combatant, or a ranting moralist, or the founder of a prosperous state. He considered rather the lilies of the field, the little children, the sparrows; even the tares among the wheat, though destined for the burning, and the hairs of a man's head were God's creatures; the harlots and the publicans were also his children. Without expecting to extirpate evil so long as this world lasted, he went about healing and forgiving. In the midst of trouble the redeemed soul might be joyful, and even the body might often be restored in sympathy with the soul. A dissolving insight, a great renunciation, might bring peace suddenly to all who accepted it. All men, all creatures, might abandon their wilfulness, disclaim their possessions, and love one another. The saints might form, even on earth, a new society without war, greed, competition, or anxiety. Poverty or disgrace might be sweet to them in its sharpness, and they might thank God for their little sister, the death of the body. If smitten on one cheek they might turn the other, and when robbed of their cloak they might offer their tunic also. Leaving their nets upon the shore and their plough in mid-furrow, they might beg food and lodging from strangers; and when these were refused, they might sit down starving by the wayside and praise God with a loud voice.

Socrates. Were such madmen and gymnosophists the men whom your Prophet loved?

The Stranger. No, as a matter of fact, his heart went out rather to children, to frank young men, to women who themselves had loved, and to the common folk in fishing hamlets and in the streets of cities.

Socrates. Then his love of mankind might have been strangely chilled if mankind had followed his precepts?

The Stranger. Such is the irony of reform. I can imagine the cold words that our saints will hear at the Last Day. And would you yourself, Socrates, have loved Alcibiades if he had resembled you, or Athens if it had been like Sparta?

Socrates. Athens and Alcibiades were constant irritants to me, cruelly reminding me of what they ought to have been. How should I not have loved even the worst vehicle of so great a revelation? There would be no irony in reform, my friend, if reform were guided by knowledge of human nature, and not by a captious imagination. Man is a natural being; if he is ill at ease in the world, it is only because he is ignorant of the world and of his own good; and the discord between man and nature would be wholly resolved if man would practise the true arts of medicine and politics. But your Prophet seems to have delivered precepts which, if ever his disciples had obeyed them, would have turned them into sanctified idiots, contemptible in his own eyes. He set before them as models other creatures, or the gods, or the ways of the universe, thereby counselling them to destroy themselves; and I see no benefit which he conferred, or even wished to confer, upon mankind.

The Stranger. Metamorphosis, I suppose, is never strictly a benefit, because it changes the standard of values and alienates the heart from its old pursuits. It is such a metamorphosis of the spirit that our religion proposes to us, although of course none occurs in most of us, and our society remains perfectly animal and heathen. Yet the other note has sounded, and is sometimes heard. If you asked me for my own opinion, I should say that there is one great gift which our Prophet has bestowed on us, and that is himself. After all, is not that the best gift which a lover has to bestow, and the only one which a lover would much care to receive? That he should have walked among us; that he should have spoken those golden words, composed those parables so rich in simplicity, tenderness, and wisdom; that he should have done those works of mercy in which the material miracle was but the spark for the new flame of charity which it kindled; that he should have dismissed with a divine scorn and a perfect disillusion all the busy vanities of this world—the Pharisees with their orthodoxy, the Sadducees with their liberalism, the scribes with their scriptures; that he should have renounced family and nation and party and riches, and any other hope or notion of paradise than this very liberation and self-surrender of the soul—that is his gift to mankind. Alone among dreaming mortals he seemed to be awake, because he knew that he was dreaming; the images and passions which bring illusion to others, although he felt them, brought no illusion to him. He had enough sympathy with blind life to understand it, to forgive it, to heal its wounds, to cover its shames, and even to foster it when innocent; yet that very understanding compelled him to renounce it all in his heart, continually draining his chalice to the dregs, and foreknowing the solitude of the cross. Thus the indwelling deity entirely transfigured without shattering his humanity, and the flame of love in him, though it rose and fell humanly as the miseries or the beauties of the world passed before his eyes, yet never had the least taint in it of impurity, moodiness, or favour. It was divine love, free from craving or decay. The saint and the blackguard alike were known to him at their true worth; in both he could see something disfigured or unattained, perhaps hidden from their own eyes, and yet the sole reason and root of their being, something simple and worthy of love beneath all their weakness or perversity; and the assurance of this divine love, so surprising and inexplicable, became to many the only warrant of their worth, and lent them courage not wholly to despise themselves, but to seek and to cleanse the pure pearl in their dung-hill, on which his own eye rested, and not without reason to call him the saviour of their souls.

Socrates. In all your words you are implying, if I understand you, that your Prophet was a god in the form of man?

The Stranger. Yes.

Socrates. That is a point of difference between him and me which may justify the difference in our maxims. A god, even if for a moment he condescends to play the mortal, holds his immortality in reserve; it is one thing to live and die in an assumed character, and another thing to live and die in the only character one has.

 **LOVE'S UNMASKING**

Erich Neumann

Central to the myth of Amor (Eros) and Psyche is the theme of love and knowledge. Psyche has been kept prisoner by the man-god Eros, who comes to seduce her always in darkness. Convinced that she is the victim of a monster, one night Psyche brings a lighted lamp to the bed where Eros sleeps, intending to kill him. The sight of Eros kindles Psyche's love, but a drop of burning oil from the lamp wakens Eros, who flees. In the end he returns to Psyche and the two are united in love.

Neumann centers on the light-bringing as the point of Psyche's death and rebirth. It marks the death of the Psyche of dependence and ignorance, of passivity and undergoing. It is an "Amazonian" act which gives birth to womanly initiative and knowledge as contributions to love. By his reference to Aristophanes' myth (Plato's Symposium*), Neumann suggests that the aim of "Amazonianism" is the fulfillment of humanhood by the contribution of essential femininity to essential masculinity.*

But the immediate effect of the appearance of the Amazon is Eros's wounding and his flight. He chose to seduce in darkness, and is burned by the light. Does this suggest something in the masculine nature which resists being known by women? Does man believe that to be known fully by woman is to fall under her power? If so, is this an accurate estimate of the Amazon, or a misconception (from what source?) which bars the way to human wholeness?

The reader is invited to compare the Psyche of darkness with woman as "second sex" in Simone de Beauvoir (see the selection, Part I).

Reprinted from *Amor and Psyche: The Psychic Development of the Feminine* by Erich Neumann; trans. Ralph Manheim, Bollingen Series LIV. Copyright 1956 by Princeton University Press. Reprinted by permission of the publisher.

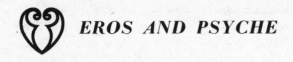 **EROS AND PSYCHE**

(EDITORS' SUMMARY OF THE MYTH AS TOLD BY APULEIUS)

Psyche, youngest of a king's three daughters, becomes so famous and adored for her exceeding beauty that she arouses the jealousy of Aphrodite herself. Aphrodite commands her son Eros (Cupid) to use his arrows to make Psyche fall in love with the vilest creature on earth. But in her rage Aphrodite has made the mistake of showing Psyche to Eros, and he is madly in love with her. He hides his love from his mother and promises to obey her command.

Meanwhile Psyche is worshipped by all, but from a distance, and no man dares to ask for her in marriage. Bewildered, her parents consult the oracle of Apollo, who says that Psyche must be dressed in mourning and left for dead upon a high crag where her destined husband, a fearful winged serpent, will come to claim her. Her parents obey, and as Psyche waits in terror she is gently lifted from atop the crag by the wind and carried to a beautiful mansion, where kind voices sing to her and wait upon her. Through the days she sees no one, but by night her husband comes to her; and though she never sees him the gentleness of his voice banishes her fear that he is the storied monster.

For a long time Psyche is happy in this life, until one day she hears her sisters mourning her on the crag where she had been left for dead. Though her husband warns gravely against it Psyche has her way and her sisters are borne by the wind to the mansion. They are awestruck by its riches and ask to meet Psyche's lord, but in keeping with her promise Psyche only tells them that he is young and handsome. Frustrated and exceedingly jealous, her sisters depart.

Shortly the sisters return again, for they have deduced from Psyche's responses that she has never seen her husband. They convince her that in fact he is the foul monster. They persuade her to place a lamp and a knife beside her bed, with which to illuminate the beast while he sleeps and slay him.

That night by lamplight the murder-intending Psyche perceives her lover. He is no monster but the handsomest of men, the god of love himself—Eros. Psyche fills with genuine love, but a drop of hot oil falls from the lamp she holds and burns Eros. Awake he is outraged by Psyche's lack of faith, and he flees, promising never to return.

Aphrodite dresses Eros's burns and is furious with him both for failing to ruin Psyche and for falling in love with her. She redoubles her resolve to destroy Psyche.

But in her desperation to find her husband again Psyche has won the sympathy of all the gods. At last she visits Aphrodite, who charges her to undergo four dangerous tests to win Eros back. Each of the tests is virtually suicidal but the gods help and Psyche passes the first three. She is on the verge of failing the fourth and sinking into eternal oblivion when Eros himself saves her. The two are united in love and live eternally thereafter in happiness with the gods.

The Psyche who approaches the bed on which Eros is lying is no longer the languorously ensnared being, bewitched by her senses, who lived in the dark paradise of sexuality and lust. Awakened by the incursion of her sisters, conscious of the danger that threatens her, she assumes the cruel militancy of the matriarchate as she approaches the bed to kill the monster, the male beast who has torn her from the upper world in a marriage of death and carried her off into darkness. But in the glow of the newly kindled light, with which she illumines the unconscious darkness of her previous existence, she recognizes Eros. *She loves.* In the light of her new consciousness she experiences a fateful transformation, in which she discovers that the separation between beast and husband is not valid. As the lightning bolt of love strikes her, she turns the knife against her own heart or (in other terms) wounds herself on Eros' arrow. With this she departs from the child-like, unconscious aspect of her reality and the matriarchal, man-hating aspect as well. Only in a squalid, lightless existence can Psyche mistake her lover for a beast, a violator, a dragon, and only as a childishly ignorant girl (but this too is a dark aspect) can she suppose that she is in love with a "higher husband" distinct from the lower dragon. In the light of irrupting love Psyche recognized Eros as a god, who is the upper and the lower in one, who connects the two.

Psyche pricks herself on Eros' arrow and bleeds. "So all unwitting, yet of her own doing, Psyche fell in love with Love." The beginning of her love was a marriage of death as dying, being-raped, and being-taken; what Psyche now experiences may be said to be a second defloration, the real, active, voluntary defloration, which she accomplishes in herself. She is no longer a victim, but an actively loving woman. She is in love, enraptured by Eros, who has seized her as a power from within, no longer as a man from without. For Eros as a man outside sleeps and knows nothing of what Psyche does and what goes on within her. And here the narrative begins to disclose a psychological acuteness that has no equal.

Psyche's act of love, in which she voluntarily gives herself to love, to Eros, is at once a sacrifice and a loss. She does not renounce the matriarchal stage of her womanhood; the paradoxical core of the situation is that in and through her act of love she raises the matriarchal stage to its authentic being and exalts it to the Amazonian level.

The knowing Psyche, who sees Eros in the full light and has broken the taboo of his invisibility, is no longer naïve and infantile in her attitude toward the masculine; she is no longer merely captivating and captivated, but is so completely changed in her new womanhood that she loses and indeed must lose her lover. In this love situation of womanhood growing conscious through encounter, knowledge and suffering and sacrifice are identical. With Psyche's love that burst forth when she "sees Eros," there comes into being within her an Eros who is no longer identical with the sleeping Eros outside her. This inner Eros that is the image of her love is in truth a higher and invisible form of the Eros who lies sleeping before her. It is the adult Eros which pertains to the conscious, adult psyche, the Psyche who is no longer a child. This greater, invisible Eros within Psyche must necessarily come into conflict with his small, visible incarnation who is revealed by the light of her lamp and burned by the drop of oil. The Eros hidden in the darkness could still be an embodiment of every image of Eros that lived within Psyche, but the Eros who has become visible is the divine, finite reality of the boy who is Aphrodite's son.[1]

And, we must not forget, Eros himself did *not* want such a Psyche! He threatened her, he fervently implored her to remain in the paradise-darkness, he warned her that she would lose him forever by her act. The unconscious tendency toward consciousness (here toward consciousness in the love relationship) was stronger in Psyche than everything else, even than her love for Eros—or so, at least, the masculine Eros would have said. But wrongly so, for though the Psyche of the paradisaical state was subservient to Eros, though she had yielded to him in the darkness, she had not loved him. Something in her, which may be designated negatively as matriarchal aggression, or positively as a tendency toward consciousness and a fulfillment precisely of her feminine nature, drove her imperiously to emerge from the darkness. It is in the light of knowledge, her knowledge of Eros, that she begins to love.

The loss of her lover in this moment is among the deepest truths of this myth; this is the tragic moment in which every feminine psyche enters upon its own destiny. Eros is wounded by Psyche's act; the drop of oil that burns him, awakens him, and drives him away is in every sense a source of pain. To him, the masculine god, she was desirable enough when she was in the dark and he possessed her in the dark, when she was the mere companion of his nights, secluded from the world, living only for him, without share in his diurnal existence, in his reality and his divinity. Her servitude was made still deeper by his insistence on his divine anonymity: she was still more "devoured" by him. This childlike girl, this "simple and gentle soul" (a masculine misunderstanding if ever there was one!), approaches the sleeper

---

[1]But for Psyche it is essential that she unify the dual structure of Eros, which is also manifested in the antithetical figures of Eros and Anteros, and transform the lower into the higher Eros. Here it is interesting to note that the twofold Eros, the Eros of Aphrodite and the Eros of Psyche, "τῆς Ἀφροδίτης καὶ τῆς ψυχῆς Ἐρωτα," is already mentioned in the Egyptian magic papyrus. See Reitzenstein, *Das Märchen von Amor und Psyche bei Apuleius*, p. 80.

with knife and lamp to slay him. Inevitably her willingness to lose him must burn and wound the masculine Eros most painfully.

Psyche emerges from the darkness and enters upon her destiny as a woman in love, for she is Psyche, that is, her essence is psychic, an existence in paradisaical darkness cannot satisfy her.[2] It is not until Psyche experiences Eros as more than the darkly ensnaring one, not until she sees him (*he* after all has always seen her), that she really encounters him. And in this very moment of loss and alienation, she loves him and consciously recognizes Eros.

With this she enacts the matriarchal sacrifice of the lover on a higher plane and with the full justification of her human claim to consciousness. By freeing herself from him with dagger and lamp, which she bears in place of the torch of Hecate and the other matriarchal goddesses, and so surpassing him and her servitude to him, she deprives Eros of his divine power over her. Psyche and Eros now confront one another as equals. But confrontation implies separateness. The uroboric[3] original unity of the embrace in the darkness is transcended, and with Psyche's heroic act suffering, guilt, and loneliness have come into the world. For Psyche's act is analogous to the deed of the hero who separated the original parents in order to produce the light of consciousness; in this case, it is Psyche and Eros themselves, during their sojourn in the paradise of darkness, who are the original parents.

But Psyche's act only appears to be a "masculine" deed resembling that of the hero. For there is one crucially and fundamentally different factor: although Psyche's act corresponds to the necessary development of consciousness, it is not an act of killing, indeed it is this very act that gives rise to Psyche's love. And whereas the masculine goes on from his act of heroic slaying to conquer the world, whereas his *hieros gamos* with the anima figure he has won constitutes only a part of his victory,[4] Psyche's subsequent development is nothing other than an attempt to transcend, through suffering and struggle, the separation accomplished by her act. On a new plane, that is, in love and full consciousness, she strives to be reunited with him who had been separated from her and make whole again by a new union what necessity had impelled her to sacrifice. Thus Psyche's act is the beginning of a development which not only embraces Psyche but must also seize hold of Eros.

Eros, as he himself relates, was wounded at the very outset by his own arrow, that is, he loved Psyche from the start, whereas Psyche, who wounds herself in accomplishing her deed, falls in love with Eros only in this mo-

---

[2]This is a repetition on a different plane of the matriarchal act of the Amazon, who sacrifices her womanhood, her breasts, not only in order to fight as a man in her struggle with the male for independence, but also in order to fortify the Great Goddess of the matriarchate. The "many-breasted" Ephesian Artemis wears a cloak of breasts, which are the symbols of the breasts sacrificed to her by the Amazons, if not these breasts themselves. Cf. Picard, "Die Ephesia von Anatolien," *EJ 1938.*

[3]The uroboros is the circular snake, biting its tail, that symbolizes the One and All.

[4]Cf. my *Origins and History of Consciousness*, pp. 195 ff.

ment. But what Eros calls "his love" and the manner in which he wishes to love her conflict with Psyche and her act. By her courageous readiness to embark on her independent development, to sacrifice him in order to know him, Psyche drives Eros and herself out of the paradise of uroboric unconsciousness. It is through Psyche's act that Eros first suffers the consequence of the arrow of love that he has aimed at himself.[5]

Here something should be said about the symbolism of the scalding oil that burns Eros. "Ah! rash, overbold lamp!" says our tale, "thou burnest the very lord of fire." The bringer of suffering is not a cutting weapon, like the arrow, but the substance that feeds the lamp, which is the principle of light and knowledge. The oil as essence of the plant world, an essence of the earth, which is accordingly used to anoint the lord of the earth, the king, is a widespread symbol. In this case it is significant as the basis of light, and to give light it must kindle and burn. Similarly in psychic life, it is the heat, the fire of passion, the flame and ardor of emotion that provide the basis of illumination, that is, of an illumined consciousness, which rises from the combustion of the fundamental substance and enhances it.

Through her act Psyche achieves consciousness of Eros and her love, but Eros is only wounded and is by no means illumined by Psyche's act of love and separation. In him only part of the necessary process is fulfilled: the basic substance is kindled, and he is burned by it. He is stricken with an affective pain, and through Psyche's act he is flung from the intoxication of blissful union into the pain of suffering. But the transformation is involuntary, and he experiences it passively.

When gods love mortals, they experience only desire and pleasure. The suffering had always been left to the mortal part, the human, who was usually destroyed by the encounter, while the divine partner went smilingly on to new adventures equally disastrous for humankind. But here something different happens: Psyche, for all her individuality a symbol of mortal woman's soul, takes an active part.

Eros, as we have seen in the beginning, was a boy, a youth, the son-lover of his great mother. He has circumvented Aphrodite's commandment and loved Psyche instead of making her unhappy—but has he really circumvented her command, has he not made her unhappy after all, has he not forced her into marriage with a monster, the "vilest of men"? In any event, he has not freed himself from the Mother Goddess but has merely deceived her behind her back. For his design was that everything should take place in darkness and secrecy, hidden from the eyes of the goddess. His "affair" with Psyche was planned as one of the many little digressions of Greek gods, far from the light of public opinion, which is typically represented by the feminine deities.

This situation with all its advantages for Eros is disturbed by Psyche.

[5]It need not concern us that this is a logical development of the mythical figure of Eros, who was originally less and more than an actual god.

Psyche dissolves her *participation mystique* with her partner and flings herself and him into the destiny of separation that is consciousness. Love as an expression of feminine wholeness is not possible in the dark, as a merely unconscious process; an authentic encounter with another involves consciousness, hence also the aspect of suffering and separation.

Psyche's act leads, then, to all the pain of individuation, in which a personality experiences itself in relation to a partner as something other, that is, as not only connected with the partner. Psyche wounds herself and wounds Eros, and through their related wounds their original, unconscious bond is dissolved. But it is this two-fold wounding that first gives rise to love, whose striving it is to reunite what has been separated; it is this wounding that creates the possibility of an encounter, which is prerequisite for love between two individuals. In Plato's *Symposium* the division of the One and the yearning to reunite what has been sundered are represented as the mythical origin of love; here this same insight is repeated in terms of the individual.

Bachofen writes: "The power that leads back together again that which has been cut apart is the egg-born god, whom the Orphic teachings call Metis, Phanes, Ericopaeus, Protogonos, Heracles, Thronos, Eros, the Lesbians Enorides, the Egyptians Osiris."[13] There the feminine is always the egg and the container, while the masculine is that which is born and that which parts the primordial unity; in our context, however, the exact opposite is true. Eros, the Eros of Aphrodite, holds Psyche captive, ensnared in the darkness of the egg, and Psyche, with knife and lamp, parts this perfect existence of the beginning; with her acts and sufferings she restores the original unity on a celestial plane.

Psyche's act ends the mythical age in the archetypal world, the age in which the relation between the sexes depended only on the superior power of the gods, who held men at their mercy. Now begins the age of human love, in which the human psyche consciously takes the fateful decision on itself.

THE LOOK

Jean-Paul Sartre

In this tour de force *of phenomenological analysis, Sartre attempts to derive the essential structure of* all human social relations *from the simplest of social facts—the look which one person directs upon another.*

Alone in a field or a park, I am master of all I survey. For as a person *I am the organizing center for my environmental world, and everything within my purview finds its meaning in relationship to me. But let another person appear and the world drains away from me to the new center, it is appropriated by the look of the other. Moreover the other's look upon me transforms me into an object, a satellite, whose being is dependent. My only recourse is to return the look, seeking to appropriate him. Thus arises a dialectic of possessor and possessed, a tug-of-war which according to Sartre constitutes the heart of social relations. On this model love is at bottom a sado-masochistic alternation, each person desiring both to possess the other and to be possessed by him.*

Sartre's theory of the person as "authentic project" is a direct derivation from Greek self-realization ethics and the Eros tradition. But Sartre is at odds with the tradition on cardinal points. Classically, self-knowledge and self-love are the preconditions of knowledge and love of others, while for the Sartre of Being *and* Nothingness *true knowledge or love of others is impossible. And whereas in classical Eros what is loved in the other is his unique possibility, Sartre sees what passes for love as an enslavement which amputates the other's possibilities.*

Sartre's estimate of the look finds clear precedent in the jungle, where the forward-directed gaze of the carnivore paralyzes its prey. Doubtless, in much of his behavior man resembles the jungle carnivores. But is it true that appropriation *is the deepest meaning of his first social gesture? We can expect strong issue to be taken with Sartre on this contention by proponents of sympathy and fellow-feeling (see Part VII). Moreover, Sartre has earlier said that man first appears in the world as the questioner (*Being and Nothingness, *Part One, Chap. One, I), which is close to Plato's and Aristotle's identification of man as* wonder. *But the attitude of the questioner would seem to be non-appropriative. It remains to determine which attitude is truly basic, and how the other derives from it.*

From *Being and Nothingness, An Essay on Phenomenological Ontology* by Jean-Paul Sartre, trans. Hazel E. Barnes (New York: Philosophical Library, 1956), pp. 253–256. Reprinted by permission of Philosophical Library, Inc.

It is in the reality of everyday life that the Other appears to us, and his probability refers to everyday reality. The problem is precisely this: there is in everyday reality an original relation to the Other which can be constantly pointed to and which consequently can be revealed to me outside all reference to a religious or mystic unknowable. In order to understand it I must question more exactly this ordinary appearance of the Other in the field of my perception; since this appearance refers to that fundamental relation, the appearance must be capable of revealing to us, at least as a reality aimed at, the relation to which it refers.

I am in a public park. Not far away there is a lawn and along the edge of that lawn there are benches. A man passes by those benches. I see this man; I apprehend him as an object and at the same time as a man. What does this signify? What do I mean when I assert that this object *is a man?*

If I were to think of him as being only a puppet, I should apply to him the categories which I ordinarily use to group temporal-spatial "things." That is, I should apprehend him as being "beside" the benches, two yards and twenty inches from the lawn, as exercising a certain pressure on the ground, *etc.* His relation with other objects would be of the purely additive type; this means that I could have him disappear without the relations of the other objects around him being perceptibly *changed.* In short, no new relation would appear *through him* between those things in my universe: grouped and synthesized *from my point of view* into instrumental complexes, they would *from his* disintegrate into multiplicities of indifferent relations. Perceiving him as a *man*, on the other hand, is not to apprehend an additive relation between the chair and him; it is to register an organization *without distance* of the things in my universe around that privileged object. To be sure, the lawn remains two yards and twenty inches away from him, but it is also *as a lawn* bound to him in a relation which at once both transcends distance and contains it. Instead of the two terms of the distance being indifferent, interchangeable, and in a reciprocal relation, the distance *is unfolded starting from* the man whom I see and *extending up to* the lawn as the synthetic upsurge of a univocal relation. We are dealing with a relation which is without *parts*, given at one stroke, inside of which there unfolds a spatiality which is not *my* spatiality; for instead of a grouping *toward me* of the objects, there is now an orientation which *flees from me.*

Of course this relation without distance and without parts is in no way that original relation of the Other to me which I am seeking. In the first place, it concerns only the man and the things in the world. In addition it is still an object of knowledge; I shall express it, for example, by saying that this man sees the lawn, or that in spite of the prohibiting sign he is preparing to walk on the grass, *etc.* Finally it still retains a pure character of probability: First, it is *probable* that this object is a man. Second, even granted that he is a man, it remains only probable that he *sees* the lawn at the moment that I perceive him; it is possible that he is dreaming of some project without exactly being aware of what is around him, or that he is blind, *etc., etc.* Nevertheless this new relation of the object-man to the object-lawn has a particular character; it is simultaneously given to me as a whole, since it is there in the world as an object which I can know (it is, in fact, an objective relation which I express by saying: Pierre has glanced at this watch, Jean has looked out the window, *etc.*), and at the same time it entirely escapes me. To the extent that the man-as-object is the fundamental term of this relation, to the extent that the relation *reaches toward him*, it escapes me. I can not put myself at the center of it. The distance which unfolds between the lawn and the man across the synthetic upsurge of this primary relation is a negation of the distance which I establish—as a pure type of external negation—between these two objects. The distance appears as a pure *disintegration* of the relations which I apprehend between the objects of my universe. It is not I who realize this disintegration; it appears to me as a relation which I aim at emptily across the distances which I originally established between things. It stands as a background of things, a background which on principle escapes me and which is conferred on them from without. Thus the appearance among the objects of *my* universe of an element of disintegration in that universe is what I mean by the appearance of a man in my universe.

The Other is first the permanent flight of things toward a goal which I apprehend as an object at a certain distance from me but which escapes me inasmuch as it unfolds about itself its own distances. Moreover this disintegration grows by degrees; if there exists between the lawn and the Other a relation which is without distance and which creates distance, then there exists necessarily a relation between the Other and the statue which stands on a pedestal *in the middle of* the lawn, and a relation between the Other and the big chestnut trees which border the walk; there is a total space which is grouped around the Other, and this space is made *with my space*; there is a regrouping in which I take part but which escapes me, a regrouping of all the objects which people my universe. This regrouping does not stop there. The grass is something qualified; it is *this* green grass which exists for the Other; in this sense the very quality of the object, its deep, raw green is in direct relation to this man. This green turns toward the Other a face which escapes me. I apprehend the relation of the green to the Other as an objective relation, but I can not apprehend the green as it appears to the Other. Thus suddenly an object has appeared which has stolen the world from me. Everything is in place; everything still exists for me; but everything is traversed by an invisible flight and fixed in the direction of a new object. The appearance of the Other in the world corresponds therefore to a fixed sliding of the whole universe, to a decentralization of the world which undermines the centralization which I am simultaneously effecting.

But *the Other* is still an object *for me*. He belongs to *my distances*; the man is there, twenty paces from me, he is turning his back on *me*. As such he is again two yards, twenty inches from the lawn, six yards from the statue; hence the disintegration of my universe is contained within the limits of this same universe; we are not dealing here with a flight of the world toward nothingness or outside itself. Rather it appears that the world has a kind of drain hole in the middle of its being and that it is perpetually flowing off through this hole. The universe, the flow, and the drain hole are all once again recovered, reapprehended, and fixed as an object. All this is there *for me* as a partial structure of the world, even though the total disintegration of the universe is involved. Moreover these disintegrations may often be contained within more narrow limits. There, for example, is a man who is reading while he walks. The disintegration of the universe which he represents is purely virtual; he has ears which do not hear, eyes which see nothing except his book. Between his book and him I apprehend an undeniable relation without distance of the same type as that which earlier connected the walker with the grass. But this time the form has closed in on itself. There is a full object for me to grasp. In the midst of the world I can say "man-reading" as I could say "cold stone," "fine rain." I apprehend a closed "Gestalt" in which the *reading* forms the essential quality; for the rest, it remains blind and mute, lets itself be known and perceived as a pure and simple temporal-spatial thing, and seems to be related to the rest of the world by a purely indifferent externality. The quality "man-reading" as the relation of the man to the book is simply a little particular crack in my universe. At the heart of this solid, visible form he makes himself a particular emptying. The form is massive only in appearance; its peculiar meaning is to be—in the midst of my universe, at ten paces from me, at the heart of that massivity—a closely consolidated and localized flight.

PART *III*
Agape

AGAPE: THE DIVINE BESTOWAL

Our principle of inquiry—that mankind's basic modes of love are accessible to each individual—blunts itself against Agape, for Christian doctrine maintains that God alone loves Agapistically. Man receives Agape but cannot know what it is to give it. Moreover, Agape in no way depends upon man's nature, hence it reveals nothing of that nature and, conversely, nothing in man's nature or experience illuminates Agape. Such is the doctrine strictly interpreted. Nor does the religionist find cause here for discomfort, for he is entirely convinced of the weakness of human understanding and ready to respond by faith to that which lies beyond it. But to the philosopher this resort is precluded, for philosophy does not smile upon mysteries. Come what may, she is pledged to the aim of understanding. If some matters lie beyond, this judgment must be made in the end, when every recourse has been exhausted, not in the beginning and by definition. With due note of the discrepancy, then, we turn to Agape in search of understanding.

Between Greek and Christian love, Eros and Agape, lies what Max Scheler calls a "reversal of movement." "The Christian view," he says, "boldly denies the Greek axiom that love is an aspiration of the lower towards the higher. On the contrary, now the criterion of love is that the nobler stoops to the vulgar, the healthy to the sick, the rich to the poor, the handsome to the ugly, the good and saintly to the bad and common, the Messiah to the sinners and publicans."

If Eros can be symbolized by an arrow aimed aloft, Agape appears as an arrow directed downward. It is a movement from the independent creature to the dependent, from superior to inferior, from advantage to disadvantage, from sufficiency to lack. This direction of movement appears in the word which Christianity chooses for the kind of human love which reflects or parallels Agape—Caritas, or "charity." Life exemplifies this direction in the "philanthropy" of the wealthy toward the poor, in the ministrations of physician and nurse to patient, in material aid by great nations to "developing" countries, in the naturalist's love for lower animals and inanimate nature. If we were to accept the widespread belief that woman's essential nature is dependent (the "second sex") upon the male, then this downward direction could be ascribed to man's love for woman. But its primary instance is the love of parent for child.

Our focus narrows considerably if we now add a second characteristic of Agape, its "unconditionality." God's Agape is unconditioned by the natures of its recipients; it flows to men and women regardless of who and what they are. Now a truly unconditional love in this sense is probably impossible as man's love for man; indeed, its very desirability is questionable. Testimony suggests that most of us wish to be loved in part at least for what we are, rather than in disregard of this. Yet a striking exception appears in a single case—that of maternal love. Many psychologists and laymen today agree that here the *ideal*, at least, is unconditional. A mother's love for her child should flow continuously and without regard for the child's "nature" or immediate behavior. She may disapprove of something the child has just done and register her disapproval, but the child must know that beneath this her love remains clear and uninterrupted.

In virtue of this paradigm, some investigators conclude that unconditional love is *essentially feminine*. In this case Christianity is armed against certain critics (psychologist Carl Jung is a notable example) who contend that its Trinity lacks all trace of the "eternal Feminine" and is crippled thereby. It can be contended that God's Agape conceals within itself the feminine principle.

By its downward direction and its unconditionality, Agape affords clear evidence of an intermixture of Greek sources with Judaic and specifically Christian. The sources are not of the Eros tradition, however, but of the mystical Neoplatonism whose foremost exponent was Plotinus (205–270 A.D.). According to Plotinus, God ("the One") created the world out of the *superabundance* of his own nature, by a process of overflow or *emanation*. Thus the sole reason for God's creativity and love is His own nature, which spontaneously overflows itself without suffering the least depletion.

Plotinus's markedly hydraulic conception of God has interesting psychological analogues in human love. Each of us knows the feelings which mark two very different conditions within himself, that of spiritual impoverishment and that of spiritual abundance. On the one hand there are periods in which our soul is miniscule and shrivelled, rattling in the cavern of our body like a dried pea. These days we are insufficient to ourselves and have nothing to give to others, shrinking from them instead. In marked contrast are other days in which our soul is voluminous and "bursting," as we say, with good feeling. Here is spiritual richness which we can dispense lavishly over the landscape without the least diminution. Now a hallmark of Agape is excess, while Eros expresses deficiency and need. Let the reader ask himself which of the two conditions most nearly represents the feelings associated with his loves. And let him be extremely careful in his answer.

That Agape is God's nature, wholly independent of man, is a principle which aligns perfectly with the Christian doctrine of Grace. In the words of the Roman Catholic philosopher, Jacques Maritain, Grace means "that God takes the first initiative in all good, that He gives both the will and the deed, that in crowning our merits He crowns His own gifts, that man alone cannot save himself, nor begin alone the work of salvation, nor alone prepare himself for it, that by himself alone he can only fall into evil and error . . ." (*True Humanism*).

Maritain speaks for the typically Roman Catholic belief that man's salvation requires the *cooperation* of human and divine wills, God taking "first initiative." Here Protestantism differs. The strict Protestant understanding of Grace precludes cooperation by denying the least efficacy to human initiative in the aim of salvation. As stated by Anders Nygren, Bishop of Lund, "there is from man's side no way at all that leads to God." (See the selection hereafter.) In the same vein Paul Tillich asserts "the negative judgment over any finite attempts to reach the infinite" (*The Dynamics of Faith*). Both statements reiterate Martin Luther's principle that salvation awaits "he who never doubts that all depends upon the will of God, [and] despairs completely of helping himself . . ." (*On the Enslaved Will*).

Here arise Agape's most resolute opponents. They are advocates of human autonomy and self-responsibility, and on the basis of the Grace-Agape linkage they are convinced that Agape conspires to keep man in the condition of childish dependence, mistrustful of himself, a lamb begging to be slaughtered. Under Agape-Grace man's prime virtue is obedience, but perfect obedience can be exacted from a dog, and hence a moral system which asserts its priority is at bottom dehumanizing. Here is the "slave morality" charge of Christianity's arch-opponent, Friedrich Nietzsche.

The philosophical question which must be decided is: does unconditional love *necessitate* dependence? Notice that it is relatively costless to dispense goodwill among our inferiors. "With the generosity of a great lord the happy lover smiles upon everything about him. But the great lord's generosity is always in moderation and involves no effort. It is not a very expansive sort of generosity; actually it originates in disdain." (Ortega y Gasset, *On Love*).

Disdain is not the origin of maternal love. But whether or not maternal love's unconditionality requires dependence is a serious question in light of the prevalence of "smother mothers" who try to preserve the dependence of their offspring, preventing growth and autonomy.

An analogue appears in racial relations when militant blacks in the United States charge that the "help" they receive from the best-intentioned whites is in fact a "charity" which preserves black dependence.

Returning to Agape, Maritain says that man receives it "precisely on condition that he does *not* make himself his own centre" (*True Humanism*). Here Agape is no longer unconditional, but flows only upon acknowledged dependence.

Critics have charged Eros, its eyes ever aloft, with the failure to provide consolation. And critics of Agape have charged, conversely, that this mode of love is all consolation with no dynamic of growth.

And what of this superabundance which is said to characterize Agape and God's nature? The classical Greeks, with their love of measure, appropriateness, and moderation, would have found it repugnant and horrifying. "Nothing in excess" applied to men and doubly so to gods. And a love which flowed upon people whether they wished it or not? It would have struck the Greeks as cosmic rape.

But an emphasis upon the antithetical natures of Agape and Eros must not obscure a crucial teaching of both together. Alike, Eros and Agape center all of the significance in loving, not in being loved. They tell us together that it is better to love than to be loved, and they advise us that the quality of the love is the measure of the lover. Strictly speaking, if Agape is love, men are incapable of it. Few Christians are pessimistic to such an extent. But if it be proposed that the capacity for real love calls for exceptional qualities which make it a rarity, shall we consider this pessimism, or realism?

THE CONTENT OF AGAPE

Anders Nygren

In the introduction to the section on Agape (immediately preceding),
some of the possible experiential sources of this conception of love have
been suggested. But from the strict Christian standpoint this procedure is
illegitimate, for Agape is God's love, and as such its nature cannot be in-
ferred from human experience. For this reason the sources which are employed by the commentators to follow are not experiential but scriptural.
By agreement the meaning of Agape emerges primarily from Paul's
"Hymn to Love" (I Corinthians 13) and from the identification of God and
Agape in the First Epistle of John (I John 4:8, 16).

From this starting-point the Christian and non-Christian interpreta-
tions of Agape spin off in every direction. To introduce some degree of
order in the bewildering array, four selections are offered which afford a
certain symmetry, serving like the points of the compass to divide the field
into quadrants. The key point at issue is the relationship of Agape and
Eros, God-centeredness and man-centeredness. Those whom we shall term
"radical" on this issue are convinced that Agape and Eros stand in irreconcilable contradiction such that to choose one is to reject the other.
Anders Nygren, Bishop of Lund, Sweden, the leading twentieth century
Protestant interpreter, is a radical who stands as a proponent of Agape.
Friedrich Nietzsche, prophet of the Übermensch and arch foe of Christianity, is a radical proponent of Eros.

Against the radicals, those whom we shall term "moderates" hold the
belief that a synthesis of Eros and Agape is both possible and necessary.
M. C. D'Arcy, S. J., is the leading Roman Catholic interpreter of our time
and a moderate proponent of Agape. The twentieth century German
philosopher Max Scheler is a moderate proponent of Eros who was a convert to Catholicism but maintained his Greek allegiance.

According to Nygren, Eros and Agape are the centers of two different
"general attitudes to life." Each of them organizes all things in the world
according to its own principle, hence to live out of one or the other is to see
everything in life in a different way. They "belong originally to two entirely separate spiritual worlds, between which no direct communication
is possible. They do not represent the same value in their respective con-

From *Agape and Eros* by Anders Nygren, trans. Philip S. Watson (Philadelphia: The
Westminster Press, 1953), pp. 75–80. Reprinted by permission of The Westminster Press
and The Society for Promoting Christian Knowledge.

texts, so they cannot in any circumstances be rightly substituted for one another" (Agape and Eros, *pp. 30–32).*

Our inquiry has now reached the point where it is possible for us briefly to describe the content of the Christian idea of love in so far as it concerns Divine love. Its main features can be summarised in the following four points:

(1) *Agape is spontaneous and "unmotivated"*. This is the most striking feature of God's love as Jesus represents it. We look in vain for an explanation of God's love in the character of the man who is the object of His love. God's love is "groundless"—though not, of course, in the sense that there is no ground for it at all, or that it is arbitrary and fortuitous. On the contrary, it is just in order to bring out the element of necessity in it that we describe it as "groundless"; our purpose is to emphasise that there are no extrinsic grounds for it. The only ground for it is to be found in God Himself. God's love is altogether *spontaneous*. It does not look for anything in man that could be adduced as motivation for it. In relation to man, Divine love is *"unmotivated"*. When it is said that God loves man, this is not a judgment on what man is like, but on what God is like.

It is this love, spontaneous and "unmotivated"—having no motive outside itself, in the personal worth of men—which characterises also the action of Jesus in seeking out the lost and consorting with "publicans and sinners." It was precisely in this action, which from the point of view of legal relationships was inexplicable and indefensible, that He knew Himself carrying out the Father's work and revealing His mind and will. When fellowship with God is conceived of as a legal relationship, Divine love must in the last resort be dependent on the worth of its object. But in Christ there is revealed a Divine love which breaks all bounds, refusing to be controlled by the value of its object, and being determined only by its own intrinsic nature. According to Christianity, "motivated" love is human; spontaneous and "unmotivated" love is Divine.

This being so, we can see why Jesus was bound to attack a religious relationship conceived in legal terms. Had He been concerned only to claim a place for the idea of *love in the most general sense* within the religious relationship, He could have secured it even within the legal scheme. There was no need to smash the legal scheme in order to do that. The love for which there is room in this scheme, however, is the "motivated" love that is directed to the righteous, to those who deserve it. But Jesus is not concerned with love in this ordinary sense, but with the spontaneous, unmotivated love that is Agape; and for this there is fundamentally no place within the framework of legal order. To go back once more to the words of Jesus in Matt. ix. 17, we may say that *Agape is the new wine which inevitably bursts the old wineskins*. Now we see also why there had to be a revolutionary change of attitude towards the righteous and the sinner. If God's love were restricted to the righteous it would be evoked by its object and not spontaneous; but just by the fact that it seeks sinners, who do not deserve it and can lay no claim to it, it manifests most clearly its spontaneous and unmotivated nature.

(2) *Agape is "Indifferent to value"*. This does not really add anything new to what has already been said; but in order to prevent a possible misunderstanding, it is necessary to give special emphasis to one aspect of the point we have just made. When Jesus makes the righteous and sinners change places, it might at first sight appear as if there were a matter of simple transvaluation, or inversion of values; but we have already said enough to show that it is a question of something far deeper. It is not that Jesus simply reverses the generally accepted standard of values and holds that the sinner is "better" than the righteous. True as it is to say that He effected a "transvaluation of all values," yet the phrase can easily give rise to a false impression. Actually, something of far deeper import than any "transvaluation" is involved here—namely, the principle that *any thought of valuation whatsoever* is out of place in connection with fellowship with God. When God's love is directed to the sinner, then the position is clear; all thought of valuation is excluded in advance; for if God, the Holy One, loves the sinner, it cannot be because of his sin, but in spite of his sin. But when God's love is shown to the righteous and godly, there is always the risk of our thinking that God loves the man on account of his righteousness and godliness. But this is a denial of Agape—as if God's love for the "righteous" were not just as unmotivated and spontaneous as His love for the sinner! As if there were any other Divine love than spontaneous and unmotivated Agape! It is only when all thought of the worthiness of the object is abandoned that we can understand what Agape is. God's love allows no limits to be set for it by the character or conduct of man. The distinction between the worthy and the unworthy, the righteous and the sinner, sets no bounds to His love. "He maketh His sun to rise on the evil and the good, and sendeth rain on the just and the unjust" (Matt. v. 45).

(3) *Agape is creative.* When we seek to analyse the structure of the idea of Agape, what first attracts our attention is its spontaneous and unmotivated character. This, as we have described it above, shows that we are dealing with a love of a quite unique kind. The deepest reason for its uniqueness, however, has not yet been stated. What is ultimately decisive for the meaning of Agape can only be seen when we observe that it is *Divine* love and therefore shares in the creativeness that is characteristic of all the life of God. Agape is creative love. God does not love that which is already in itself worthy of love, but on the contrary, that which in itself has no worth acquires worth just by becoming the object of God's love. Agape has nothing to do with the kind of love that depends on the recognition of a valuable quality in its object; Agape does not recognise value, but creates it. Agape loves, and imparts value by loving. The man

who is loved by God has no value in himself; what gives him value is precisely the fact that God loves him. *Agape is a value-creating principle.*

We have now reached the deepest and ultimately decisive feature of the idea of Agape—a feature which it must be said has been very much obscured in modern theology. Ever since Ritschl's time it has been common for theologians to speak of "the infinite value of the human soul" as one of the central ideas of Christianity, and to connect it with the idea of "God's fatherly love." Thus A. von Harnack, in *Das Wesen des Christentums*, claims that the teaching of Jesus as a whole can be grouped under three heads, each of such a nature as to contain the whole; and one of these he entitles "God the Father and the infinite value of the human soul." To this, however, we can rightly object that the idea of "the infinite value of the human soul" is by no means a central idea of Christianity. Only a false exegesis has made it possible to find support for this idea in the oft-quoted passage: "What doth it profit a man, to gain the whole world, and forfeit his life (A. V. soul)? For what should a man give in exchange for his life (A. V. soul)?" (Mark viii. 36 f.). Moreover, Harnack's statement that "all who bear a human face are of more value than the whole world" shows very clearly that the thought of an infinite value of this kind as belonging to man by nature has its roots elsewhere than in Christianity.

What chiefly interests us here, however, is the destructive effect that this idea has had on the conception of Divine love. The suggestion that man is by nature possessed of such an inalienable value, easily gives rise to the thought that it is this matchless value on which God's love is set. Even though the Divine spark may seem to have been wholly quenched in a man sunk in sin, it is none the less present in "all who bear a human face," and its potentialities are capable of being actualised in everyone. Viewed in this light, God's forgiveness of sins means merely that He disregards the manifold faults and failings of the outward life and looks only at the inward, imperishable value which not even sin has been able to destroy. His forgiving love means that He sees and values the pearl of great price, regardless of the defilement that happens at present to cling to it. He overlooks the defects and imperfections and concentrates on the essence of the personality which wins His approbation.

If this interpretation of Divine forgiveness and love were correct, God's love would not in the last resort be spontaneous and unmotivated but would have an adequate motive in the infinite value inherent in human nature. The forgiveness of sins would then imply merely the recognition of an already existing value. But it is evident enough that this is not the forgiveness of sins as Jesus understands it. When He says, "Thy sins are forgiven thee," this is no merely formal attestation of the presence of a value which justifies the overlooking of faults; it is the bestowal of a gift. Something really new is introduced, something new is taking place. The forgiveness of sins is a *creative work of Divine power* (ἐξουσία) which Jesus knows Himself called to carry out on earth, and which can be put on a level with other Divine miracles, such as His healing of the paralytic (Mark ii. 5-12).

(4) *Agape is the initiator of fellowship with God.* Not only does Agape determine the essential and characteristic content of Christian fellowship with God, but in virtue of its creative nature it is also important for the initiation of that fellowship. In the relations between God and man the initiative in establishing fellowship lies with Divine Agape. If we consider the implications of the idea of Agape, it becomes very plain that all the other ways by which man seeks to enter into fellowship with God are futile. This is above all true of the righteous man's way of meritorious conduct, but it is no less true of the sinner's way of repentance and amendment. Repentance and amendment are no more able than righteousness to move God to love.

In this connection also the advent of Agape is completely revolutionary. Hitherto the question of fellowship with God had always been understood as a question of the way by which man could come to God. But now, when not only the way of righteousness but also that of self-abasement and amendment is rejected as incapable of leading to the goal, it follows that *there is from man's side no way at all that leads to God.* If such a thing as fellowship between God and man nevertheless exists, this can only be due to God's own action; God must Himself come to meet man and offer him His fellowship. There is thus no way for man to come to God, but only a way for God to come to man: the way of Divine forgiveness, Divine love.

AGAPE AND HUMAN INITIATIVE

Martin C. D'Arcy, S. J.

Closely following the synthesis of Greek philosophy and Christian theology achieved by St. Thomas Aquinas, Father D'Arcy contends that the man who truly fulfills his own nature is at the same time obeying God's will, hence Eros and Agape are harmonious. According to the Thomistic doctrine of natural law, every man seeks his own good by "inclination" (closely resembling the Eros of Greek self-realization) and this natural law is a reflection of divine law. The man who fulfills his own natural end in this way will subsequently be freed from the bonds of human nature by God's Agape, hence fulfillment of the human is followed by transcendence of the human.

As thus stated man's salvation would appear to call for a partnership of human and divine initiative, but is this the case? According to Thomism the initiative in natural law, both in establishing it and in making it known, is entirely God's. To a naturalistic humanist this "reconciliation" in fact empties Eros of all content, resting man's self-realization on obedience to an initiative not his own.

Similarly with Agape. It has two forms, God's love and our love for our neighbour. It is theocentric; indeed, God is Agape, and there is no self-love. It is banished. In Nygren's summary Agape is a self-giving; it comes down from above; it is a free gift; it is unselfish: it freely gives and spends; it is sovereign and independent with regard to its object; hence it is spontaneous, "uncaused," and creates value in its object. Finally, "Agape lives by God's life . . . is primarily God's own love," and "when it appears in man, is a love that takes its form from God's own love." Now in this description there is no mention of any distinction between grace and nature, the supernatural and the natural, and to the medieval and modern Catholic theologian, who is criticized by Nygren, this is a grave omission. The very theologian who lays such stress on the value of a properly ordered self-love, when writing on human nature, will with reserve use, when writing of grace, a language closely resembling that of Nygren's Agape. He will hold that it only causes confusion to neglect the fundamental Christian distinction of grace and nature. He will also go on to say that the real problem is not what Nygren indicates, but the relation of grace to nature, and the conciliation of much that can be called Eros with Agape. The point made here is that grace does not destroy all that is human; it perfects it and elevates it to a new dynamic, and the real problem is to work out how both nature and the supernatural life survive in their integrity in the Christian order. Nygren cuts the knot and sunders self-love and grace, nature and the supernatural completely. This does not make a peace between the two, but only a solitude in which Agape withers.

All is not however well with Agape, even though it is given the entire rule in the Christian kingdom. Nygren would have it that the Gospels proclaim his doctrine of Agape. But is this so? He quotes the Prodigal Son to prove that Agape is spontaneous and has nothing to do with deserts. But he makes no mention of the elder son, to whom most comforting words are addressed at the end of the parable on account of his long-standing fidelity. He cites the parable of the vineyard and the equal payment of all the labourers, whether they entered at an early hour or at a late hour. But here again the fact is ignored that they did offer themselves and that all did some labour. Their lot is quite different from those who remained outside. There is no need, however, to press the argument from the Gospels. Such an extreme form of the Agape theory will not work out. God is Agape, and we should naturally expect someone to be the beneficiary of that love, and as beneficiary to respond. But if this theory is taken literally there is no one to respond. There is no need of that intercommunication which is essential to love. We are told that no Eros (in Nygren's sense) should enter in in man's return of love, that it should be all Agape. But as we have seen, God is Agape. There is nothing human or personal in the response, nor can there be on this interpretation. In the elimination of Eros man has been eliminated. Of this consequence Nygren seems to be uncomfortably aware, for he says that man's return of love must be Agape and not Eros, and then goes on to say that we can hardly speak of man's response as Agape; it should rather be called faith. Agape, that is, God's love, should be used, perhaps, exclusively of man's love of his neighbour. In line with the same reasoning he suggests in one place that the "deep truth of predestination" fits in with this interpretation. Yes, indeed, if we take "predestination" as meaning that God arbitrarily constrains those whom He wills to be saved without any human response or act of free will on their part. That this is what Nygren really means seems to be clear from his remark following on his reference to predestination. "Man is to love God, not because he finds fuller and completer satisfaction of his need in God than in any other object of desire, but because God's 'uncaused' love has over-powered him and constrained him, so that he can do nothing else than love God."

This image of "overpowering" and "constraining" sounds like an echo of the old Dionysiac frenzy and the constraining of Persephone by the god of the dark world. It occurs frequently in the experience of the mystery religions. The classical instance is to be found in the Sixth book of Virgil: "But the prophetess, not yet Phoebus' willing slave, is storming with giant frenzy in her cavern, as though she hoped to unseat from her bosom the mighty god. All the more sharply he plies her mouth with his bit till its fury flags, tames her savage soul, and moulds her to his will by strong constraint." Such a constraint is the antipodes to the Christian revelation of God. Yet if we remove this last spasm of human activity and freedom we are left with a theology which may be called Christian, but is, in fact, hardly if at all discernible from pantheism or monism. If the Agape be an act which proceeds from man and at the same time has nothing human or free in it, how can that act, which is expressly declared to be divine, be anything less. And if man is literally divine, then we are back at the monism of the ancient Gnostic cult.

This is not to deny that in the Christian teaching there is a deep mystery and that much of what Nygren says of Agape is drawn from the New Testament. There is indeed a problem which can be stated in terms of Eros and Agape, but it has been wrongly formulated by Nygren; so wrongly formulated that the way out, whether by Eros or by Agape, is barred. Neither Eros nor Agape can function in Nygren's formulation. The proper way of stating the problem is surely this: that God must act with sovereign power and freedom, and we know from the New Testament and all Christian teaching that God has freely offered to man a way of life which is His own, the way of what Nygren calls Agape. God, therefore, has the initiative and by His grace does lift man up into an order of love which is above that which Nygren delineates in terms of Eros. But God does this without constraint or defiance of what is best in human nature; He makes man a co-heir with His own Divine son without destruction of his freedom or his human personality. Grace perfects nature and does not undo it. How this can be so is precisely the mystery. No Procrustean solution will do; no Pelagian overemphasis on the natural or Eros will serve, nor again an overlordship of Agape so peremptory that it leaves no room for human value. This puzzle has its repercussions in all debates about love, whether they concern grace and nature or the love of self and the love of others, personal rights and duties and duties to the State, community or motherland. There is a desire of the self to give its all and a desire to be oneself and be perfect. The principle of give and take has to be harmonized in all phases of love. This is the problem which vexed the medieval thinkers—a problem which is the same as that confronting us in Nygren's pages, but seen from another angle, and in the next chapter we must consider it. . . .

A reader of Nygren's work might easily pick up a wrong impression of the difference between his view of "caritas" and that of the main body of Catholic writers. He holds that caritas or Agape is entirely gratuitous, that God gives the initiative and the increase, in fact, that without God's grace man can do nothing. He contrasts with this a view that caritas is

God's response to human merit, that human desire, the rapacious and levelling intellect and self-love have all a place in caritas, and in general that man's natural virtue counts and that man works with God and is graced as he deserves. Such an interpretation of the Latin Fathers and the great Scholastic writers is gravely mistaken, and seems to ignore the fundamental distinction which they all make between the natural and the supernatural, between nature and grace. In the text I have avoided emphasizing this distinction in order not to complicate the issue. For a proper understanding of caritas it is, however, essential to begin with this distinction. Caritas is essentially a grace, and therefore supernatural, and if this be misunderstood, the whole of Catholic teaching will be misunderstood. Very shortly, the meaning of the supernatural can be stated as follows: God is infinitely perfect; man belongs to a finite order of being, an order in which matter and spirit meet. Man is highest in the animal world and lowest in the world of spirit. But because he is spiritual he has a far-off kinship with God in that with his mind he meets truth and with his love he desires goodness—and God is truth and goodness and knows and loves perfectly. This means that friendship, an exchange of love, is possible between man and God. But as man's mind is so feeble and his will so contrary to have any close friendship with God would be impossible if he had to rely on his own strength. Now God might have so helped man, as an inspiring teacher draws the best out of a pupil or a great lover evokes a new responsiveness in the beloved—that man would have loved Him to the limit of his natural capacity. What we learn from the New Testament is that God did more than this. His design was and is so to animate man with His own love that man, in and through God's love or grace, should have a kind of equality of friendship, such that he could know God as God knows Himself, and love God as God loves Himself in the Blessed Trinity. This is to give man, as it were, a new dimension, to raise him far above his natural capacity. Not even God could do this to a material thing; it would crack under the strain and cease to be itself. But a being who has a mind and a spiritual will and power to love can submit to this Divine pressure on it without destruction. The reason is that a mind, as such, has no limitation, and, as I suggest, a person in being a person is *for* himself and *to* another; that is to say, he is both a living self-contained being and a living relation. On both counts a human being can remain himself while acting above his natural capacity. He is energized by the love of God; that love is diffused in his heart by the Holy Ghost so that he can say: "Abba, Father," and enjoy equal terms of friendship with the Son of God.

Now it is this mysterious elevation of man above himself which is described in the technical language of the supernatural and of grace. The Epistles of St. Paul abound in attempts to describe it. He calls it grace, adoption, regeneration, membership in Christ. St. John's favourite name for it is "sonship." Furthermore, as is obvious, man can do nothing of himself to deserve this gift, to begin this life or to live it. The early Christians were told over and over again that of themselves they could do nothing. "So then it is not of him that willeth nor of him that runneth, but of God that showeth mercy." And again: "For by grace you are saved through faith, and that not of yourselves, for it is the gift of God; not of works, that no man may glory. For we are his workmanship, created in Christ Jesus in good works, which God hath prepared that we should walk in them." These are but two examples of what is a constant refrain in the New Testament and in early Christian literature. So far from there being any hesitation about this or going back upon it, Councils laid it down as an essential of the Christian faith, and the later Scholastic theologians accepted it as a First principle.

The main and orthodox Catholic tradition, as represented by the Fathers and the great Scholastic writers, is, therefore, entirely at one with Nygren in maintaining the gratuity of God's gifts of grace and charity. Their doctrine of the "supernatural" insures the concomitant doctrine that man can do nothing of himself to deserve God's Agape or exercise it. Nygren unwittingly misrepresents that view and sets up a false contrast between the pure doctrine of Agape and the diluted half-human and half-divine version of it which he thinks St. Augustine canonized and St. Thomas Aquinas developed. The point of difference between their view and that of Nygren does not lie here. They both start from the same tests, but whereas Nygren so exalts Agape that no place is left for any properly human response and co-operation, the great Scholastic thinkers held on to the principle that in all friendships two are concerned and not one. Even though man's love in the new covenant of friendship with God is supernatural, that is to say, beyond his natural capacity, he does not become an automaton; he is not forced, not taken hold of willy nilly and made to love. The whole purpose of God's action is to give and not to take away, to restore and increase the dignity of the human person. This means that man must be left his freedom, his power to accept or refuse, and his power, consequently, to merit by cooperation with Divine love. As Nygren ignores man's part he oversimplifies the problem of grace and charity. He has to leave out the second half of a sentence such as that from the Book of Revelation: "they shall walk with me in white, because they are worthy." The real problem, as the great Catholic thinkers saw it, was to allow for the full force of grace and Agape and also for man's participation in the new supernatural friendship. It is only when this is understood that we can appreciate the care and thought given to such problems as that of grace and freewill, man's divine sonship and his ever-continuing finite status and selfhood.

So far I have used the words "grace" and "charity" as if they were equivalent. Some great theologians, like Scotus and Bellarmine and

Lessius, have argued for the identity, but the majority make a distinction. They hold with St. Augustine that "grace precedes charity," that charity, which is an active habit, presupposes the "new birth" of which St. Paul speaks. This question, interesting as it is in itself, does not concern us. What is more relevant is the proper definition of caritas and its relation with that love of God which does lie within our human capacity. One well-known definition of supernatural charity runs as follows: it is the love which refers all things to God and sets God above all things, even man himself. This is a more technical paraphrase of the command by Christ that we should love God with our whole strength and with our whole mind. St. Thomas sums up the difference between natural and supernatural love in an answer to an objection: "God, in so far as he is the general good from whom all natural good depends, is loved with a natural love by everyone; in so far, however, as He is the good who makes all happy in supernatural bliss, he is loved with a supernatural love." The point of this is that with our natural knowledge we can have some idea of the goodness of God; we can see that all good and lovely things are but a reflection of His goodness and that they come from Him. But in the Christian Revelation we learn a new lesson about God; we are given the power to understand that God is Our Father, that His nature is love, and that He intends to share His love with us and give us a vision of His essential loveliness. The act with which we respond to this invitation is supernatural charity.

The question here debated by the theologians about the difference between natural and supernatural charity may, as they frame it, seem a little unreal. The reason for this is that, in order to make their contrasts clear, they take a theoretical example from the natural order. The God who is loved as the "general good from whom all natural good depends" is undoubtedly very different from the God of the New Testament. But the problem is much more difficult when we appeal to experience and try from experience to make a clear demarcation. The effect of the Christian teaching has been very widespread and is not confined to those who are confessedly of the Christian faith. Pagans, too, show a love both in word and in act which seems to pass far beyond the limits of the love as laid down, for example, by St. Thomas. Lastly there are many whose mind does not seem to run with their deeds. They prove a very high degree of love by their acts, though in word they seem not to know what they are doing. Modern psychology has proved, if proof were needed, how badly a man may mistake his own motives and shy away from truth which he has been shocked into fearing. Again, we have to allow for many uncovenanted graces from God, Who desires all to enjoy His friendship. Many a man, it may be, owing to his heredity and environment and upbringing is so fixed in a certain way of viewing God and the world that it would need an extraordinary shaking up of his personality for him to see the full truth. God may, to use the vivid words of Gerard Hopkins, prefer to work within the "burl of being" of the individual man and change "the cleave" of it. The one law is that the man should be moved by supernatural charity.

On this relation of the natural to the supernatural not all follow St. Thomas in his clear-cut distinction. He holds that there is a substantial difference in the two kinds of love. A man cannot love God above all things and more than himself with a real and efficacious love without grace; if he appears to do so, then it is only the semblance of the real love, a pious dream or ineffective fancy. Against St. Thomas many teach that there is no such substantial difference, that a difference in mode suffices, as a child of a family might love its parents very much, but unless its love had that special quality which belongs to family affection, it would be wanting in that mode of love which is appropriate to parents and brothers and sisters. Such delicate but vital differences in love are not easy to tabulate, nor again the relation of charity to the other virtues. Some theologians so stress the importance of charity that they seem loath to give any value to other virtues, such as courage or justice or purity, unless they explicitly fall under that of charity. They quote the great saying of St. Paul that "if I should distribute all my goods to feed the poor, and if I should deliver my body to be burnt, and have not charity, it profiteth me nothing." They cannot, however, mean that we must always explicitly refer what we do to the love of God, and once we admit that a virtue has an intrinsic excellence of its own and that only some kind of overruling principle of life or motive is needed, the edge of the difficulty is removed. All our actions are to some extent affected by our central love; when a man is selfish at heart even his virtues are slightly tinged by this attitude, and it is a common experience to find that a man who has changed his convictions, undergone a testing and shaking experience and survived it, without permanent harm, talks, speaks and acts as a "different person." The whole man is in each of our acts, and that is why love does have some say as to the dress in which we clothe our virtues and our vices. The same truth can be illustrated in a more general way in the rise and decline of a culture. New beliefs which are accepted and loved influence the style and idiom in art, literature, customs and morals, and when the belief begins to fade both the appreciation and practice of the moral virtues begins to evaporate. There is a remarkable parallel between the love of a living God and the chivalry, the "lowliness and loyalty" of our social relations. (I am thinking of the lines in Piers Plowman: "Love and lowliness and loyalty, these shall be Lords in the land, truth to save.") The ideal of womanhood and marriage, for instance, is girt about with dogmas; she is the image of God, she reflects the beauty of the Virgin Mother of God, the union of marriage is like to that of the soul with Christ and the Church with its Head, her fidelity is like to that of God's suffering fidelity and covenant with man. Once these dogmas began to lose their sway the ideal of the virgin, the wife and the mother also grow dim, the moral customs and laws of purity and marriage are changed, and love is regulated by business and convenience.

The difference caused by the absence of the supernatural is unmistakable, and can easily be seen, for example, in a comparison of two such novels as Sigrid Undset's *Kristin Lavransdatter* and Galsworthy's *Forsyte Saga*. In both men and women toil and suffer, love and grow estranged, and evil seems to conquer, as the seasons come and go year after year; but in the one the sin and suffering and death take place under a living Providence, and the ravages of time are redeemed in some mystery of love; whereas in the other there is no hope. But it is in such biographies as those of Emma Goldman and Jan Valtin's *Out of the Night* that the contrast is most clearly presented. All the details described may not have happened, but the life lived and the persons are drawn from their experience. In both stories we read of superlative acts of courage and resolution, astounding endurance and self-sacrifice, but the violence and the treachery, the ruthlessness regarding others' bodies and lives, fill one with pity and horror. Here is naturalism, naked and exposed, without grace. And even the virtues in this underworld without light look like the "splendid vices" of St. Augustine. They cannot but excite admiration, for they make one understand how marvellous is the nature of man with its pride and determination and its willingness to sacrifice everything. Why these two should remain with man to the last will, I hope, become plain when the nature of the two loves by which man is driven is sketched out in the later chapters of this book.

However difficult, therefore, it may be to put one's finger on the boundary line between natural love and the supernatural, there can be no doubt of the unhappy condition of the natural when the supernatural is withdrawn. In his essay on Christianity and the Supernatural, Baron Von Hügel tries to indicate some of the positive effects of grace. He says that "decency is carried up into devotedness and homeliness into heroism. . . . Simple justice and average fairness are transfigured into genial generosity and over-flowing self-devotion. Competition is replaced by co-operation, indeed even by vicarious work and suffering. And now the desire for a simple survival of the natural activities and of the natural happiness, and of a dim and discursive sense of God, is replaced by thirst for the full expansion and the final establishment of the human personality in an endless life of such self-devotion and of a vivid, intuitive vision of God, supreme Author and End of all Nature and Supernature."

Von Hügel then mentions seven virtues: courage, purity, unlimited compassion, humility, truthfulness, self-abandonment in the hands of God and spiritual joy, and gives some very touching examples in the practice of them of a supernatural quality. I will quote one of these examples as it bears on the nature of love. "There is an Irish Roman Catholic washerwoman with whom I had the honour of worshipping some thirty years ago in our English Midlands. She had twelve children, whom she managed to bring up most carefully, and a drunken husband, an Englishman of no religion, openly unfaithful to herself. The constant standing of many years at last brought on some grave internal complications: a most delicate operation would alone save her life. Whilst resting in hospital against the coming ordeal, with the experts thoroughly hopeful of success, a visiting surgeon came round, really the worse for drink, and insisted with trembling hands upon an examination there and then. This doomed the patient to a certain death, which duly came a week later. Yet from the first moment of the fatal change to the last instant of her consciousness (so the priest who attended her throughout declared to me after all was over) she was absorbed in seeking to respond, with all she was, to this great grace of God, this opportunity of utter self-abandonment to Him, and this although she dearly loved her children, and although she knew well that her eyes would hardly be closed before their father would marry a bad woman and give her full authority over this, their mother's darling little flock. All possible plans were made by the dying woman for each of her children, and from the first moment she spontaneously exacted from the priest a promise to prevent any prosecution of the fuddled surgeon—she never stopped to consider his offence even to forgive it; it was God, and the utter trust in Him, and in the wisdom, the love of His Will, that swallowed up all the pain, physical and mental, and all possible conflicts and perplexities."

Lastly, Von Hügel points to certain implications, which, as he thinks, are characteristic of the Supernatural. The last of these points to the distinction between all natural appreciation of God and the full Christian faith and love. "Qualities, such as reality, transcendance, presence, existence—these are not apprehended as floating in the air, or fancied in the mind; such qualities, or the impressions of such qualities, are, however confusedly, however unuttered even to itself by the apprehending mind, felt and loved as effects and constituents of a Reality distinct from the apprehender, and yet a Reality sufficiently like the human spirit when thus supernaturally sustained and sublimated, to be recognized by this human spirit with rapt, joyous adoration as its living source, support and end." Other religions have, he says, something similar, but "it remains a fact that, given the truth of Theism, Christianity brings to this truth a depth of roots, a breadth of inclusions and utilizations, and a penetrative delicacy of applications matched only very partially and sporadically elsewhere. For in Christianity its faith in God is the culmination and resolution of the other four convictions and tensions—of the belief in the natural-supernatural character of human experience as a whole; of the insight into the social-solitary quality of all religion; of the apprehension that the supernatural endowment is very unequal amongst men, and that there exists one supremely rich, uniquely intimate union with God, in one particular human mind and will; and of the experience that an element of Suffering enters into every Serenity. Thus everything beautiful, true and good, of whatever degree or kind, is indeed included within Christian Theism, but it is included therein according to certain very definite principles; the whole is thus not a guess or a jumble, a fog or a quicksand; it is a certainty as rock-firm as it is rich and elastic, a certainty groped after and confirmed by all that is virile, pure, humble, truthful, tender, self-immolating and deeply joyous in the depths of man's longings and attempts."

The full meaning of "caritas" cannot, however, be understood without some reference to the doctrine of "incorporation" in Christ. As we say of a child: "How like his father"—so an Apostle, if he were alive now would say of a Christian acting with supernatural charity: "How he reminds me of the Lord!"

> For Christ plays in ten thousand places,
> Lovely in limbs, and lovely in eyes not his
> To the Father through the features of man's faces.

AGAPE AS RESENTMENT AND SUPPRESSION

Friedrich Nietzsche

Nietzsche's charges against Judeo-Christianity are two: that it expresses the resentment of inferior for superior, and that it is a "slave morality" which binds man in ignorance and servitude.

The earliest Jews were ragged nomads wandering the fringe of the desert and surrounded by cultures which surpassed them by thousands of years. To gain the advantage they used their only distinction—their inferiority. They made themselves the chosen people by inventing a god who preferred weakness, deficiency, infirmity.

The subsequent institutionalization of Agape by Christianity is directed at keeping man in the state of dependence, preventing his development of intelligence, initiative, and autonomy. It does this by making virtues of weakness, humility, self-disgust, poverty, chastity. It has thus inverted all of the values of classical humanism, and Nietzsche calls for the overthrow of Christianity by a return to the heroic code and a resumption of classical striving for the Übermensch—*the fully realized man.*

Together with Nygren, Nietzsche sees Eros and Agape as contradictory and irreconcilable life-styles. But Agape to Nietzsche is not unconditional, flowing to all men alike in complete disregard of their natures. As suggested by the Beatitudes and by Paul's inversion of Greek values in 1 Corinthians, Agape flows to disadvantage before advantage.

. . .The problem I set in this work is not what will replace mankind in the order of living beings (—Man is an *end*—); but, what type of man must be *reared,* must be *willed,* as having the highest value, as being the most worthy of life and the surest guarantee of the future.

This more valuable type has appeared often enough already: but as a happy accident, as an exception, never as *willed.* He has rather been precisely the most feared; hitherto he has been almost the terrible in itself;—and from out the very fear he provoked there arose the will to rear the type which has now been reared, *attained*: the domestic animal, the gregarious animal, the sick animal man,—the Christian. . . .

We must not deck out and adorn Christianity: it has waged a deadly war upon this *higher* type of man, it has set a ban upon all the fundamental

From *The Antichrist* by Friedrich Nietzsche. *The Complete Works of Friedrich Nietzsche*, ed. Oscar Levy (London: George Allen & Unwin Ltd; New York: The Macmillan Company, 1911), Vol. 16, trans. Anthony M. Ludovici, pp. 128–135. Reprinted by permission of The Macmillan Company.

instincts of this type, and has distilled evil and the devil himself out of these instincts:—the strong man as the typical pariah, the villain. Christianity has sided with everything weak, low, and botched; it has made an ideal out of *antagonism* towards all the self-preservative instincts of strong life: it has corrupted even the reason of the strongest intellects, by teaching that the highest values of intellectuality are sinful, misleading and full of temptations. The most lamentable example of this was the corruption of Pascal, who believed in the perversion of his reason through original sin, whereas it had only been perverted by his Christianity.

A painful and ghastly spectacle has just risen before my eyes. I tore down the curtain which concealed mankind's *corruption*. This word in my mouth is at least secure from the suspicion that it contains a moral charge against mankind. It is—I would fain emphasise this again—free from moralic acid: to such an extent is this so, that I am most thoroughly conscious of the corruption in question precisely in those quarters in which hitherto people have aspired with most determination to "virtue" and to "godliness." As you have already surmised, I understand corruption in the sense of *decadence*. What I maintain is this, that all the values upon which mankind builds its highest hopes and desires are *decadent* values.

I call an animal, a species, an individual corrupt, when it loses its instincts, when it selects and *prefers* that which is detrimental to it. A history of the "higher feelings," of "human ideals"—and it is not impossible that I shall have to write it—would almost explain why man is so corrupt. Life itself, to my mind, is nothing more nor less than the instinct of growth, of permanence, of accumulating forces, of power: where the will to power is lacking, degeneration sets in. My contention is that all the highest values of mankind *lack* this will,—that the values of decline and of *nihilism* are exercising the sovereign power under the cover of the holiest names.

Christianity is called the religion of *pity*.—Pity is opposed to the tonic passions which enhance the energy of the feeling of life: its action is depressing. A man loses power when he pities. By means of pity the drain on strength which suffering itself already introduces into the world is multiplied a thousandfold. Through pity, suffering itself becomes infectious; in certain circumstances it may lead to a total loss of life and vital energy, which is absurdly out of proportion to the magnitude of the cause (—the case of the death of the Nazarene). This is the first standpoint; but there is a still more important one. Supposing one measures pity according to the value of the reactions it usually stimulates, its danger to life appears in a much more telling light. On the whole, pity thwarts the law of development which is the law of selection. It preserves that which is ripe for death, it fights in favour of the disinherited and the condemned of life; thanks to the multitude of abortions of all kinds which it maintains in life, it lends life itself a sombre and questionable aspect. People have dared to call pity a virtue (—in every *noble* culture it is considered as a weakness—); people went still further, they exalted it to *the* virtue, the root and origin of all virtues,—but, of course, what must never be forgotten is the fact that this was done from the standpoint of a philosophy which was nihilistic, and on whose shield the device *The Denial of Life* was inscribed. Schopenhauer was right in this respect: by means of pity, life is denied and made *more worthy of denial,*—pity is the *praxis* of Nihilism. I repeat, this depressing and infectious instinct thwarts those instincts which aim at the preservation and enhancement of the value life: by *multiplying* misery quite as much as by preserving all that is miserable, it is the principal agent in promoting decadence,—pity exhorts people to nothing, to *nonentity!* But they do not say "*nonentity,*" they say "Beyond," or "God," or "the true life"; or Nirvana, or Salvation, or Blessedness, instead. This innocent rhetoric, which belongs to the realm of the religio-moral idiosyncrasy, immediately appears to be *very much less innocent* if one realises what the tendency is which here tries to drape itself in the mantle of sublime expressions—the tendency of hostility to life. Schopenhauer was hostile to life: that is why he elevated pity to a virtue . . . . Aristotle, as you know, recognized in pity a morbid and dangerous state, of which it was wise to rid one's self from time to time by a purgative: he regarded tragedy as a purgative. For the sake of the instinct of life, it would certainly seem necessary to find some means of lancing any such morbid and dangerous accumulation of pity, as that which possessed Schopenhauer (and unfortunately the whole of our literary and artistic decadence as well, from St. Petersburg to Paris, from Tolstoi to Wagner), if only to make it *burst.* . . . Nothing is more unhealthy in the midst of our unhealthy modernity, than Christian pity. To be doctors *here*, to be inexorable *here*, to wield the knife effectively *here*,—all this is our business, all this is *our* kind of love to our fellows, this is what makes *us* philosophers, us hyperboreans!——

It is necessary to state whom we regard as our antithesis:—the theologians, and all those who have the blood of theologians in their veins—the whole of our philosophy. . . . A man must have had his very nose upon this fatality, or better still he must have experienced it in his own soul; he must almost have perished through it, in order to be unable to treat this matter lightly (—the free-spiritedness of our friends the naturalists and physiologists is, in my opinion, a *joke,*—what they lack in these questions is passion, what they lack is having suffered from these questions—). This poisoning extends much further than people think: I unearthed the "arrogant" instinct of the theologian, wherever nowadays people feel themselves idealists,—wherever, thanks to superior antecedents, they claim the right to rise above reality and to regard it with suspicion. . . . Like the priest the idealist has every grandiloquent concept in his hand (—and not only in his hand!), he wields them all with kindly contempt against the "understanding," the "senses," "honours," "decent living," "science"; he regards such things as *beneath* him, as detrimental and seductive forces, upon the face of which, "the Spirit" moves in pure absoluteness:—as if humility, chastity, poverty, in a word *holiness,* had not done incalculably more harm to life hitherto, than any sort of horror and vice. . . . Pure spirit is pure falsehood. . . . As long as the priest, the *professional* denier, calumniator and poisoner of life, is considered as the *highest* kind of man, there can be no answer to the question, what *is* truth? Truth has already been turned topsy-turvy, when the conscious advocate of nonentity and of denial passes as the representative of "truth."

It is upon this theological instinct that I wage war. I find traces of it everywhere. Whoever has the blood of theologians in his veins, stands from the start in a false and dishonest position to all things. The pathos which grows out of this state, is called *Faith*: that is to say, to shut one's eyes once and for all, in order not to suffer at the sight of incurable falsity. People convert this faulty view of all things into a moral, a virtue, a thing of holiness. They endow their distorted vision with a good conscience,—they claim that no *other* point of view is any longer of value, once theirs has been made sacrosanct with the names "God," "Salvation," "Eternity." I unearthed the instinct of the theologian everywhere: it is the most universal, and actually the most subterranean form of falsity on earth. That which a theologian considers true, *must* of necessity be false: this furnishes almost the criterion of truth. It is his most profound self-preservative instinct which forbids reality ever to attain to honour in any way, or even to raise its voice. Whithersoever the influence of the theologian extends, *valuations* are topsy-turvy, and the concepts "true" and "false" have necessarily changed places: that which is most deleterious to life, is here called "true," that which enhances it, elevates it, says Yea to it, justifies it and renders it triumphant, is called "false." . . . If it should happen that theologians, *via* the "conscience" either of princes or of the people, stretch out their hand for power, let us not be in any doubt as to what results therefrom each time, namely:—the will to the end, the *nihilistic* will to power. . . .

The Christian concept of God—God as the deity of the sick, God as a spider, God as spirit—is one of the most corrupt concepts of God that has ever been attained on earth. Maybe it represents the low-water mark in the evolutionary ebb of the godlike type. God degenerated into the *contradiction of life*, instead of being its transfiguration and eternal Yea! With God war is declared on life, nature, and the will to life! God is the formula for every calumny of this world and for every lie concerning a beyond! In God, nonentity is deified, and the will to nonentity is declared holy!

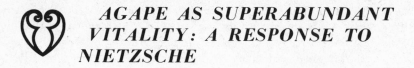

AGAPE AS SUPERABUNDANT VITALITY: A RESPONSE TO NIETZSCHE

Max Scheler

Scheler gives full credit to Nietzsche's discovery that resentment *is the source of many human value judgments, and he admits the seepage of resentment into Christianity. "We distinctly feel," he says, "how the ressentiment-laden man transfers to God the vengeance he himself cannot wreak upon the great." But Scheler insists that resentment is not the essential motive of Christianity but only a corrupting admixture.*

Under Scheler's scrutiny Christian Agape reveals itself as a corrective to Greek Eros based upon a profounder psychology and an apprehension of deeper values. Love, for Scheler, seeks the maximization of value, and in this aim Eros and Agape are at one. But Agape, which is directed downward (from sufficiency to deficiency), sees deeper into man's nature. It is not directed at sickness and poverty but at what is behind *them. Here Scheler contends that the "highest and ultimate personality values" are independent of contrasts such as rich and poor, sick and healthy. Overlooked by Eros, these underlying values are recognized by Christian Agape.*

More, Agape means maximization of value in the lover, marking "a blissful ability to stoop, born from an abundance of force and nobility." As such it derives from "a profound and secret confidence in life's own vigor *and . . . an inner security from the mechanical accidents which may befall it."*

Scheler thus equates Eros and Agape as seeking higher value and then commends Agape as the profounder in the common quest. But has Scheler understood Agape? His preoccupation with heightened value, man's nobility, "vital plenitude" and the like are reverberations from the Eros tradition, and it becomes hard not to conclude that Scheler has exchanged Agape for a profounder Eros, transforming Jesus into a Greek hero and God into a human ideal. Specifically, Scheler's value-directed Agape contradicts the principle of Agape's "unconditionality," while his rooting of Agape in life's "profound confidence" in its own vigor appears anthropocentric, consonant with the priority of self-love, but contradicted by Agape's total absence of self-love.

. . . Let us compare this with the Christian conception. In that conception there takes place what might be called a *reversal in the movement of love*.

From *Ressentiment* by Max Scheler, trans. William W. Holdheim, ed. Lewis A. Coser (New York: The Free Press of Glencoe, 1961), pp. 86–97. Reprinted by permission of The Free Press of Glencoe.

The Christian view boldly denies the Greek axiom that love is an aspiration of the lower towards the higher. On the contrary, now the criterion of love is that the nobler stoops to the vulgar, the healthy to the sick, the rich to the poor, the handsome to the ugly, the good and saintly to the bad and common, the Messiah to the sinners and publicans. The Christian is not afraid, like the ancient, that he might lose something by doing so, that he might impair his own nobility. He acts in the peculiarly pious conviction that through this "condescension," through this self-abasement and "self-renunciation" he gains the highest good and becomes equal to God. The change in the notion of God and his fundamental relation to man and the world is not the cause, but the *consequence* of this reversal in the movement of love. God is no longer the eternal unmoving goal—like a star —for the love of all things, moving the world as "the beloved moves the lover." Now the very *essence* of God is to love and serve. Creating, willing, and acting are derived from these original qualities. The eternal "first mover" of the world is replaced by the "creator" who created it "out of love." An event that is monstrous for the man of antiquity, that is absolutely paradoxical according to his axioms, is supposed to have taken place in Galilee: God spontaneously "descended" to man, became a servant, and died the bad servant's death on the cross! Now the precept of loving good and hating evil, loving one's friend and hating one's enemy, becomes meaningless. There is no longer any "highest good" independent of and beyond the *act* and movement of love! Love itself is the highest of all goods! The *summum bonum* is no longer the value of a thing, but of an act, the value of love itself *as love*—not for its results and achievements. Indeed, the achievements of love are only symbols and proofs of its *presence in the person*. And thus God himself becomes a "person" who has no "idea of the good," no "form and order," no λόγο above him, but only below him—through his deed of love. He becomes a God who loves— for the man of antiquity something like a square circle, an "imperfect perfection"! How strongly did Neo-Platonic criticism stress that love is a form of "need" and "aspiration" which indicates "imperfection," and that it is false, presumptuous, and sinful to attribute it to the deity! But there is another great innovation: in the Christian view, love is a non-sensuous act of the *spirit* (not a mere stage of feeling, as for the moderns), but it is nevertheless not a striving and desiring, and even less a need. These acts consume themselves in the realization of the desired goal. Love, however, *grows* in its action. And there are no longer any rational principles, any rules or justice, higher than love, independent of it and preceding it, which should guide its action and its distribution among men according to their value. All are worthy of love—friends and enemies, the good and the evil, the noble and the common. Whenever I see badness in another, I must feel partly guilty, for I must say to myself: "Would that man be bad if you had loved him enough?" In the Christian view, *sensuous* sympathy— together with its root in our most powerful impulse—is not the source, but the partial *blockage* of love. Therefore not only positive wrongdoing, but even the failure of love is "guilt." Indeed, it is *the* guilt at the bottom of all guiltiness.

Thus the picture has shifted immensely. This is no longer a band of men and things that surpass each other in striving up to the deity. It is a band in which every member looks back toward those who are further removed from God and comes to resemble the deity by helping and serving them—for this great urge to love, to serve, to bend down, is God's own essence.

I do not here analyze the constructive forms which this emotional reversal has taken in dogma, theology, and religious worship, though the task is tempting—especially in the cases of Paul and Augustine. Confining myself to the essential, I ask: whence this reversal? Is *ressentiment* really its mainspring?

The more I reflected on this question, the more clearly I realized that the root of Christian love is entirely *free* of *ressentiment*, but that *ressentiment* can very easily use it for its own purposes by simulating an emotion which corresponds to this idea. This simulation is often so perfect that even the sharpest observer can no longer distinguish real love from *ressentiment* which poses as love.

There are two fundamentally different ways for the strong to bend down to the weak, for the rich to help the poor, for the more perfect life to help the "less perfect." This action can be motivated by a powerful feeling of security, strength, and inner salvation, of the invincible fullness of one's own life and existence. All this unites into the clear awareness that one is *rich enough* to share one's being and possessions. Love, sacrifice, help, the descent to the small and the weak, here spring from a spontaneous overflow of force, accompanied by bliss and deep inner calm. Compared to this natural readiness for love and sacrifice, all specific "egoism," the concern for oneself and one's interest, and even the instinct of "self-preservation" are signs of a blocked and weakened life. Life is essentially expansion, development, growth in plenitude, and not "self-preservation," as a false doctrine has it. Development, expansion, and growth are not epiphenomena of mere preservative forces and cannot be reduced to the preservation of the "better adapted." We do believe that life itself can be sacrificed for values higher than life, but this does not mean that all sacrifice runs counter to life and its advancement. There is a form of sacrifice which is a free renunciation of one's own vital abundance, a beautiful and natural overflow of one's forces. Every living being has a natural instinct of sympathy for other living beings, which increases with their proximity and similarity to himself. Thus we sacrifice ourselves for beings with whom we feel united and solidary, in contrast to everything "dead." This sacrificial impulse is by no means a later acquisition of life, derived from originally egoistic urges. It is an *original* component of life and *precedes* all those particular "aims" and "goals" which calculation, intelligence, and reflection impose upon it later. *We have an urge to sacrifice* before we ever know why, for what, and for whom! Jesus' view of nature and life, which sometimes shines through his speeches and parables in fragments and hidden allusions, shows quite clearly that he understood this fact. When he tells us not to worry about eating and drinking, it is not because he is indifferent to life and its preservation, but because he sees also a *vital* weakness in all "worrying" about the next day, in all concentration on one's own physical well-being. The ravens with neither storehouse nor barn, the lilies which do not toil and spin and which God still arrays more gloriously than Solomon (Luke 12:24 and 27)—they are symbols of that profound total impression he has of life: all voluntary concentration on one's own bodily well-being, all worry and anxiety, hampers rather than furthers the creative force which instinctively and beneficently governs all life. "And which of you with taking thought can add to his stature one cubit?" (Luke 12:25). This kind of indifference to the external *means* of life (food, clothing, etc.) is not a sign of indifference to life and its value, but rather of a profound and secret confidence in life's own *vigor* and of an inner security from the mechanical accidents which may befall it. A gay, light, bold, knightly indifference to external circumstances, drawn from the depth of life itself—that is the feeling which inspires these words! Egoism and fear of death are signs of a declining, sick, and broken life. Let us remember that the fear of death was so widespread in antiquity that some schools of philosophy, that of the Epicureans among others, see the aim of philosophy in freeing man from it. The periods of greatest vitality were indifferent to life and its end. Such indifference is itself a state of mind which has vital value.

This kind of love and sacrifice for the weaker, the sick, and the small springs from inner security and vital plenitude. In addition to this vital security, there is that other feeling of bliss and security, that awareness of safety in the fortress of ultimate being itself (Jesus calls it "kingdom of God"). The deeper and more central it is, the more man can and may be almost playfully "indifferent" to his "fate" in the peripheral zones of his existence—indifferent to whatever is still accessible to "happiness" and "suffering," "pleasure" and "displeasure," "joy" and "pain."

When a person's spontaneous impulse of love and sacrifice finds a specific goal, an opportunity for applying itself, he does not welcome it as a chance to plunge into such phenomena as poverty, sickness, or ugliness. He does not help this struggling life because of those negative values, but *despite* them—he helps in order to develop whatever may still be sound and positive. He does not love such life *because* it is sick, poor, small, and ugly, and he does not passively dwell upon these attributes. The positive vital values (and even more, of course, the spiritual personal values of that individual) are completely *independent* of these defects and lie much deeper.

Therefore his own fullness of life can (and therefore "should") overcome his natural reaction of fearing and fleeing them, and his love should help-fully develop whatever is positive in the poor or sick man. He does not love sickness and poverty, but what is *behind* them, and his help is directed *against* these evils. When Francis of Assisi kisses festering wounds and does not even kill the bugs that bite him, but leaves his body to them as a hospi-table home, these acts (if seen from the outside) could be signs of perverted instincts and of a perverted valuation. But that is not actually the case. It is not a lack of nausea or a delight in the pus which makes St. Francis act in this way. He has overcome his nausea through a deeper feeling of life and vigor! This attitude is completely different from that of recent modern realism in art and literature, the exposure of social misery, the description of little people, the wallowing in the morbid—a typical *ressentiment* phe-nomenon. Those people saw something bug-like in everything that lives, whereas Francis sees the holiness of "life" even in the bug.

In the ancient notion of love, on the other hand, there is an element of *anxiety*. The noble fears the descent to the less noble, is afraid of being infected and pulled down. The "sage" of antiquity does not have the same firmness, the same inner certainty of himself and his own value, as the genius and hero of Christian love.

A further characteristic! Love in Jesus' sense helps energetically. But it *does not consist* in the desire to help, or even in "benevolence." Such love is, as it were, immersed in positive value, and helping and benevolence are only its consequences. The fake love of *ressentiment* man offers no real help, since for his perverted sense of values, evils like "sickness" and "poverty" have become goods. He believes, after all, that "God giveth grace to the humble" (I Peter, 5:5), so that raising the small or curing the sick would mean *removing* them from their salvation. But this does not mean that the value of love in the genuine Christian sense lies in the use-fulness of its helping deed. The usefulness may be great with little love or none at all, and it may be small while love is great. The window's mites (Mark 12:42-4) are more to God than the gifts of the rich—not because they are only "mites" or because the giver is only a "poor widow," but because her action reveals *more love*. Thus the increase in value originally always lies on the side of him who loves, *not* on the side of him who is helped. Love is no spiritual "institution of charity" and is not in contrast to one's own bliss. In the very act of self-renunciation, the person eternally wins him-self. He is blissful in loving and giving, for "it is more blessed to give than to receive" (Acts 20:35). Love is not valuable and does not bestow distinc-tion on the lover because it is just one of the countless forces which further human or social welfare. No, the value is love *itself*, its penetra-tion of the whole person—the higher, firmer, and richer life and existence of which its movement is the sign and the gem. The important thing is not the amount of welfare, it is that there should be a *maximum of love* among men. The act of helping is the direct and adequate *expression* of love, not its meaning or "purpose." Its meaning lies in itself, in its illumination of the soul, in the nobility of the loving soul in the act of love. Therefore nothing can be further removed from this genuine concept of Christian love than all kinds of "socialism," "social feeling," "altruism," and other subaltern modern things. When the rich youth is told to divest himself of his riches and give them to the poor, it is really not in order to help the "poor" and to effect a better distribution of property in the interest of general welfare. Nor is it because poverty as such is supposed to be better than wealth. The order is given because the *act* of giving away, and the spiritual freedom and abundance of love which manifest themselves in this act, ennoble the youth and make him even "richer" than he is.

This element is also present in the metaphysico-religious conceptions of man's relation to God. The old covenant between God and man, which is the root of all "legality," is replaced by the love between God and his children. And even the love "for God" is not to be founded on his works alone, in gratitude for his constant gifts, his care and maintenance. All these experiences of God's actions and works are only means to make us look up to "eternal love" and to the infinite abundance of value of which these works are but the proof. They should be admired and loved only because they are works of love! This conception was still very strong among the best medieval Christians. Thus Hugo de Saint Victor, in his *Soliloquy on the Earnest Money of the Soul (Soliloquium de arrha animae)*, refers to a love which is founded only on God's works and good deeds as "a love like a whore"! But already in Solomon's proverb "When I have *you*, I do not ask for heaven or earth" we find this strict opposition to the idea of the covenant—an idea which contains the germs of that love based on gratitude which typifies all average religiosity. We should not love God because of his heaven and earth: we should love heaven and earth because they are God's, and because they adumbrate eternal love by means of sensible *expression* rather than as a purposive idea. The same is true for the concept of God. Antiquity believed that the forces of love in the universe were limited. Therefore they were to be used sparingly, and everyone was to be loved only according to his value. The idea that love has its origin in God himself, the infinite Being, that he himself is infinite love and mercy, naturally entails the precept of loving both the good and the bad, the just and the sinners, one's friends and one's enemies. Genuine love, transcending the natural sphere, is manifested most clearly when we love our enemy. The ancient precept of loving the good and the just, and of hating the evil and the unjust, is now rejected as "pharisaism." Indeed, in a wider metaphysical context, God is not only the "creator" (instead of a mere ideal, a perfect being, the goal of the world's upward movement), but even the "creator out of love." His creation, the "world" itself, is nothing but the momentary coagulation of an infinitely flowing gesture of love. The deity of Greek metaphysics is the ideal of the "sage" in its absolute form: a logical egoist, a being closed in itself, self-observing and self-thinking (νόησις νόησεως), who cares little about the course of earthly events and is not truly responsible for the world. The Christian deity is a *personal* God who created the "world" out of an infinite overflow of love—not because he wanted to help anyone or anything, for "nothing" existed before, but only to express his superabundance of love. This new notion of the deity is the conceptual theological expression of the changed attitude toward life.

There is not a trace of *ressentiment* in all this. Nothing but a blissful ability to stoop, born from an abundance of force and nobility!

But there is a completely different way of stooping to the small, the lowly, and the common, even though it may seem almost the same. Here love does not spring from an abundance of vital power, from firmness and security. Here it is only a euphemism for *escape*, for the inability to "remain at home" with oneself (*chez soi*). Turning toward others is but the secondary consequence of this urge to flee from oneself. One cannot love anybody without turning away from oneself. However, the crucial question is whether this movement is prompted by the desire to turn toward a positive value, or whether the intention is a radical escape from oneself. "Love" of the second variety is inspired by self-hatred, by hatred of one's own weakness and misery. The mind is always on the point of departing for distant places. Afraid of seeing itself and its inferiority, it is driven to give itself to the other—not because of his worth, but merely for the sake of his "otherness." Modern philosophical jargon has found a revealing term for this phenomenon, one of the many modern substitutes for love: "altruism." This love is not directed at a previously discovered positive value, nor does any such value flash up in the act of loving: there is nothing but the urge to turn away from oneself and to lose oneself in other people's business. We all know a certain type of man frequently found among socialists, suffragettes, and all people with an ever-ready "social conscience"—the kind of person whose social activity is quite clearly prompted by inability to keep his attention focussed on himself, on his own tasks and problems. Looking away from oneself is here mistaken for love! Isn't it abundantly clear that "altruism," the interest in "others" and their lives, has nothing at all to do with love? The malicious or envious person also forgets his own interest, even his "preservation." He only thinks about the other man's feelings, about the harm and the suffering he inflicts on him. Conversely, there is a form of genuine "self-love" which has nothing at all to do with "egoism." It is precisely the essential feature of egoism that it does not apprehend the full value of the isolated self. The egoist sees himself only with regard to the others, as a member of society who wishes to possess and acquire *more* than the others. Self-directedness or other-directedness have no essential bearing on the specific quality of love or hatred. These acts are different *in themselves*, quite independently of their direction.

Thus the "altruistic" urge is really a form of hatred, of self-hatred, *posing* as its opposite ("Love") in the false perspective of consciousness. In the same way, in *ressentiment* morality, love for the "small," the "poor," the "weak," and the "oppressed" is really disguised hatred, repressed envy, an impulse to detract, etc., directed against the opposite phenomena: "wealth," "strength," "power," "*largesse.*" When hatred does not dare to come out into the open, it can be easily expressed in the form of ostensible love—love for something which has features that are the opposite of those of the hated object. This can happen in such a way that the hatred remains secret. When we hear that falsely pious, unctious tone (it is the tone of a certain "socially-minded" type of priest), sermonizing that love for the "small" is our first duty, love for the "humble" in spirit, since God gives "grace" to them, then it is often only hatred posing as Christian love. We clearly feel how the sight of these phenomena fills the mind with secret "satisfaction" and how they themselves are loved, not the higher values which may lie behind them. Nor can the helping deed be the important thing in this perspective, since it would make the "small" less agreeable to God and would therefore be an expression of hatred. The whole value lies in *dwelling* upon these phenomena. And when we are told, in the same tone, that these people will be rewarded in "heaven" for their distress, and that "heaven" is the exact reverse of the earthly order ("the first shall be last"), we distinctly feel how the *ressentiment*-laden man transfers to God the vengeance he himself cannot wreak on the great. In this way, he can satisfy his revenge at least in imagination, with the aid of an other-worldly mechanism of rewards and punishments. The core of the *ressentiment* Christian's idea of God is still the avenging Jehovah. The only difference is that revenge is now masked as sham love for the "small." There is no longer any organic and experienced bond between the "kingdom of God" and the visible realm, so that the values and laws of retaliation of the former have ceased to be simply a purer and more perfect expression of those which already appear in life. The "kingdom of God" has become the "other world," which stands mechanically beside "this world"—an opposition unknown to the strongest periods of Christianity. It is merely a plane of being where the shadows of the people and events we experienced carry on a dance led by *ressentiment*, according to a rhythm which is simply opposite to that of the earth.

PART *IV*

Tristanism and Chivalric Love

TRISTANISM:
PASSION CHOOSES DEATH

In Tristanism passion finds its hottest flame, ultimately consuming the lovers. If, as de Rougemont says, "happy love has no history," the world's fascination for unfulfilled love under the sentence of death has bestowed immortality upon the legend of Tristan and Iseult.

Following an oral history in the British Isles, the legend became written literature in the twelfth century at the hands of Eilhart von Oberge of Germany, Thomas of Britain, and Beroul of France. It rose quickly to cultural significance, influencing the chivalric and courtly love forms of medieval Europe. And it has been continually with us thereafter, achieving consummate musical expression by Richard Wagner, and reverberating today from such sources as the Broadway musicals "Camelot" and "West Side Story," the lyrics of Leonard Cohen, and the love-philosophy of our self-determined social exiles, the hippies.

The durability of the theme points to the presence of its seed in the heart of everyman, but on the face of it this would seem uniquely improbable in Tristanism's case. This love pits purest passion against the world in mortal combat, knowing that the world must win. Moreover Tristanism's ambition—the total union of two individuals—is manifestly impossible. Then is this not a form of pathology calling for a cure?

But let us look more closely. If we separate Tristanism's elements, one by one they stand up and move closer to us. For example, consider the love philtre: in the legend the two lovers are bound together irredeemably because they have innocently drunk a magical potion which produces this result. Symbolically this expresses the idea that love is something over which the lovers have no control, something which befalls them despite themselves and "carries them away." This conception finds no fewer adherents today than it did in the Middle Ages. Indeed, universal appeal lies in the moral holiday thus afforded, by which love means release from the wearisome burden of self-responsibility. Love takes over and controls us, hence it is not we who are accountable for what we do, but the power of love. We are lifted out of ourselves to become something else. Just what it is that we become does not matter for the moment. Is not merely the "something else" a seductive siren song? For wherever we go and however we live, the one thing that is always with us is our self; it is the pack on our back that cannot be laid down. Are there not times when this condition rankles us and we long for someone who will take this burden from us?

A second feature of Tristanism is its exclusivism. Isolde and Tristan take each other, not within the world, but against the world and in preference to it. In Gottfried von Strassburg's telling, Tristan's heart is "sealed and locked from all the world save her alone." This defiance is the lovers' doom, for the world is the stronger and will avenge itself. But the death implications go still deeper, for, shorn of the world, the beloved is deprived of the medium which sustains her life. Thus Simone de Beauvoir extracts from the legend the meaning that "two lovers destined solely for each other are already dead: they die of ennui, of the slow agony of a love that feeds only on itself" (*The Second Sex*, Chap. 23).

Tristanism's defiance of the world seems histrionic, gratuitous. Does society not willingly accommodate love, paying it abundant tribute? But look carefully. What society accommodates is a thoroughly domesticated and docile kind of love, a love yoked to society's service. The fire, so to speak, has been banked, vented, and made to do the cooking. And this is a far cry from passion. Passion is a flaming fidelity to the beloved which betrays everything else. Indeed, it utilizes social prohibitions to exalt itself. Here is the significance of the *obstacle* which Tristanism requires— King Mark in the legend, or physical distance, or the law, or sometimes the scruples of the lovers themselves, or even the disinterest of the beloved (in the love songs of the courts, nothing so uplifted the lover as the disdain of the beloved). Tristanian passion is a hemorrhage through a wall, requiring resistance to achieve its pressure.

If passion is tolerated by society, this is thanks to passion's notorious impermanence. It is here today but gone tomorrow, whereupon society can handily reassert itself. But Tristan's mission is precisely to remedy this defect, making passion endure. Here he joins Don Juan as an *enfant terrible*, flying in the face of life's lessons. But the strategies of the two figures are very different. To preserve passion Don Juan manipulates time, compressing it to point-instants; he sustains novelty by his maxim, "To horse and to spur!" On the other hand Tristan works with space, preserving passion by maintaining distance between himself and his beloved. In de Rougemont's words the two lovers "never miss a chance of getting parted."

Tristanism, *amour courtois*, and chivalric love are alike in the requirement of distance. The chivalric code prescribed the *minnedienst*, or love service. Under it the lady could test a suitor by demanding of him a feat of valor and ingenuity, the mythical favorite being the tracking down and slaying of a predatory monster. In this way the *minnedienst* put distance between lady and lover. And as we would expect, vanity stretched the distance—greater feats being thought to measure greater love—until it reached infinity and heroic love went unfulfilled. Meanwhile in the French and German courts, troubadours were celebrating the lady by such an extravagance of idealization as to distance her beyond mortal reach.

"Beyond mortal reach" is a clue to a core trait of Tristanism—its sense of the sacred. The sacred must be preserved from contact with the profane. To prevent her contamination the lady must be shielded from the world. And this means—bittersweet pill!—that she must be preserved against the lover's own touch. Thus the Tristanism in Romeo's first words to Juliet: "If I profane with my unworthiest hand this holiest shrine . . ." It is a double bind; the lover's sense of the sacred bars his love's fulfillment. This is the feature which opens Tristanism to parody by more robust inclinations (e.g., the opening pages of Tirso de Molina's "Trickster of Seville," which explain Don Juan's success by the frustrations of women who are worshipped by Tristanian lovers).

But if we turn within ourselves, kinship with Tristan may be discoverable. Surely the reader has at some time striven for a distant goal which radiated its preciousness from afar, but lost its value upon attainment. As high school freshmen we looked upon seniors as the epitome of *savoir faire*, but when we ourselves had risen to that office the *savoir faire*—was it not so?—had fled elsewhere. Given several such occasions and we put questions to ourselves. Are values illusory? Or are they destroyed by our touch? Is it in the nature of value to reside only in what is distant from ourselves? An affirmative answer to the first of these questions constitutes nihilism; to the second throws us into the labors of Sisyphus, forever pushing the value on ahead; and to the third marks our kinship with Tristan.

The reader is thus invited to identify each of Tristanism's essential features, making use of the commentaries provided in the following pages. If, thus equipped, he will delve deep within himself, we think that Tristanism's seeming remoteness will give way to insight into some enduring propensities of mankind.

TRISTANISM: THE LOVE OF LOVE

Denis de Rougemont

Following his synopsis of the legend, de Rougemont here derives a number of the key features of Tristanian love—its compulsiveness, its narcissism, its inherent death wish, its need of obstacles in order to sustain itself.

What does not appear in the selections and requires to be added is de Rougemont's complete identification of Tristanism with passion and thereby with romantic love. But is romantic love in truth a reciprocal death wish? What of the "natural teleology of love" which is the desire for children (see the Schopenhauer selection, Part One); and what of Ortega's and Scheler's contentions that love seeks the "maximization of value" in the other? The reader is invited to question whether romantic love deserves to be rescued from de Rougemont's pessimism, and by what means.

WHAT THE TRISTAN ROMANCE[1] SEEMS TO BE ABOUT

Amors par force vos demeine!—BEROUL.

Tristan is born in misfortune. His father has just died, and Blanchefleur, his mother, does not survive his birth. Hence his name, the sombre hue of his life, and the lowering stormy sky that hangs over the legend. King Mark of Cornwall, Blanchefleur's brother, takes the orphan into his castle at Tintagel and brings him up there.

Tristan presently performs an early feat of prowess. He vanquishes the Morholt. This Irish giant has come like a Minotaur to exact his tribute of Cornish maidens or youths. Tristan is of an age for knighthood—that is, he has just reached puberty—and he obtains leave to fight him. The Morholt is killed, but not before he has wounded Tristan with a poisoned barb. Having no hope of recovery, Tristan begs to be put on board a boat that is cast adrift with neither sail nor oar. He takes his sword and harp with him.

Reprinted from *Love in the Western World,* revised and augmented edition, by Denis de Rougemont; trans. Montgomery Belgion. Copyright 1940, 1956 by Pantheon Books, Inc. Reprinted by permission of the publisher.

[1]In summing up the chief episodes of the Romance, I shall make use (except here and there) of M. Bédier's *Concordance* (contained in his study of Thomas's poem) for the five twelfth-century versions—those by Béroul, Thomas and Eilhart together with *La Folie Tristan* and *Le Roman en prose.* The later versions by Gottfried of Strasbourg, or by German, Italian, Danish, Russian, Czech, and other imitators, are all derived from those five. I also take into account the more recent critical undertakings of Messrs. E. Muret and E. Vinaver.

He lands in Ireland. There is only one remedy that can save him, and, as it happens, the Queen of Ireland is alone in knowing its secret. But the giant Morholt was this queen's brother, and so Tristan is careful not to disclose his name or to explain how he has come by his wound. Iseult, the queen's daughter, nurses him and restores him to health. That is the Prologue.

A few years later a bird has brought to King Mark a golden hair. The king determines to marry the woman from whose head the hair has come. It is Tristan whom he selects to go in quest of her. A storm causes the hero to be cast ashore once again in Ireland. There he fights and kills a dragon that was threatening the capital. (This is the conventional motif of a virgin delivered by a young paladin.) Having been wounded by the dragon, Tristan is again nursed by Iseult. One day she learns that the wounded stranger is no other than the man who killed her uncle. She seizes Tristan's sword and threatens to transfix him in his bath. It is then that he tells her of the mission on which he has been sent by King Mark. And Iseult spares him, for she would like to be a queen. (According to some of the authors, she spares him also because she then finds him handsome.)

Tristan and the princess set sail for Cornwall. At sea the wind drops and the heat grows oppressive. They are thirsty. Brengain, Iseult's maid, gives them a drink. But by mistake she pours out the 'wine of herbs' which the queen, Iseult's mother, has brewed for King Mark and his bride after they shall have wed. Tristan and Iseult drink it. The effect is to commit them to a fate from 'which they can never escape during the remainder of their lives, *for they have drunk their destruction and death.*' They confess that they are now in love, and fall into one another's arms.

(Let it be noted here that according to the archetypal version, which Béroul alone has followed, the effect of the love-potion is limited to three years.[2] Thomas, a sensitive psychologist and highly suspicious of marvels, which he considers crude, minimizes the importance of the love-potion as far as possible, and depicts the love of Tristan and Iseult as having occurred spontaneously. Its first signs he places as early as the episode of the bath. On the other hand, Eilhart, Gottfried, and most of the others attribute unlimited effect to the magic wine. Nothing could be more significant than these variations, as we shall see.)

Thus the fault is perpetrated. *Yet Tristan is still in duty bound to fulfil the mission with which King Mark has entrusted him.* So, notwithstanding

---

[2] Verses 2137–2140:

> A conbien fu determinez
> Li lovendrins, li vin herbez:
> La mere Yseut, qui le bolli,
> A trois anz d'amistié le fist.

The quotation is from Béroul, as are those below. I follow A. Ewert's text (*The Romance of Tristan* (Oxford, Blackwell, 1939)), which is later than E. Muret, and I am also indebted to Ewert's glossary for my translations. 'For how long was the love potion, the herb wine? Mother Yseut, who brewed it, made it to three years of love.'—Translator's note.

his betrayal of the king, he delivers Iseult to him. On the wedding night Brengain, thanks to a ruse, takes Iseult's place in the royal bed, thus saving her mistress from dishonour and at the same time expiating the irretrievable mistake she made in pouring out the love-potion.

Presently, however, four 'felon' barons of the king's go and tell their sovereign that Tristan and Iseult are lovers. Tristan is banished to Tintagel town. But thanks to another trick—the episode of the pine-tree in the orchard—Mark is convinced of his innocence and allows him to return to the castle. Then Frocin the Dwarf, who is in league with the barons, lays a trap in order to establish the lovers' guilt. In the spear-length between Tristan's bed and the queen's he scatters flour, and persuades Mark to order Tristan to ride to King Arthur at Carduel the next morning at dawn. Tristan is determined to embrace his mistress once more before he rides away. To avoid leaving his foot-marks in the flour he leaps across from his own bed to the queen's. But the effort reopens a wound in his leg inflicted the previous day by a boar. Led by Frocin, the king and the barons burst into the bedchamber. They find the flour blood-stained. Mark is satisfied with this evidence of adultery. Iseult is handed over to a party of a hundred lepers, and Tristan is sentenced to the stake. On the way to execution, however, he is allowed to go into a chantry on the cliff's edge. He forces a window and leaps over the cliffs, thus effecting his escape. He rescues Iseult from the lepers, and together they go and hide in the depths of the Forest of Morrois. There for three years they lead a life 'harsh and hard.' It happens one day that Mark comes upon them while they are asleep. But on this occasion Tristan has put between Iseult and himself his drawn sword. Moved by this evidence of innocence, as he supposes it to be, the king spares them. Without waking them, he takes up Tristan's sword and sets his own in its place.

At the end of three years the potency of the love-potion wears off (according to Béroul and the common ancestor of the five versions). It is only then that Tristan repents, and that Iseult wishes she were a queen again. Together they seek out the hermit Ogrin, through whom Tristan offers peace to the king, saying he will surrender Iseult. Mark promises forgiveness. As the royal procession approaches, the lovers part. But before this happens Iseult has besought Tristan to stay in the neighbourhood till he has made certain that Mark is treating her well. Then, with a final display of feminine wiles, she follows up her advantage in having persuaded Tristan to agree to this, and declares she will join him at the first sign he makes, for nothing shall stop her from doing his will, 'neither tower, nor wall, nor stronghold.'

They have several secret meetings in the hut of Orri the Woodman. But the felon barons are keeping watch and ward over the queen's virtue. She asks and is granted 'a Judgement of God.' Thanks to a subterfuge, the ordeal is a success. Before she grasps the red-hot iron which will not harm one who has spoken the truth, she swears that no man has ever held her in his arms except the king and a poor pilgrim who has just carried her ashore from a boat. And the poor pilgrim is Tristan in disguise.

However, fresh adventures carry Tristan far away from Iseult, and he then comes to suppose that she no longer loves him. So he agrees to marry 'for her beauty and her name'[3] another Iseult, Iseult 'of the White Hand.' And indeed this Iseult remains unstained, for after their marriage Tristan still sighs for 'Iseult the Fair.'

At last, wounded by a poisoned spear and about to die, Tristan sends for the queen from Cornwall, she who alone can save his life. She comes, and as her ship draws near it hoists a white sail as a sign of hope. But Iseult of the White Hand has been on the look-out, and, tormented by jealousy, she runs to Tristan and tells him that the sail is black. Tristan dies. As he does so, Iseult the Fair lands, and on arriving at the castle, she lies down beside her dead lover and clasps him close. Then she dies too.

SOME RIDDLES

Thus summarized, and with all the 'charm' destroyed, the most absorbing of poems appears, on cool consideration, to be straightforward neither in its matter nor in its progression. I have passed over numerous accessory episodes, but over none of the motives alleged for the central action. Indeed, these motives I have rather stressed. They have been seen not to amount to much. Tristan delivers up Iseult to the king, *because* bound by the fealty of a knight. At the end of the three years spent in the forest, the lovers part, *because* the love-potion has lost its potency. Tristan marries Iseult of the White Hand *'for her beauty and her name.'* If these 'reasons' are discounted—although we shall return to them—the Romance turns out to depend on a series of puzzling contradictions.

I have been struck by the passing comment of one recent editor of the legend. All through the Romance Tristan is made to appear the physical superior of all his foes and particularly of the king. It follows that no external power prevents him from carrying off Iseult and thus fulfilling his fate. The manners of the time sanctioned the rights of the stronger; they made these rights divine without qualification; and this was especially the case with a man's rights over a woman. *Why does Tristan not take advantage of these rights?*

Put on the alert by this first question, our critical suspicions lead us to discover other riddles, no less curious and obscure. *Why has the sword of chastity been placed between the two sleepers in the forest?* The lovers have already sinned, and they refuse to repent just then. Furthermore, they do not expect that the king will discover them. Yet in all five versions

[3]'Pur belté e pur nun d'Isolt' (Thomas).

there is neither a line nor a word to explain the sword.[4] Again, *why does Tristan restore the queen to Mark*, even in those versions where at that time the love-potion is still active? If, as some say, the lovers part because they now sincerely repent, why do they promise one another to meet again in the moment they undertake to part? And why later does Tristan go forth upon fresh adventures when he and Iseult have made a tryst in the forest? Why does the guilty queen ask for 'a Judgement of God'? She must know that the ordeal is bound to go against her. It is only successful thanks to a trick improvised at the last moment; and this trick, it is implied, deceives God Himself, since the miracle ensues.[5] Moreover, the judgement having gone in the queen's favour, her innocence is thereupon taken for granted. But if she is innocent, so is Tristan; and it becomes quite impossible to see what prevents his return to the king's castle, and *hence to Iseult's side*.

At the same time it is surely very odd that thirteenth-century poets—so punctilious in matters of honour and suzerain fealty—should let pass without a word of comment so much thoroughly indefensible behaviour. How can they hold up Tristan as a model of chivalry when he betrays his king with the most shameless cunning, or the queen as a virtuous lady when she is not only an adulteress, but does not shrink from committing an astute blasphemy? On the other hand, why do they call 'felons' the four barons who defend Mark's honour and who, even if actuated by jealousy, neither deceive nor betray (which is more than can be said of Tristan)?

Even the validity of what few motives are mentioned remains open to question. For if the rule of suzerain fealty required that Tristan should deliver to Mark the betrothed he had been to fetch,[6] his compliance with this rule must seem both very belated and hardly sincere, inasmuch as once he has delivered up Iseult he knows no rest till he has contrived to get back into the castle and is with her again. And as the love-potion was brewed for Mark and his queen, it must be wondered why its potency is not permanent. Three years of married bliss are not much. And when Tristan marries

---

[4]It is true that in Bédier's edition of Thomas's poem (Vol. I, p. 240), the king's huntsman is said to have gone to the lovers' retreat, where he has seen 'Tristan' lying asleep, and across the cave was Iseult. The lovers were resting from the great heat, and lay apart from one another because. . . .' At this point the text breaks off! And Bédier notes: 'An unintelligible passage.' What diabolical agency can have partly destroyed *the one text* likely to have solved the riddle?

[5]Gottfried of Strasbourg brazenly insists:

'Twas thus made manifest
And averr'd before all
That Christ most glorious
Will mould like cloth for garments.
. . . He complies with ev'ry one's wish,
Whether honest or deceitful.
He ever is as we would have Him be.

[6]But to whom he had won a full title *himself* by delivering her from the dragon, as Thomas does not omit to stress.

another Iseult 'for her beauty and her name,' but does not touch her, it is surely obvious that nothing has compelled him either to marry or to be guilty of his insulting chastity, and that by marrying a woman whom he cannot make his wife he has put himself into a position from which the only way out is death.

CHIVALRY V. MARRIAGE

The Romance of *Tristan and Iseult* brings home to us the antagonism which grew up in the second half of the twelfth century between the rule of chivalry and feudal custom. Perhaps the extent to which the Arthurian romances reflect and foster this antagonism has not hitherto attracted the notice it deserves. In all likelihood, courtly chivalry was never more than an ideal. The earliest writers to mention it commonly lament its decay, but in doing so they overlook that in the form which they would like it to assume it has only just come into existence in their dreams. It is of the essence of an ideal that its decay should be lamented in the very moment it is clumsily striving for fulfilment. Moreover, to contrast the *fiction* of some ideal of living with tyrannical reality is precisely something possible in a romance. A preliminary answer to several of the riddles propounded by the legend can be sought in this direction. Once it is granted that Tristan's experience was intended to illustrate a conflict between chivalry and feudal society—and hence a conflict between two kinds of *duty* and even between two 'religions'—a number of episodes are made intelligible. At any rate, even if not disposing of every difficulty, the hypothesis significantly delays a solution.

Arthurian romance, which supplanted the *chanson de geste* with astonishing swiftness in the middle of the twelfth century, differs from this *chanson* in that it allots to woman the part formerly taken by a suzerain. An Arthurian knight, exactly like a troubadour of the South, regarded himself as the vassal of some chosen Lady, when, actually, he remained the vassal of a lord; and this gave rise to a number of conflicting claims of which the Romance supplies examples.

Let me go back to the three 'felon' barons. According to feudal morals, it was the duty of a vassal to warn his lord of anything that might endanger the latter's rights or honour. He was a 'felon' if he did not. Now, in *Tristan* the barons go and tell King Mark how Iseult is behaving. They should therefore be considered feal and true. If, then, the author refers to them as 'felons', he must evidently do so in virtue of some other code, which can only be the code of southern chivalry. For instance, according to a well-known judgement delivered by the Gascon courts of love, whosoever discloses the secrets of courtly love is a felon. The single instance is enough to show that the authors of the different versions of the Romance were deliberately siding with 'courtly' chivalry against feudal law. But there are further grounds for thinking so. Alone the view of fidelity and of marriage that was adopted in courtly love will explain some of the striking contradictions in the tale.

According to the theory officially received, courtly love arose as a reaction to the brutal lawlessness of feudal manners. It is well known that the nobles in the twelfth century made of marriage simply a means of enriching themselves, either through the annexation of dower estates or through expectations of inheritance. When a 'deal' turned out badly, the wife was repudiated. The plea of incest was exploited in curious ways, and in the face of it the Church was powerless. To allege a consanguinity of even the fourth degree, no matter on what slender evidence, was enough to secure an annulment. In order to counteract these abuses, which led to much quarrelling and to warring, courtly love established a *fealty* that was independent of legal marriage and of which the sole basis was love. It was even contended—for example, in the famous judgement delivered by a court of love in the house of the Countess of Champagne[7]—that love and marriage were incompatible. If such is the view of both Tristan and the author of the Romance, the sense given to the terms 'felony' and 'adultery' is thereby justified—indeed, more than justified, extolled, inasmuch as it implies an intrepid loyalty to the higher law of the *donnoi* or courtly love. (*Donnoi*, or *domnei*, is the Provençal name for the vassal-relation set up between a knight-lover and his lady, or *domina*.)

As has been said, this loyalty was incompatible with the fidelity of marriage. The Romance misses no opportunity of disparaging the social institution of marriage and of humiliating husbands—e.g. the king with horse's ears who is always being so easily deceived—as well as of glorifying the virtue of men and women who love outside, and in despite of, marriage. This courtly loyalty, however, displays one curious feature. It is opposed to the 'satisfaction' of love as much as to marriage. 'Of *donnoi* he knows truly nothing who wants fully to possess his lady. *Whatever turns into a reality is no longer love.*'[8] Here is something that puts us on the track of a preliminary explanation of such episodes as that of the sword of chastity, of Iseult's return to her lord after staying in the Forest of Morrois, and even of Tristan's nominal marriage.

The 'claims of passion', as understood today, would entitle Tristan to carry off Iseult as soon as he and she had drunk the love-potion. Instead

[7]The judgement reads as follows: 'We declare and affirm, by the tenour of these presents, that love cannot extend its rights over two married persons. For indeed lovers grant one another all things mutually and freely, without being impelled by any motive of necessity, whereas husband and wife are held by their duty to submit their wills to each other and to refuse each other nothing.

'May this judgement, which we have delivered with extreme caution, and after consulting with a great number of other ladies, be for you a constant and unassailable truth, Delivered in this year 1174, on the third day before the Kalends of May, Proclamation VII.'

[8]Claude Fauriel, *Histoire de la poésie provençale* (Paris, 1846), I, p. 512.

he delivers her to Mark, and he does so because the rule of courtly love did not allow a passion of this kind 'to turn into a reality', to result in the 'full possession of his lady'. Accordingly, Tristan chooses to respect feudal fealty, which is thus made to disguise and equivocally to abet courtly fealty. He chooses quite freely; for, as was noted above, being stronger than the king and the barons, he could—*on the feudal plane upon which he puts himself*—resort to the right of force.

What a strange love (it will be thought) that thus conforms to laws whereby it stands condemned in order the better to preserve itself! Whence arises this preference for whatever *thwarts* passion, hinders the lovers' 'happiness', and parts and torments them? To reply that so courtly love required is only to reply superficially; for this still leaves it to be ascertained why love of this kind is preferred to the other, the love that gets 'fulfilled' and 'satisfied'. With the help of the highly plausible theory that the Romance illustrates a conflict between 'religions', we have been able to specify and set forth the main difficulties raised by the plot; but really we have only succeeded in deferring a solution of the problem.

THE LOVE OF THE ROMANCE

In my summary of the legend, one thing in particular must have struck us. The two codes that come into play—chivalry and feudal morals—are respected by the author *only in those situations where his respecting them makes it possible for the tale to move forward again.*[9] In itself this explains nothing. It is all too easy to dispose of every one of our questions by saying: Events happen thus because *otherwise* there would be no story. Such a reply will appear convincing only owing to a lazy custom of literary criticism. Actually, it answers nothing. It simply raises the fundamental question: Why has there to be a story? And *this* story in particular? There is an unconscious wisdom in calling such a question ingenuous, for it is not asked without peril. In fact, it carried us into the heart of the problem; and undoubtedly it involves far more than the particular case of this myth.

If, by an effort of abstraction, we place ourselves outside the process common to both novelist and reader so that we can over-hear the intimate dialogue that goes on between them, we see that a tacit convention, or, rather, a mutual *encouragement*, unites them. They both wish the novel to go on, or, as the saying is, to rebound. Suppress that *wish*, and there can be no verisimilitude whatsoever. This is exemplified in scientific history. The reader of a 'serious' book is all the more exacting for being aware that

[9] I should make this quite clear. 1. The codes are respected each in turn as the result of a secret calculation; for if either was chosen to the entire exclusion of the other, the situation would be resolved too soon. 2. The codes are not always respected: for instance, when the lovers sin together as soon as they have drunk the love-potion they are committing a sin according to courtly love just as much as according to Christian and feudal morality. But were it not for that first fault there would be no romance at all.

neither his wishes nor the author's fancies can govern the sequence of events. Suppose, instead, these wishes to operate unchecked, and then nothing is too far-fetched. That is the situation for fiction. Between the two extremes there are as many levels of verisimilitude as there are plots. Or, if you like, what shall be verisimilitude in any given piece of literary fiction is intended to please. In short, a reader pays no heed to distortions or to twistings of the 'logic' of current observation so long as the licence thus taken produces the *pretexts* necessary to the passion which he longs to feel. Hence it is in the kind of 'tricks of the trade' employed by the author that the real plot of a given piece of fiction is disclosed, and a reader condones these tricks precisely to the extent that he shares the author's intentions.[10]

I have shown that the external barriers to the fulfilment of Tristan's love are in one sense arbitrary, and, after all, only fictional contrivances. And it follows from what has just been said about verisimilitude that it is precisely the arbitrary character of the obstructions introduced into a tale that may show what this tale is really about and what is the real nature of the passion it is concerned with. In this respect everything, it must be realized, is symbolical. Everything holds together and is connected after the manner of a *dream*, and not in accordance with our lives. This is equally true of the pretexts devised by the author, the conduct of his two leading characters, and the secret inclinations which he assumes to exist in his reader. The events narrated are but images or projections of a longing and of whatever runs counter to this longing, excites it, or merely protracts it. Everything the knight and princess do betrays that they act in virtue of a necessity they are unaware of—and that perhaps the author has been unaware of too—but *that is stronger than the need of their happiness*. Objectively, not one of the barriers to the fulfilment of their love is insuperable, and yet each time they give up. It is not too much to say that they never miss a chance of getting parted. When there is no obstruction, they invent one, as in the case of the drawn sword and of Tristan's marriage. They invent obstructions as if on purpose, notwithstanding that such barriers are their bane. Can it be in order to please author and reader? It is all one; for the demon of courtly love which prompts the lovers in their inmost selves to the devices that are the cause of their pain is the very demon of *the novel* as we in the West like it to be.

What, then, is the legend really about? The partings of the lovers? Yes, but in the name of passion, and for love of the very love that agitates them, in order that this love may be intensified and transfigured—at the cost of their happiness and even of their lives.

---

[10]The twentieth-century detective story is the best illustration of this. Veri-similitude there becomes a function of the amateur's 'technical' pleasure and is nothing else.

The secret and disturbing significance of the myth is beginning to loom out—the *peril* it at once expresses and veils, the passion to which to yield is like a swoon. But it is too late to turn away. We are affected, we are under the spell, we grow alive to the 'exquisite anguish'. It would be idle to condemn; swooning cannot be condemned. But is it not a philosopher's passion to meditate in the act of swooning? Perhaps knowledge is but the effort of a mind that resists the headlong fall and holds back in the midst of temptation.

THE LOVE OF LOVE

'De tous les maux, le mien diffère; il me plaît; je me réjouis de lui; mon mal est ce que je veux et ma douleur est ma santé. Je ne vois donc pas de quoi je me plains; car mon mal me vient de ma volonté; c'est mon vouloir qui devient mon mal; mais j'ai tant d'aise à vouloir ainsi que je souffre agréablement, et tant de joie dans me douleur que je suis malade avec delicés.'—CHRESTIEN DE TROYES.[11]

It is only 'silly' questions that can enlighten us; for behind whatever seems obvious lurks something that is not. Let us then boldly ask: Does Tristan care for Iseult, and she for him? The lovers do not seem to be brought together in any normal *human* way. On the contrary, at their first encounter they confine themselves to having ordinary polite relations; and later, when Tristan returns to Ireland to fetch Iseult, the politeness, it will be remembered, gives place to open hostility. Everything goes to show that they would never have chosen one another were they acting *freely*. But no sooner have they drunk the love-potion than passion flares between them. Yet that any fondness supervenes to unite them as a result of the magic spell I have found, among the thousands of lines of the Romance, only a single indication. When, following Tristan's escape, it has been told how they have gone to live in the Forest of Morrois, there occur these lines:

> Aspre vie meinent et dure:
> Tant s'entraiment de bone amor
> L'un por l'autre ne sent dolor.[12]

If it should be imagined that poets in the Middle Ages were less emotional than we have grown to be and felt no need to insist on what goes without saying, let the account of the three years in the forest be read attentively. Its two finest passages—which are no doubt also the most profound pas-

[11]'From all other ills doth mine differ. It pleaseth me; I rejoice at it; my ill is what I want and my suffering is my health. So I do not see what I am conplaining about; for my ill comes to my by my will; it is my willing that becomes my ill; but I am so pleased to want thus that I suffer agreeably, and have so much joy in my pain that I am sick with delight.'
[12]'Harsh life led they and hard, so entertaining good love for one another. One by the other was ne'er exposed to pain.'

sages in the whole legend—describe the lovers' two visits to the hermit Ogrin. The first time they go to see him, it is in order to make confession. But instead of confessing their sin and asking for absolution, they do their best to convince him that they are not to blame for what has befallen, since after all *they do not care for one another*!

> Q'el m'aime, c'est par la poison
> Ge ne me pus de lié partir,
> N'ele de moi—[13]

So speaks Tristan, and Iseult says after him:

> Sire, por Deu omnipotent,
> Il ne m'aime pas, ne je lui,
> Fors par un herbé dont je bui
> Et il en but: ce fu pechiez.[14]

They are thus in a thrillingly contradictory position. They love, but not one another. They have sinned, but cannot repent; for they are not to blame. They make confession, but wish neither to reform nor even to beg forgiveness. Actually, then, like all other great lovers, they imagine that they have ravished 'beyond good and evil' into a kind of transcendental state outside ordinary human experience, into an ineffable absolute irreconcilable with the world, but that they feel to be *more real than the world*. Their oppressive fate, even though they yield to it with wailings, obliterates the antithesis of good and evil, and carries them away beyond the source of moral values, beyond pleasure and pain, beyond the realm of distinctions —into a realm where opposites cancel out.

Their admission is explicit enough: 'Il ne m'aime pas, ne je lui.' Everything happens as if they could neither see nor recognize one another. They are the prisoners of 'exquisite anguish' owing to something which neither controls—some alien power independent of their capacities, or at any rate of their conscious wishes, and of their being in so far as they are aware of being. Both characters, the man as much as the woman, are depicted physically and psychologically in an entirely conventional and rhetorical manner. He is 'the strongest'; she, 'the most beautiful'; he, the knight; she, the princess; and so on. It is impossible to believe that any human feeling can grow between two such rudimentary characters. The friendship mentioned in connexion with the length of time the effect of the lovepotion lasts is the opposite of a true friendship; and, what is still more striking, if moral friendship does at last appear, it is at the moment their passion declines. And the immediate consequence of their nascent friend-

---

[13]'If she loves me, it is by the poison which holds me from leaving her and her from leaving me.'

[14]'Lord, by almighty God, he loves me not, nor I him; except for a herb potion which I drank and which he drank; it was a sin.'

ship, far from being to knit them more closely together, is to make them feel that they have everything to gain from a separation. This last point deserves to be considered more closely.

> L'endemain de la saint Jehan
> Aconpli furent li troi an.[15]

Tristan is out in the forest after game. Suddenly he is reminded of the world. He sees in his mind's eye King Mark's castle. He signs for 'the vair and grey' and for the pomp of chivalry. He thinks of the high rank he might hold among his uncle's barons. He thinks too of his beloved—apparently for the first time! But for him she might be 'in fine rooms . . . hung with cloth of silk'. Simultaneously Iseult is filled with similar regrets. In the evening they are together and they confess to one another what is newly agitating them—'en mal uson nostre jovente'. It does not take them long to agree to part. Tristan talks of making off to Brittany. But first they will seek out Ogrin the Hermit and beg his forgiveness—and at the same time King Mark's forgiveness of Iseult.

It is at this point that there occurs a highly dramatic short dialogue between the hermit and the two penitents:

> Amors par force vos demeine![16]
> Conbien durra vostre folie?
> Trop avez mené ceste vie.

So Ogrin admonishes them.

> Tristan li dist: or escoutez[17]
> Si longuement l'avons menee
> Itel fu nostre destinee.

On top of this comes one more feature. When Tristan hears that the king agrees to Iseult's return:

> Dex! dist Tristan, quel departie![18]
> Molt est dolenz qui pert s'amie!

It is with his own pain that he commiserates; not a thought for 's'amie'! And she too, we are made to feel, finds it much more pleasant to be back with the king than she ever did with her lover—happier in the unhappiness of love than she ever was in the life they led together in the Morrois.

[15]'On the morrow of St John's Day, the three years were accomplished.'
[16]'Love by force dominates you. How long will your folly last? Too long you have been leading this life.' *Amors par force vos demeine*—the most poignant description of passion ever penned by a poet! We must pause to admire it. In a single line the whole of passion is summed up with a vigour of expression making all romanticism look pallid! Shall we ever recover this sturdy 'dialect of the heart'?
[17]'Tristan quoth to him: "Now harken, if for long we have been leading this life, that is because it was our destiny." '
[18]'God!' quoth Tristan, 'What a fate! Wretched he who loseth his mistress.'

For that matter, later on—as we have seen—passion seizes the lovers again, notwithstanding that the effect of the love-potion has worn off, and this time they are so carried away that they die—'he by her, she by him'. The seeming *selfishness* of their love is enough to account for the many 'chance' happenings and tricks of fate that obstruct their attainment of happiness. But this selfishness, in its profound ambiguity, still wants explaining. Selfishness, it is said, always ends in death. But that is as a final defeat. Theirs, on the contrary, requires death for its perfect fulfilment and triumph. To the problem this raises there is only one answer worthy of the myth.

Tristan and Iseult do not love one another. They say they don't, and everything goes to prove it. *What they love is love and being in love.* They behave as if aware that whatever obstructs love must ensure and consolidate it in the heart of each and intensify it infinitely in the moment they reach the absolute obstacle, which is death. Tristan loves the awareness that he is loving far more than he loves Iseult the Fair. And Iseult does nothing to hold Tristan. All she needs is her passionate dream. Their need of one another is in order to be aflame, and they do not need one another as they are. What they need is not one another's presence, but one another's absence. *Thus the partings of the lovers are dictated by their passion itself*, and by the love they bestow on their passion rather than on its satisfaction or on its living object. That is why the Romance abounds in obstructions, why when mutually encouraging their joint dream in which each remains solitary they show such astounding indifference, and why events work up in a romantic climax to a fatal apotheosis.

The duality is at once irrevocable and deliberate. 'Mot est dolenz qui pert s'amie,' Tristan sighs: and yet he then already sees, glimmering in the depths of the approaching night, that hidden flame which absence rekindles.

THE LOVE OF DEATH

But we must push on further still. Augustine's *amabam amare* is a poignant phrase with which he himself was not content. I have repeatedly referred to *obstruction*, and there is the way in which the passion of the two lovers *creates obstruction*, its effects coinciding with those of narrative necessity and of the reader's suspense. Is this obstruction not simply a *pretext* needed in order to enable the passion to progress, or is it connected with the passion in some far more profound manner? If we delve into the recesses of the myth, we see that this obstruction is what passion really *wants*—its true object.

I have shown that the Romance is given its motive power by the repeated partings and reunions of the lovers. For convenience, here once more, briefly, is what happens. Tristan, having landed in Ireland, meets Iseult and then parts from her without being in love. He turns up in Ireland again, and this time Iseult wants to kill him. They take ship together and drink the love-potion, and then sin. Next, Iseult is delivered up to Mark, and Tristan is banished from the castle. He and Iseult meet under a pine-tree, their talk being overheard by Mark. Tristan comes back to the castle, and Frocin and the barons discover evidence of his crime. They are parted. They meet again, and for three years go to live in the forest. Then, once more, they part. They meet at the hut of Orri the Woodman. Tristan goes away. He comes back, disguised as a poor pilgrim. He goes away again. The separation this time is prolonged, and he marries Iseult of the White Hand. Iseult the Fair is about to rejoin him when he dies. She dies too. More briefly still: They have one long spell together ('L'aspre vie'— 'The harsh life'), to which corresponds a lengthy separation—and Tristan's marriage. First, the love-potion; lastly, the death of both. In between, furtive meetings.

They are led to part so often either by adverse external circumstances or by hindrances which Tristan devises; and it is to be noted that Tristan's behaviour varies according to which kind of cause is operating. When social circumstances—for example, Mark's presence, the barons' sus-piciousness, the Judgement of God—threaten the lovers, Tristan leaps over the obstruction (this is symbolized by his leap from his own bed to the queen's). He then does not mind pain (his wound reopens) nor the danger to his life (he knows he is being spied upon). Passion is then so violent— so brutish, it might be said—that in the intoxication of his *déduit* (or delight) he is oblivious to pain and perils alike. Nevertheless, the blood flowing from his wound betrays him. This is the 'red stain' that apprises the king of what is happening. And it also apprises the reader of the lovers' secret—that they are seeking peril for its own sake. But so long as the peril comes from without, Tristan's prowess in overcoming it is an affirmation of life. At this stage Tristan is simply complying with the feudal practice of knights. He has to prove his 'valour' and show he is either the stronger or the more wily. We have seen that if he persevered in this direction he would carry off the queen, and that established law is only respected here because this gives the tale an excuse to rebound.

But the knight's demeanour becomes quite different when nothing external any longer separates the two lovers. Indeed, it becomes the opposite of what it has been. When Tristan puts his drawn sword between himself and Iseult although they are lying down fully clothed, this is again prowess, but on this occasion against himself, *to his own cost*. Since he himself has set up the obstruction, it is no longer one *he can overcome!* It must not be overlooked that the hierarchy of events corresponds closely to the hierarchy of both the story-teller's and the reader's *preferences*. The most serious obstruction is thus the one preferred above all. It is the one most suited to intensifying passion. At this extreme, furthermore, the wish to part assumes an emotional value *greater than that of passion itself*. Death, in being the goal of passion, kills it.

Yet the drawn sword is not the ultimate expression of the dark desire and of the actual *end* of passion (in both senses of the word 'end'). The admirable episode of the exchange of swords makes this clear. When the king comes upon the lovers lying asleep in the cave, he substitutes his own sword for that of his rival. The meaning of this is that in place of the obstruction which the lovers have wanted and have deliberately set up he puts the sign of the social prerogative, a legal and objective obstruction. Tristan accepts the challenge, and thereby enables the *action* of the tale to rebound. At this point the word 'action' takes on a symbolical meaning. Action prevents 'passion' from being complete, for passion is 'what is suffered'— and its limit is death. In other words, the action here is a fresh postponement of passion, which means a delaying of Death.

There is the same shift as regards the two marriages in the Romance, that of Iseult the Fair to the king and that of Iseult of the White Hand to Tristan. The first is an obstruction in fact. The concrete existence of a *husband* symbolizes its character, husbands being despised in courtly love. Making the obstruction that leads to adultery a husband is unimaginative, the excuse most readily thought of, and most in keeping with everyday experience.[19] See how Tristan shoves the husband aside, and enjoys making sport of him! But for the existence of a husband, the love of Tristan and Iseult would not have lasted beyond three years! And old Béroul showed his good sense in limiting the effect of the love-potion to that length of time:

> La mere Yseut, qui le bolli,
> A trois anz d'amistié le fist.

But for the existence of a husband, the lovers would have had to get married; and it is unbelievable that Tristan should ever be in a position to marry Iseult. She typifies the woman a man does not marry; for once she became his wife she would no longer be what she is, and he would no longer love her. Just think of a Mme Tristan! It would be the negation of passion—at least of the passion we are concerned with here. The spontaneous ardour of a love crowned and not thwarted is essentially of short duration. It is a flare-up doomed not to survive the effulgence of its fulfilment. But its *branding* remains, and this is what the lovers want to prolong and indefinitely to renew. That is why they go on summoning fresh perils. But these the knight's valour drives him to overcome, and so he has to go away, in quest of more profound and more intimate—and it even seems, more interior—experiences.

When Tristan is sighing quietly for his lost Iseult, the brother of Iseult of the White Hand thinks his friend must be in love with his sister. This confusion—produced by identity of name—is the sole 'cause' of Tristan's marrying. It is obvious that he could easily have cleared up the misunder-

---

[19]Romanticism was later on to devise more refined excuses.

standing. But here again honour supervenes—of course, as a mere pretext—to prevent him from drawing back. The reason is that he foresees, in this new ordeal which is *self-imposed*, the opportunity of a decisive advance. This merely formal marriage with a woman he finds beautiful is an obstruction which he can remove only by achieving a victory *over himself* (as well as over the institution of marriage, which he thus damages from within). This time his prowess goes against him. His chastity now he is married corresponds to the placing of the drawn sword between himself and the other Iseult. But a self-imposed chastity is a symbolical suicide (here is the hidden meaning of the sword)—a victory for the courtly ideal over the sturdy Celtic tradition which proclaimed its pride in life. It is a way of purifying desire of the spontaneous, brutish, and active elements still encumbering it. 'Passion' triumphs over desire. Death triumphs over life.

Hence Tristan's inclination for a *deliberate obstruction* turns out to be a desire for death and an advance in the direction of Death! But this death is for love, a deliberate death coming at the end of a series of ordeals thanks to which he will have been purified; a death that means transfiguration, and is in no way the result of some violent chance. Hence the aim is still to unite an external with an internal fate, which the lovers deliberately embrace. *In dying for love they redeem their destiny and are avenged for the love-potion.* So that at the last the struggle between passion and obstruction is inverted. At this point the obstruction is no longer serving irresistible passion, but has itself become the goal and end wished for for its own sake. Passion has thus only played the part of a purifying ordeal, it might almost be said of a penance, in the service of this transfiguring death. Here we are within sight of the ultimate secret.

The love of love itself has concealed a far more awful passion, a desire altogether unavowable, something that could only be 'betrayed' by means of symbols such as that of the drawn sword and that of perilous chastity. Unawares and in spite of themselves, the lovers have never had but one desire—the desire for death! Unawares, and passionately deceiving themselves, they have been seeking all the time simply to be redeemed and avenged for 'what they have suffered'—the passion unloosed by the love-potion. In the innermost recesses of their hearts they have been obeying the fatal dictates of a wish for death; they have been in the throes of *the active passion of Darkness....*

UNHAPPY MUTUAL LOVE

Passion means suffering, something undergone, the mastery of fate over a free and responsible person. To love love more than the object of love, to love passion for its own sake, has been to love to suffer and to court suffering all the way from Augustine's *amabam amare* down to modern romanticism. Passionate love, the longing for what sears us and annihilates us in its triumph—there is the secret which Europe has never allowed to be given away; a secret it has always repressed—and preserved! Hardly anything could be more tragic; and the way passion has persisted through the centuries should cause us to look to the future with deep despondency.

Here let me note a feature which will presently call for consideration. Both passion and the longing for death which passion disguises are connected with, and fostered by, a particular notion of how to reach understanding which in itself is typical of the Western *psyche*. Why does Western Man wish to suffer this passion which lacerates him and which all his common sense rejects? Why does he yearn after this particular kind of love notwithstanding that its effulgence must coincide with his self-destruction? The answer is that he reaches self-awareness and tests himself only by risking his life—in suffering and on the verge of death. The third act of Wagner's drama represents far more than a romantic disaster; it represents the *essential disaster* of our sadistic genius—the repressed longing for death, for self-experience to the utmost, for the revealing shock, a longing which beyond question manifests the most tenacious root of the war instinct we nourish.

From the tragic extreme—illustrated, avowed, and evidenced by the myth in its pristine purity—let us step down to passionate experience as men undergo it today. The tremendous success of the Tristan Romance shows, whether we like it or not, that we have a secret preference for what is unhappy. According to the sturdiness of our spirit, this unhappiness may be the 'delightful sadness' and spleen of nineteenth-century decadence, a transfiguring torment, or a challenge which the mind flings down to the world. But in any case, what we pursue is what promises to uplift and excite us, so that in spite of ourselves we shall be transported into the 'real life' spoken of by poets. But this 'real life' is an impossible one. What is heralded by the sky with high-riding clouds and by the empurpled heroic sunset is not Day; it is Night! 'Real life is *elsewhere*,' Rimbaud said. 'Real life' indeed is but another name for Death, and the only name we have dared *to invoke* it by—even while we were pretending to fend it off. Why is it that we delight most of all in some tale of impossible love? Because we long for the *branding*; because we long to grow *aware* of what is on fire inside us. Suffering and understanding are deeply connected; death and self-awareness are in league;[20] and European romanticism may be compared to a man for whom sufferings, and especially the sufferings of love, are a privileged mode of understanding.

Of course, this is only true of the best romantics among us. Most people do not bother about understanding or about self-awareness; they merely go after the kind of love that promises the most *feeling*. But even this has to be a love delayed in its happy fulfilment by some obstruction.

[20]On this alliance Hegel was able to ground a general explanation of the human mind, and also of human history.

Hence, whether our desire is for the most self-conscious or simply for the most intense love, secretly we desire obstruction. And this obstruction we are ready if needs be to invent or imagine.

This seems to me to explain much of our psychological nature. Unless the course of love is being hindered there is no 'romance'; and it is romance that we revel in—that is to say, the self-conciousness, intensity, variations, and delays of passion, together with its climax rising to disaster—not its sudden flaring. Consider our literature. The happiness of lovers stirs our feelings only on account of the unhappiness which lies in wait for it. We must feel that life is imperilled, and also feel the hostile realities that drive happiness away into some beyond. What moves us is not its presence, but its nostalgia and recollection. Presence is inexpressible and has no perceptible duration; it can only be a *moment* of grace—as in the duet of Don Giovanni and Zerlina. Otherwise we lapse into a picture-postcard idyll. Happy love has no history—*in European literature*. And a love that is not mutual cannot pass for a true love. The outstanding find made by European poets, what distinguishes them first and foremost among the writers of the world, what most profoundly expresses the European obsession by suffering as a way to understanding is the secret of the Tristan myth; passionate love at once shared and fought against, anxious for a happiness it rejects, and magnified in its own disaster— *unhappy mutual love*.

Let us pause at this description of the myth.

The love is *mutual* in the sense that Tristan and Iseult 'love one another', or, at least, believe that they do. Certainly their mutual fidelity is exemplary. But *unhappiness* comes in, because the love which 'dominates' them is not a love of each for the other as that other really is. They love one another, but each loves the other *from the standpoint of self and not from the other's standpoint*. Their unhappiness thus originates in a false reciprocity, which disguises a twin narcissism. So much is this so that at times there pierces through their excessive passion a kind of hatred of the beloved. Long before Freud and modern psychology Wagner saw this. 'By me chosen, lost by me!' Isolde sings in her frantic love. And the sailor's opening song from the mast-head predicts the inevitable fate of them both:

Westward sweeps the eye, eastward on we fly.
The wind so wild blows homeward now:
my Irish child, where tarriest thou?
Sighs from thy heart ascending,
help to our sails are lending!
Sigh, ah sigh, wind so wild!
Sigh, ah sigh now, my child!
O Irish maid, thou wayward, winsome maid!

Their passion is twice unhappy in that it flees from both reality and the Norm of Day. The essential unhappiness of this love is that what they desire they have not yet had—this is Death—and that what they had is now being lost—the enjoyment of life. And yet, far from this loss being felt as privation, the couple imagine that they are now more fully alive than ever and are more than ever living dangerously and magnificently. The approach of death acts as a goad to sensuality. In the full sense of the verb, it aggravates desire. Sometimes even, it aggravates desire to the point of turning this into a wish to kill either the beloved or oneself, or to founder in a twin downrush.

> Here now my will, ye craven winds! [Isolde begins by singing]
> come forth to strife and stress of the storm!
>   to turbulent tempests' clamour and fury!
> Drive from her dreams this slumbering sea;
> wake from the depths all her envious greed!
> Destroy now this insolent ship,
> let its wreck be sunk in her waves!
> All that hath life and breath upon it,
> I leave to you winds as your prize!

Drawn to a death remote from the life that has been spurring them on, the lovers are doomed to become the voluptuous prey of conflicting forces that will cast both into the same headlong swoon. For they can never be united till, bereft of all hope and of all possible love, they reach the heart of utter obstruction and experience the supreme exaltation which is destroyed in being fulfilled.

CONVENTIONS OF CHIVALRIC LOVE

Johan Huizinga

Fidelity, compassion, justice—the virtues of the chivalric code were both religious and erotic in their aim. Dutch historian Johan Huizinga (1872–1945) uncovers their deep-seated unity in the medieval ideal of sacred love.

Historians sometimes disparage the chivalric code because of the crying disparity between its lofty idealism and the savagery of medieval life in fact. The knight who so worshipped his lady as to preclude his own touch might rape an unknown woman encountered in the forest without pang of conscience. But Huizinga rescues the significance of chivalry by pointing out that while some ideals are representative, others are compensatory. The first type simply amplifies and extends life as it is, while ideals of the second type serve to describe all that the world lacks, and longs for. Viewed in this way, chivalric love is no less expressive of man's nature and desires than are those ideals which bespeak their historical setting directly.

A conception of military life resembling that of medieval chivalry is found nearly everywhere, notably with the Hindus of the *Mahâbhârata* and in Japan. Warlike aristocracies need an ideal form of manly perfection. The aspiration to a pure and beautiful life, expressed in the *Kalokagathia* of the Hellenes, in the Middle Ages gives birth to chivalry. And during several centuries that ideal remains a source of energy, and at the same time a cloak for a whole world of violence and self-interest.

The ascetic element is never absent from it. It is most accentuated in the times when the function of knighthood is most vital, as in the times of the early crusades. The noble warrior has to be poor and exempt from worldly ties. "This ideal of the well-born man without possessions"—says William James—"was embodied in knight-errantry and templardom, and, hideously corrupted as it has always been, it still dominates sentimentally, if not practically, the military and aristocratic view of life. We glorify the soldier as the man absolutely unincumbered. Owning nothing but his bare life, and willing to toss that up at any moment when the cause commands him, he is the representative of unhampered freedom in ideal directions." Medieval chivalry, in its first bloom, was bound to blend with

Reprinted from *The Waning of the Middle Ages* by J. Huizinga by permission of St. Martin's Press, Inc. and Edward Arnold Publishers, Ltd.

monarchism. From this union were born the military orders of the Templars, of Saint John, of the Teutonic knights, and also those of Spain. Soon, however, or rather from the very beginning, reality gives the lie to the ideal, and accordingly the ideal will soar more and more towards the regions of fantasy, there to preserve the traits of asceticism and sacrifice too rarely visible in real life. The knight-errant, fantastic and useless, will always be poor and without ties, as the first Templars had been.

It would thus be unjust to regard as factitious or superficial the religious elements of chivalry, such as compassion, fidelity, justice. They are essential to it. Yet the complex of aspirations and imaginings, forming the idea of chivalry, in spite of its strong ethical foundation and the combative instinct of man, would never have made so solid a frame for the life beautiful if love had not been the source of its constantly revived ardour.

These very traits, moreover, of compassion, of sacrifice, and of fidelity, which characterize chivalry, are not purely religious; they are erotic at the same time. Here, again, it must be remembered that the desire of bestowing a form, a style, on sentiment, is not expressed exclusively in art and literature; it also unfolds in life itself: in courtly conversation, in games, in sports. There, too, love incessantly seeks a sublime and romantic expression. If, therefore, life borrows motifs and forms from literature, literature, after all, is only copying life. The chivalrous aspect of love had somehow to make its appearance in life before it expressed itself in literature.

The knight and his lady, that is to say, the hero who serves for love, this is the primary and invariable motif from which erotic fantasy will always start. It is sensuality transformed into the craving for self-sacrifice, into the desire of the male to show his courage, to incur danger, to be strong, to suffer and to bleed before his lady-love.

From the moment when the dream of heroism through love has intoxicated the yearning heart, fantasy grows and overflows. The first simple theme is soon left behind, the soul thirsts for new fancies, and passion colours the dream of suffering and of renunciation. The man will not be content merely to suffer, he will want to save from danger, or from suffering, the object of his desire. A more vehement stimulus is added to the primary motif: its chief feature will be that of defending imperilled virginity—in other words, that of ousting the rival. This, then, is the essential theme of chivalrous love poetry: the young hero, delivering the virgin. The sexual motif is always behind it, even when the aggressor is only an artless dragon; a glance at Burne-Jones's famous picture suffices to prove it.

One is suprised that comparative mythology should have looked so indefatigably to meteorological phenomena for the explanation of such an immediate and perpetual motif as the deliverance of the virgin, which is the oldest of literary motifs, and one which can never grow antiquated. It may from time to time become stale from overmuch repetition, and yet it will reappear, adapting itself to all times and surroundings. New romantic types will arise, just as the cowboy has succeeded the corsair.

The Middle Ages cultivated these motifs of a primitive romanticism with a youthful insatiability. Whereas in some higher genres of literature, such as lyrical poetry, the expression of desire and fulfilment became more refined, the romance of adventure always preserved it in its crude and naïve form, without ever losing its charm to its contemporaries. We might have expected that the last centuries of the Middle Ages would have lost their relish for these childish fancies. We are inclined to suppose that *Méliador*, the super-romantic novel by Froissart, or *Perceforest*, those belated fruits of chivalrous romance, were anachronisms even in their own day. They were no more so than the sensational novel is at present. Erotic imagination always requires similar models, and it finds them here. In the hey-day of the Renaissance we see them revive in the cycle of Amadis of Gaul. When, a good while after the middle of the sixteenth century, Francois de la Noue affirms that the novels of Amadis had caused "un esprit de vertige" among his generation—the generation of the Huguenots, which had passed through humanism with its vein of rationalism—we can imagine what must have been the romantic susceptibility of the ill-balanced and ignorant generation of 1400.

Literature did not suffice for the almost insatiable needs of the romantic imagination of the age. Some more active form of expression was required. Dramatic art might have supplied it, but the medieval drama in the real sense of the word treated love matters only exceptionally; sacred subjects were its substance. There was, however, another form of representation, namely, noble sports, tourneys and jousts. Sportive struggles always and everywhere contain a strong dramatic element and an erotic element. In the medieval tournament these two elements had so much got the upper hand, that its character of a contest of force and courage had been almost obliterated by its romantic purport. With its bizarre accoutrements and pompous staging, its poetical illusion and pathos, it filled the place of the drama of a later age.

The life of aristocracies when they are still strong, though of small utility, tends to become an all-round game. In order to forget the painful imperfection of reality, the nobles turn to the continual illusion of a high and heroic life. They wear the mask of Lancelot and of Tristram. It is an amazing self-deception. The crying falsehood of it can only be borne by treating it with some amount of raillery. The whole chivalrous culture of the last centuries of the Middle Ages is marked by an unstable equilibrium between sentimentality and mockery. Honour, fidelity and love are treated with unimpeachable seriousness; only from time to time the solemn rigidity relaxes into a smile, but downright parody never prevails. Even after the *Morgante* of Pulci and the *Orlando Innamorato* of Boiardo had made the heroic pose ridiculous, Ariosto recaptured the absolute serenity of chivalrous sentiment.

In French circles, of about 1400, the cult of chivalry was treated with perfect gravity. It is not easy for us to understand this seriousness, and not to be startled by the contrast between the literary note of a Boucicaut and the facts of his career. He is represented as the indefatigable defender of courtesy and of chivalry, serving his lady according to the old rules of courteous love. "He served all, he honoured all, for the love of one. His speech was graceful, courteous and diffident before his lady." During his travels in the Near East in 1388, he and his companions in arms amuse themselves by composing a poetical defence of the faithful and chaste love of a knight—the *Livre des Cent Ballades*. One might have supposed him cured of all chivalrous delusions after the catastrophe of Nicopolis. There he had seen the lamentable consequences of statecraft recklessly embarking on an enterprise of vital import in the spirit of a chivalrous adventure. His companions of the *Cent Ballades* had perished. That would suffice, one would think, to make him turn his back on old-fashioned forms of courtesy. Yet he remains devoted to them and resumes his moral task in founding the order "de la dame blanche à l'escu vert."

Like all romantic forms that are worn out as an instrument of passion, this apparatus of chivalry and of courtesy affects us at first sight as a silly and ridiculous thing. The accents of passion are heard in it no more save in some rare products of literary genius. Still, all these costly elaborated forms of social conduct have played their part as a decoration of life, as a framework for a living passion. In reading this antiquated love poetry, or the clumsy descriptions of tournaments, no exact knowledge of historical details avails without the vision of the smiling eyes, long turned to dust, which at one time were infinitely more important than the written word that remains.

Only a stray glimmer now reminds us of the passionate significance of these cultural forms. In the *Voeu du Héron* the unknown author makes Jean de Beaumont speak:

> "Quant sommes ès tavernes, de ces fors vins buvant,
> Et ces dames delès qui nous vont regardant,
> A ces gorgues polies, ces coliés tirant,
> Chil œil vair resplendissent de biauté souriant,
> Nature nous semont d'avoir cœur desirant,
> ... Adonc conquerons-nous Yaumont et Agoulant
> Et li autre conquierrent Olivier et Rollant.
> Mais, quant sommes as camps sus nos destriers courans,
> Nos escus à no col et nos lansses bais(s)ans,
> Et le froidure grande nous va tout engelant,
> Li membres nous effondrent, et derrière et devant,
> Et nos ennemies sont envers nous approchant,

Adonc vorrièmes estre en un chélier si grant
Que jamais ne fussions veu tant ne quant."[1]

Nowhere does the erotic element of the tournament appear more clearly than in the custom of the knight's wearing the veil or the dress of his lady. In *Perceforest* we read how the lady spectators of the combat take off their finery, one article after another, to throw them to the knights in the lists. At the end of the fight they are bareheaded and without sleeves. A poem of the thirteenth century, the work of a Picard or a Hainault minstrel, entitled *Des trois Chevaliers et del Chainse*,[2] has worked out this motif in all its force. The wife of a nobleman of great liberality, but not very fond of fighting, sends her shirt to three knights who serve her for love, that one of them at the tournament which her husband is going to give may wear it as a coat-armour, without any mail underneath. The first and the second knights excuse themselves. The third, who is poor, takes the shirt in his arms at night, and kisses it passionately. He appears at the tournament, dressed in the shirt and without a coat of mail; he is grievously wounded, the shirt, stained with his blood, is torn. Then his extraordinary bravery is perceived and he is awarded the prize. The lady gives him her heart. The lover asks something in his turn. He sends back the garment, all blood-stained, to the lady, that she may wear it over her gown at the meal which is to conclude the feast. She embraces it tenderly and shows herself dressed in the shirt as the knight had demanded. The majority of those present blame her, the husband is confounded, and the minstrel winds up by asking the question: Which of the two lovers sacrificed most for the sake of the other?

The Church was openly hostile to tournaments; it repeatedly prohibited them, and there is no doubt that the fear of the passionate character of this noble game, and of the abuses resulting from it, had a great share in this hostility. Moralists were not favourably disposed towards tournaments, neither were the humanists. Where do we read, Petrarch asks, that Cicero or Scipio jousted? The burghers thought them useless and ridiculous. Only the world of the nobility continued to cultivate all that regarded tournaments and jousts, as things of the highest importance. Monuments were erected on the sites of famous combats, as the Pélerine Cross near Saint Omer, in remembrance of the Passage of Arms of la Pélerine, and of the exploits of the bastard of Saint Pol and a Spanish knight. Bayard

[1] When we are in the tavern, drinking strong wines, And the ladies pass and look at us, With those white throats, and tight bodices, Those sparkling eyes resplendent with smiling beauty, Then nature urges us to have a desiring heart, . . . Then we could overcome Yaumont and Agoulant And the others would conquer Oliver and Roland. But when we are in camp on our trotting chargers, Our bucklers round our necks and our lances lowered, And the great cold is congealing us altogether, And our limbs are crushed before and behind, And our enemies are approaching us, Then we should wish to be in a cellar so large That we might never be seen by any means.
[2] Of the three knights and the shirt.

piously went to visit this cross, as if on a pilgrimage. In the church of Notre Dame of Boulogne were preserved the decorations of the Passage of Arms of the Fontaine des Pleurs, solemnly dedicated to the Holy Virgin.

The warlike sports of the Middle Ages differ from Greek and modern athletics by being far less simple and natural. Pride, honour, love and art give additional stimulus to the competition itself. Overloaded with pomp and decoration, full of heroic fancy, they serve to express romantic needs too strong for mere literature to satisfy. The realities of court life or a military career offered too little opportunity for the fine make-belief of heroism and love, which filled the soul. So they had to be acted. The staging of the tournament, therefore, had to be that of romance; that is to say, the imaginary world of Arthur, where the fancy of a fairy-tale was enhanced by the sentimentality of courtly love.

A Passage of Arms of the fifteenth century is based on a fictitious case of chivalrous adventure, connected with an artificial scene called by a romantic name, as, for instance, *La fontaine des pleurs, L'arbre Charle-magne.* A fountain is expressly constructed, and beside it a pavilion, where during a whole year a lady is to reside (in effigy, be it understood), holding a unicorn which bears three shields. The first day of each month knights come to touch the shields, and in this way to pledge themselves for a combat of which the "Chapters" of the Passage of Arms lay down the rules. They will find horses in readiness, for the shields have to be touched on horseback: Or, in the case of the *Emprise du dragon*, four knights will be stationed at a cross-road where, unless she gives a gage, no lady may pass without a knight breaking two lances for her. There is an unmistakable connection between these primitive forms of warlike and erotic sport and the children's play of forfeits. One of the rules of the "Chapters" of the *Fontaine des pleurs* runs thus: he who, in a combat, is unhorsed, will during a year wear a gold bracelet, until he finds the lady who holds the key to it and who can free him, on condition that he shall serve her.

The nobles liked to throw a veil of mystery and melancholy over the procedure. The knight should be unknown. He is called "le blanc chevalier," "le chevalier mesconnu," or he wears the crest of Lancelot or Palamedes. The shields of the Fount of Tears are white, violet and black, and overspread with white tears; those of the Tree of Charlemagne are sable and violet, with gold and sable tears. At the *Emprise du dragon*, celebrated on the occasion of the departure of his daughter Margaret for England, King René was present, dressed all in black, and his whole out-fit, caparison, horse and all, down to the wood of his lance, was of the same colour. . . .

When in the twelfth century unsatisfied desire was placed by the troubadours of Provence in the centre of the poetic conception of love, an important turn in the history of civilization was effected. Antiquity, too, had sung the sufferings of love, but it had never conceived them save as the expectation of happiness or as its pitiful frustration. The sentimental point of Pyramus and Thisbe, of Cephalus and Procris, lies in their tragic end; in the heart-rending loss of a happiness already enjoyed. Courtly poetry, on the other hand, makes desire itself the essential motif, and so creates a conception of love with a negative ground-note. Without giving up all connection with sensual love, the new poetic ideal was capable of embracing all kinds of ethical aspirations. Love now became the field where all moral and cultural perfection flowered. Because of his love, the courtly lover is pure and virtuous. The spiritual element dominates more and more, till towards the end of the thirteenth century, the *dolce stil nuovo* of Dante and his friends ends by attributing to love the gift of bringing about a state of piety and holy intuition. Here an extreme had been reached. Italian poetry was gradually to find its way back to a less exalted expression of erotic sentiment. Petrarch is divided between the ideal of spiritualized love and the more natural charm of antique models. Soon the artificial system of courtly love is abandoned, and its subtle distinctions will not be revived, when the Platonism of the Renaissance, latent, already, in the courtly conception, gives rise to new forms of erotic poetry with a spiritual tendency.

In France the evolution of erotic culture was more complicated. The idea of courtly love was not to be supplanted so easily there. The system is not given up; but the forms are filled by new values. Even before Dante had found the eternal harmony of his *Vita Nuova*, the *Roman de la Rose* had inaugurated a novel phase of erotic thought in France. The work, begun before 1240 by Guillaume de Lorris, was finished, before 1280, by Jean Chopinel. Few books have exercised a more profound and enduring influence on the life of any period than the *Romaunt of the Rose*. Its popularity lasted for two centuries at least. It determined the aristocratic conception of love in the expiring Middle Ages. By reason of its encyclopedic range it became the treasure-house whence lay society drew the better part of its erudition.

The existence of an upper class whose intellectual and moral notions are enshrined in an *ars amandi* remains a rather exceptional fact in history. In no other epoch did the ideal of civilization amalgamate to such a degree with that of love. Just as scholasticism represents the grand effort of the medieval spirit to unite all philosophic thought in a single centre, so the theory of courtly love, in a less elevated sphere, tends to embrace all that appertains to the noble life. The *Roman de la Rose* did not destroy the system; it only modified its tendencies and enriched its contents.

To formalize love is the supreme realization of the aspiration to the life beautiful, of which we traced above both the ceremonial and the heroic expression. More than in pride and in strength, beauty is found in love. To formalize love is, moreover, a social necessity, a need that is the more imperious as life is more ferocious. Love has to be elevated to the height of a rite. The overflowing violence of passion demands it. Only by constructing a system of forms and rules for the vehement emotions can barbarity be escaped. The brutality and the licence of the lower classes was always fervently, but never very efficiently, repressed by the Church. The aristocracy could feel less dependent on religious admonition, because they had a piece of culture of their own from which to draw their standards of conduct, namely, courtesy. Literature, fashion and conversation here formed the means to regulate and refine erotic life. If they did not altogether succeed, they at least created the appearance of an honourable life of courtly love. For, in reality, the sexual life of the higher classes remained surprisingly rude.

In the erotic conceptions of the Middle Ages two diverging currents are to be distinguished. Extreme indecency showing itself freely in customs, as in literature, contrasts with an excessive formalism, bordering on prudery. Chastellain mentions frankly how the duke of Burgundy, awaiting an English embassy at Valenciennes, reserves the baths of the town "for them and for all their retinue, baths provided with everything required for the calling of Venus, to take by choice and by election what they liked best, and all at the expense of the duke." Charles the Bold was reproached with his continence, which was thought unbecoming in a prince. At the royal or princely courts of the fifteenth century, marriage feasts were accompanied by all sorts of licentious pleasantries—a usage which had not disappeared two centuries later. In Froissart's narrative of the marriage of Charles VI with Isabella of Bavaria we hear the obscene grinning of the court. Deschamps dedicates to Antoine de Bourgogne an epithalamium of extreme indecency. A certain rhymer makes a lascivious ballad at the request of the lady of Burgundy and of all the ladies.

Such customs seem to be absolutely opposed to the constraint and the modesty imposed by courtesy. The same circles who showed so much shamelessness in sexual relations professed to venerate the ideal of courtly love. Are we to look for hypocrisy in their theory or for cynical abandonment of troublesome forms in their practice?

We should rather picture to ourselves two layers of civilization superimposed, coexisting though contradictory. Side by side with the courtly style, of literary and rather recent origin, the primitive forms of erotic life kept all their force; for a complicated civilization like that of the closing Middle Ages could not but be heir to a crowd of conceptions, motives, erotic forms, which now collided and now blended.

 **COURTLY LOVE**

John Jay Parry

Parry here catalogues the chief attributes of the medieval ideal known as "courtly love." Originating in the twelfth century revival of Ovid's The Art of Love, *the themes set forth here were carried through the European courts by troubadours and served as the radiating center of a distinctive perspective upon life and the world.*

The careful reader will discern a direction which courtly love shares with chivalric love and Tristanism. Together they move toward the celebration of a chaste love which ennobles the lover. To a robust sensibility the puzzle is how so "unnatural" an ideal could exert such pervasive influence. But recall that on Freudian principles "sublimation" (blockage and redirection of sexual energy) is responsible for civilization.

Of the *Treatise on Love*[1] of Andreas the Chaplain (Andreas Capellanus) a recent French scholar has written, "It is, like Brunetto Latini's *Trésor* or the *Speculum Majus* of Vincent of Beauvais, one of those capital works which reflect the thought of a great epoch, which explain the secret of a civilization."[2] It is from this point of view that a translation of the work is here presented. Andreas is not a great literary figure like his friend and fellow citizen Chrétien de Troyes, but perhaps for that very reason he brings us closer to the actual life of the time than does Chrétien. From his work we get a vivid picture of life in a medieval court like that of Troyes or Poitiers; to the student of medieval manners such a picture is especially valuable, because in these courts was taught, and probably also practiced, that strange social system to which Gaston Paris has given the name of "courtly love."[3] This developed in the twelfth century among the

From John Jay Parry's introduction to *The Art of Courtly Love* by Andreas Capellanus, trans. John Jay Parry (New York: Frederick Ungar, 1959), pp. 3–12. Reprinted by permission of Columbia University Press.

[1] Sometimes called *The Art of Courtly Love* (De arte honeste amandi).

[2] Robert Bossuat, *Drouart la Vache, traducteur d'André le Chapelain* (Paris: Champion, 1926), p. 31.

[3] "L'Amour courtois," in *Romania, XII* (1883), 519. Other discussions of the system are to be found in : Lewis Freeman Mott, *The System of Courtly Love* (Boston: Athenaeum Press, 1896); Joseph Anglade, *Les Troubadours* (2d ed., Paris: Colin, 1919), chap. iv.; Tom Peete Cross and William Albert Nitze, *Lancelot and Guenevere: a Study on the Origins of Courtly Love* (Chicago: University of Chicago Press, 1930), chap. iv; Alfred Jeanroy, *La Poesie lyrique des troubadours* (Toulouse: Privat, 1934), I, 90–100, II, 94–113; C. S. Lewis, *The Allegory of Love* (Oxford: Clarendon Press, 1936), chap. I; Ramon Menéndez-Pidal, "El Amor cortés," *Bull. Hisp., XL* (1938), 401–406; Sidney Painter,

troubadours of southern France, but soon spread into the neighboring countries and in one way or another colored the literature of most of western Europe for centuries. Its influence did not cease with the Renaissance, and even today, although it would scarcely be correct to speak of courtly love in our present-day society, some phases of it still linger on in our modern attitude toward romance.[4]

For all practical purposes we may say that the origin of courtly love is to be found in the writings of the poet Ovid who lived in Rome in the time of the Emperor Augustus. Among his poems are *The Art of Love* (Ars amatoria), *The Cure for Love* (Remedia amoris), and the *Amours* (Amores), all dealing, as their names imply, with the subject of love. *The Art of Love* was a sort of parody on the technical treatises of Ovid's day—a bit of fooling which should never have been taken seriously, but often was. The *Amours* supplement this with accounts of some of Ovid's own experiences in the art, and *The Cure for Love* shows those who are anxious to terminate a love affair how they may do so. Ovid does not present his ideas as a formal system (although he does speak of his "system"),[5] but from his writings men in later times derived the materials to make a system.

Love as Ovid conceived it is frankly sensual[6] ("merry sensuality" Lewis calls it[7]), and there is little or no trace in his work of the romantic affection of later times. It is extramarital and does not contemplate matrimony as its object.[8] Ovid is careful to say that the love he has in mind is not that of maidens or married women, but only such as modesty and the laws permit,[9] and much ingenuity has been expended[10] in showing that his doctrine is really not very immoral according to our present standards. But in the Middle Ages it was assumed as a matter of course that the *vir* who must be deluded, and whom Ovid delighted to delude, was the woman's husband,[11] and his statements that husbands and wives cannot love each other[12] and that even Penelope may be seduced if one is persistent[13] and his approving accounts of how Venus and Helen deceived their husbands[14] helped to confirm the impression. Whatever may have been Ovid's real meaning—and his sincerity on this point is not beyond question—the men

---

French Chivalry (Baltimore: Johns Hopkins Press, 1940), chap. iv; Thomas A. Kirby, *Chaucer's Troilus, a Study of Courtly Love* (University, La.: Louisiana State Univ. Press, 1940), chaps. i-iv. Some of these works do not distinguish sufficiently between the system as it existed in the time of Andreas and the system as it later developed.
[4]Lewis, *op. cit.*, pp. 3–4.
[5]"What used to be an impulse is now a system (*ratio*)": *The Cure for Love*, 1.
[6]*The Art of Love* III. 27; *The Cure for Love*, 11. 385–86.
[7]Op. cit., p. 4.
[9]Ibid. I. 31–34; II. 599–600.   [8]*The Art of Love* III. 585–86.
[10]For example by F. A. Wright in *Ovid: the Lover's Handbook*, 2d ed., pp. 72–83.
[11]*Amours* I. iv; *The Art of Love* I. 577 ff.; *The Cure for Love*, 1. 34.
[12]*The Art of Love* II. 153–55; III. 585–86.
[13]Ibid. I. 477.   [14]*Ibid.* II. 359 ff.; 562 ff.; *Amours* II. v. 28.

of the Middle Ages thought that they had his approval for the dictum that the best partner in a love affair is another man's wife. Ovid does not restrict either men or women to one affair at a time, but he does point out that the matter is greatly complicated if one woman learns of her lover's affair with another.[15] Trouble arises, too, if the lady's husband learns that she is in love with another man, so there is good reason for keeping such an affair secret; moreover, the very fact that it is secret makes it much pleasanter.[16]

Other ideas of Ovid which influenced the conception of courtly love are: Love is a kind of warfare, and every lover is a soldier. Cupid is the generalissimo,[17] and under him are the women whose power over the men is absolute. A man should deceive a woman, if he can, but he must never appear to oppose her slightest wish.[18] To please her he must watch all night before her doors,[19] undergo all sorts of hardships,[20] perform all sorts of absurd actions.[21] For love of her he must become pale and thin and sleepless.[22] No matter what he may do, or from what motives, he must persuade her that it is all done for her sake.[23]If in spite of all these demonstrations of affection she still remains obdurate, he must arouse her jealousy; he must pretend to be in love with some other woman, and when the first one thinks she has lost him, she will probably capitulate and he can clasp her sobbing to his breast.[24]

Of the circulation of Ovid's poems in the early Middle Ages we know comparatively little. But in the twelfth and thirteenth centuries so popular was his work[25] that Ludwig Traube used to call this period the *aetas Ovidiana*, as the two preceding periods were the *aetas Vergiliana* and the *aetas Horatiana*.[26] In this revival the *Art of Love* had its full part. It circulated both in Latin and in the vernaculars, and it was rewritten to adapt it to the changed conditions of medieval society. Much of the literature of France and England was colored by its ideas,[27] although a certain amount of the sensuality was glossed over. Even if courtly love had never

[15]*The Art of Love* II. 387 ff. [16]*Ibid.* I. 275.
[17]*Amours* I. ix. I. [18]*The Art of Love* I. 629 ff.
[19]*Ibid.* II. 523 ff.; *Amours* II. xix. 21 ff.
[20]*The Art of Love* II. 233–50; *Amours* I. ix.
[21]*The Art of Love* II. 198 ff. [22]*Ibid.* I. 727–36; *Amours* I. vi. 5–6, ix. 8.
[23]The Art of Love II. 288 ff.
[24]Ibid. II. 433 ff.; compare III. 593–94.
[25]Arturo Graf, *Röma nella memoria . . . del medio evo* (Torine: Loescher, 1882), II, 296–315; Max Manitius, "Beitrage zur Geschichte des Ovidius und anderer römischer Schriftsteller im Mittelalter," *Philologus,* Supplementband VII (1899), 723–58; J. E. Sandys, *A History of Classical Scholarship* (3d ed., Cambridge: Cambridge University Press, 1921), I, 638–41; Rudolph Schevill, "Ovid and the Renascence in Spain," pp. 6–27; Lester K. Born, "Ovid and Allegory," *Speculum,* IX (1934), 362–79.
[26]Edward Kennard Rand, *Ovid and His Influence* (New York: Longmans, 1928), pp. 12–23; Born, *op. cit.*, p. 363.
[27]Cross and Nitze, *op. cit.*, chap. iv; Urban Tigner Holmes, Jr., *A History of Old French Literature from the Origins to 1300* (Chapel Hill: Linker, 1937), pp. 302 ff.; Karl Voretzsch, *Introduction to the Study of Old French Literature* (translated by Francis M. Dumont, Halle: Niemeyer, 1931), pp. 244 ff., 450 ff.

developed, Ovid's influence would have been profound. Among the troubadours of southern France, however, this influence took on a special character. The Ovidian material was combined with other elements, and the whole combination was infused with a new spirit. It is to this new combinaton as it developed in the south and as it spread to other lands that we refer when we speak of "courtly love." No one of the troubadours produced even an approach to a treatise on the art;[28] we have to get our idea of it from their lyric poems. Yet in spite of individual differences and of the changes that took place with time, we can get a fairly coherent picture of the system.

The basis of it is the familiar material: love is an art and has its rules; lovers take service in the army of Cupid, and in this service they become pale and thin and sleepless; one cannot love one's own wife but must love the wife of some other man, so of necessity the affair must be kept secret; love cannot exist apart from jealousy. But the spirit that connects these ideas is wholly different from that of Ovid. The lover and his lady are no longer playing a game of mutual deceit. She is now his feudal suzerain, and he owes allegiance to her, or to Cupid through her. Her status is far above his, and although in theory he holds to the precept of Ovid that love levels all ranks, in practice he seldom dares to presume upon this equality, and his addresses to the lady are full of the deepest humility.[29] This difference in tone is a not unnatural result of the great social differences between Rome in Ovid's day and France in the twelfth century. The source of the other modifications of Ovid's doctrine is not so easy to discover. The matter is still in dispute, but of the various possibilities that have been suggested[30] the most reasonable seems to be that the troubadours were influenced by the culture of Moslem Spain, where many of these elements can be found before they appear among the Christians.[31]

After the fall of the Califate of Cordova in 1031 the territory of the Moors was divided among twenty petty kings whom the Spanish historians in derision have called "kings of parts" (*reyes de taïfas*).[32] Until the coming of the Almoravides from Africa in 1086 there was no religious fanaticism, and Moslems and Christians lived side by side on practically an equal footing. The period was one of pleasure and luxury, of wine and love, but it was also a period of culture. Because among the Arabs the encouragement of literature was one of the traditional manifestations of royal power, each of these petty kings had his court poets. The smaller towns and villages also produced their own poets, who came from all walks of life.

[28]*Las Leys d'amors* is a text book on grammar and the art of poetry, not a treatise on love.
[29]Jeanroy, *op. cit.*, I, 90–93.
[30]*Ibid.*, I, 64–80, and Holmes, *op. cit.*, pp. 171–73, and the authorities there cited.
[31]Opposition to the theory of Arabic influence seems to be due largely to the reluctance of the modern school of French scholars to admit that French literature is indebted to any source outside its own country and ancient Rome.
[32]The following sketch is based largely upon "La Poésie andalouse du XIe siècle," by Georges Marcais in *Journal des Savants*, 1939, pp. 14–30.

All these poets were trained in the classical Arabic tradition—some even went to Arabia to perfect themselves in the art—but the life they depicted in their poems was Spanish. For the traditional camp in the desert they substituted the gardens of Andalusia, and they described with care and interest the beauties of their own country. Their poetry has the classical Arabic emphasis upon form, but it is at the same time both national and popular.

Communication between these Moslem states, with their Mozarabic subjects, and the adjoining Christian states was both easy and frequent. Often the poets themselves were the mediums of communication. Because they had been trained in the art of saying things well, they were often employed on missions both to Mohammedan and to Christian sovereigns. Secretaries and ambassadors were often chosen from among their ranks. But such employment was precarious, and many of them changed masters either through necessity or in the hope of bettering their condition. A set of wandering poets came into existence, who passed from one court to another or sometimes found shelter with some bourgeois lover of verse. The situation is very much like that which developed a century later in France.

Not only does Moslem Spain show us a type of civilization which may well have given the impetus to that in Provence and Limousin, but even the metrical forms and the themes of the Spanish poets are like those that were later used by the troubadours.[33] The metrical similarities do not concern us here, except that they fill in the picture; but the similarities in content do, for here we find almost all the elements which, when combined with the ideas of Ovid, give us courtly love. We find among the Arabs two different attitudes toward the subject of love: they have a sensual tradition, perhaps native although colored by the work of Ovid, and another more spiritual tradition, which appears to be based upon the work of Plato as it had come down through the commentaries of Arabic scholars. As a presentation of this second point of view we may consider the book called *The Dove's Neck-Ring,* which was written about the year 1022 by the Andalusian Ibn Hazm at the request of a friend who had asked him for a discussion of the subject.[34]

Ibn Hazm admits that the ways of the Bedouins and of the ancients, in the matter of love, "are different from ours" (4), and even in his own day there was a great deal of dispute and much lengthy discussion about its nature (7). He is familiar with the Ovidian conventions that the lover must sigh and weep and become pale and thin and that he cannot eat or sleep

[33]Menendez-Pidal in *Revista cubana,* VI (1937), 5–33, and in *Bulletin hispanique,* XL (1938), 337–423; A. R. Nykl, *A Book Containing the Risala Known as The Dove's Neck-Ring about Love and Lovers composed by Abu Muhammed 'Ali ibn Hazm al-Andalusi* (Paris: Geuthner, 1931), pp. lxxviii-ciii.
[34]Nykl, *op. cit.* Roman numerals refer to pages of Nykl's introduction, and Arabic numerals to the paging of Petrof's text, which Nykl retains in his translation. On pp. ciii ff. he gives a brief summary of earlier works in the same Platonic tradition.

(xxvi, 14–15), and he adds to these the sudden trembling in the presence of the loved one (12), but he thinks that the lengths to which the Arabs have carried these conventions are absurd (143). He agrees with Ovid that the very secrecy of a love affair helps to make it pleasant, and he is in practical agreement with him as to the effect of jealousy, although he speaks of it under the heading "avoidance brought about by coquetry" (65). In a later book, *Kitab-alakhlaq*, he says definitely, "When jealousy fades out you can be sure that love has faded out," but here he thinks of jealousy as the result of love rather than its cause (xxv).

Ibn Hazm's concept of love, however, is in its main aspects very different from Ovid's and more resembles that of Plato. He defines love as a reunion of parts of souls which were separated in the creation (7). Its usual cause is an outwardly beautiful form, "because the soul is beautiful and passionately desires anything beautiful, and inclines toward perfect images" (9). This kind of love cannot be felt for more than one person although the other type, which is really passion and is improperly called love, may (24–25). True love does not ignore the physical aspect (58), but the union of souls is a thousand times finer in its effects than that of bodies (92). True love is not forbidden by religious law, and it makes the lover better in many ways, for he tries with all his power to do what he was incapable of doing before, in order to show his good qualities and to make himself desirable. "And how many a stingy one became generous, and a gloomy one became bright-faced, and a coward became brave, and a grouchy-dispositioned one became gay, and an ignoramus became clever, and a slovenly one in his personal appearance 'dolled up,' and an ill-shaped one became handsome" (12–13). Ibn Hazm does not say specifically, as Andreas does, that love ennobles the character, but this seems clearly implied by his definition of love and by such remarks as, "Among the praiseworthy natural gifts and noble character and excellent characteristics in love and elsewhere is faithfulness" (71–72). Certainly in his system true love and nobility of character go hand in hand.

This type of love may be felt for a woman who is powerful and of high rank (22, 50), or it may be felt for a slave girl (75, 78, 85),—the position of slave girls in Moslem society was one which seems very strange to us today.[35] In its purely spiritual aspect such a love may exist between two men without blame, but the question is complicated for us by the fact that among the Arabs public opinion required that if the beloved was a woman she must, "for decency's sake," be spoken of as a man and referred to by masculine pronouns, adjectives, and verbs.[36] Ibn Hazm disapproves of the practice which some poets indulged in of addressing their love

---

[35]There is some doubt as to whether the word *garija* always means "slave girl," although in most cases it certainly does. *Archivum Romanicum*, XIX (1935), 235.

[36]See the authorities cited by Nykl, *op. cit.*, p. cxviii. There may be some connection between this convention and the practice of the troubadour of addressing his lady as "my lord" (*midons* or *senhor*). Jeanroy, *op. cit.*, I, 91; Nykl, *op. cit.*, pp. cii f.

poems to the daughters of their lords (35), and upon one point he is most emphatic—one must not make love to a married woman; "Moslems have come together on this point unanimously, only heretics not fulfilling it" (128).

Whether the beloved was of high or of low rank, the lover was always abject before her. "The surprising thing which happens in love is the submissiveness of the lover to his beloved" (39–40). "I have [trod] the carpets of khalifs and [seen] circles of kings, and I never saw a timid respect which would equal that of a lover toward his beloved" (66). If the woman's soul, wrapped in its earthly veil, does not recognize its other half (8, 24) and she is not favorable to him, or if circumstances prevent the union of the lovers, the man seeks for contentment in what he has and hopes for more favors later (89). When he does receive anything, he is filled with joy; but he does not pretend, as the troubadours sometimes did, that he finds joy in the mere fact that his devotion is not rewarded. There are differences between Ibn Hazm's conception of love and that of the troubadours, but there is no justification for the statement of Jeanroy that "there is no trace, for example, in Ibn Hazm of the ennobling power of love, nor of the amorous vassalage, nor of the superiority of the lady over her lover, that is to say, of the courtly theories."[37] There is much more than a trace of each of these.

In his view of love Ibn Hazm is by no means unique among the Arabs. We find similar ideas in the works of the philosophers who preceded him, and we find them over and over again in the works of the poets of the eleventh century.[38] There was a definite school among them which advocated what Pérès calls "platonic love," but which resembles more closely what Andreas (p. 122) designates as "pure love." These poets taught that a man shows his good character and his good breeding by practicing a chaste love (*al-hawa al-'udri*) rather than a sensual love.[39] But true love, whether "pure" or "mixed," had an ennobling influence upon the lover, making a man of the humblest birth the equal of the noble lady whom he addressed (p. 427), for among the Arabs courtly manners were not the exclusive prerogative of the upper class (p. 425). But the lover, whether of higher or lower rank than his beloved, speaks of himself as her slave—a form of slavery which does honor to him (pp. 411 ff.); he addresses the lady as "my lord" (*sayyidi*) or "my master" (*mawlaya*) (p. 416) and loves her even when she tortures him. He finds contentment when she rejects him and joy when she shows him any kindness (415). One poet, Ibn 'Ammar, even says that love's delights are made of its burning torments (427), a form of

[37]*Op. cit.,* II, 367. He is answered by Nykl in *Archivum Romanicum,* XIX (1935), 227 ff.
[38]Henri Pérès, *La Poésie andalouse en arabe classique au XIe siècle* (Paris: Maisonneuve, 1937), see especially pp. 397–431, "La Femme et l'amour." Pérès says (p. 411) that the material is so abundant that he finds it difficult to select.
[39]For more specific details see Pérès, *loc. cit.* This institution should be compared with that of the *subintroducta* among the early Christians.

expression which is almost identical with that of some of the later Christian poets.

In spite of what Ibn Hazm says about the fact that Moslems avoided love affairs with married women, we find that some of the poets did address their amatory verses to the wives of other men, and Pérès believes that this was not due to pure fancy, but that the verses reflect the actual social condition of the time (419). There are abundant evidences of the freedom which women, even married women, enjoyed in Andalusia at this period (398 ff.). We even know that Wallada, daughter of the Caliph Al-Mustakfi, established, after her father's death, a sort of salon which was a gathering place for literary men and other people of prominence. She was criticized, it is true, but the fact that such a state of things was tolerated at all shows a great deal about the freedom of the Mohammedan women (399).

PART *V*
Friendship

FRIENDSHIP: "BECAUSE IT WAS HE, BECAUSE IT WAS I"

Among mankind's many modes of love, it is the value of friendship which is least disputed. Many accord it sovereignty over all other forms, as did Horace, for example, and Montaigne. Thus Montaigne contrasts it with romantic love, which he says is "more precipitant, fickle, moving and inconstant; a fever subject to intermissions and paroxysms, that has seized upon but one part of us. Whereas in friendship, 'tis a general and universal fire, but temperate and equal, a constant established heat, all gentle and smooth, without poignancy or roughness" ("Of Friendship"). In the end, even the hard-bitten Schopenhauer, glorifying lofty solitude, at least longs for the friendship which he believes that the man upon the heights is denied.

And when we set about to uncover the essential meaning of friendship, here too we are helped by more agreement among previous investigators than is to be found in other forms of love. A brief sketch of some points of considerable accord will be offered here as an introduction to the readings.

First of all, while the rest of life uses us piecemeal, friendship is uniquely the situation in which *whole persons* are invited forth.

Suppose we are just now approaching a street crossing and our glance takes in the policeman who is stationed there, directing traffic. Now if we only knew it, he is having a miserable day. Last night his teenage daughter quit the home; morning's mail brought news that IRS disputes a large deduction on his last year's tax return; and in the past hour no fewer than three automobiles have tried to amputate random parts of him. But we do not know these things and we do not want to know them. We insist that none of this show in his demeanor at the crossing, for it is extraneous to the single function we expect of him. He is no more than a blue uniform with hand motions, and must be kept so.

While it is exaggerated, this situation is nonetheless a model of human relations. The same basic terms appear among club members, between teacher and student, doctor and patient, host and guest, parent and child— yes, and husband and wife. By all such relations the individual is in some degree partitioned, portions of him being inadmissable. And the process appears with a vengeance in intellectual circles. A speaker on Einstein praises his physics but condemns his theology; a commentator on Immanuel Kant endorses this philosopher's first *Critique* but is personally embarrassed by the two subsequent *Critiques*, which he rather wishes the philosopher had not written. Nor is it different with each of us among our acquaintances; in each of them we pick and choose, accepting this, rejecting that, ignoring the rest. But to put it bluntly, what is left is a field of carrion in which we ourselves are the only living thing (and meanwhile we are carrion in others' fields). Mincemeat is not a person, and a person is not an agglomeration of pieces which can be picked apart without any loss. Instead, the word "person" denotes the unifying center of heterogeneous experience, the power which transforms heterogeneity into homogeneity, and it is this unification which is lost by partitioning. When Einstein's theology is disregarded, Einstein's physics is no longer Einstein's, and the man himself vanishes.

It is sheer sentimentalism to believe that we can all be whole human beings in our daily relations. It is *necessary* that the traffic policeman be merely a uniform. It is *necessary* to abstract those portions of what we read and hear which serve our purposes. Abstraction is the very meaning of purpose, and without the one we would be without the other. But is it not also necessary that amid our piecemal amputations a place exist where the absolute significance of personal wholeness be affirmed and encouraged? Such a place is made by love, and within the domain of love by that sanctuary which we call friendship.

For other forms of love do not give equal assurance of this capacity. Romantic love, Montaigne says, seizes on "but one part of us". Fellow feeling deals only in what is common to all. Comradeship often seems to entail a *loss* of personality, the sacrifice of anything that does not conduce to the group purpose. Is it not friendship alone which aims directly at the person, for no reason but that "he is he and I am I" (Montaigne)?

In this sense the symbol of friendship appears in the Greek myth of Philoctetes, immortalized in Sophocles' play. Philoctetes is possessed of a magic bow, given him by Heracles, that never misses its mark. But he also has an incurable, festering wound, which gives off so horrible an odor that he must live in exile on the island of Lemnos. But now the Greeks are hardpressed in the battle of Troy; they need his bow but are unwilling to accept his wound, and try to gain the bow by trickery. Only Neoptolemus, the young son of Achilles, knows that the wound must be accepted with the bow. Thus Neoptolemus becomes the symbol of friendship, which embraces the whole man.

By embracing the whole person, friendship reveals its necessarily *a priori* character. If we wait to *see* the whole man before declaring friendship we shall wait forever. Always in friendship, then, the heart must outrun the evidence and say, He is my friend come what may. Notice that this introduces an impetuous note—something that a strict prudence would disallow—into the very heart of friendship. Have not most of us at some time felt an intense interest in another person almost at the moment of first meeting, an interest aroused perhaps by a gesture or manner or unusual phrasing which suggests that the world as it appears to this person would be well worth knowing? Would we be wrong to call this "friendship at first sight?"

If the *a priori* necessity in friendship is its risk, it is also its joy, for it points to an exploration of the other which is never-ending and of equal reward to both parties. Friendship is the unique setting for reciprocal realization of two people as whole persons.

We conclude with a word about friendship's acceptance of the other. This feature has a highly significant function. It forcibly knocks us out of our native parochialism—a parochialism so severe that but for friendship no escape could be made. Imagine a child who is reared in a household which has a definite life-style. Let us say it is American middle-class, Protestant, white, Republican, educated, and kept scrupulously clean (any other set of factors would serve the illustration as well). These features constitute his home ground, his security, and his identity. Moreover, they will be sure to generate overt or subtle moral tones—"a tidy house means a tidy mind," and so on. As the child encounters differences he can always justify his familiar terms as "best." (Ford is the best kind of car "because my father owns one.") He is free to do so with perfect impunity until it occurs that he *first* makes a friend and *thereafter* discovers that his friend is Roman Catholic, or lives in a messy house. In this situation his resort to retrenchment is barred by his friendship. He can use it only by declaring the friendship a mistake. But the friendship possesses an intrinsic tenacity. If he is unwilling to dissolve it, then he finds himself impelled to say, "Catholicism (or messiness) cannot be bad, for it has helped to produce my friend." In this way he is forcibly pried out of his burrow by friendship, toward the discovery of new values.

Facing another whose life-style differs from their own, too many adults can do nothing but retrench and disparage the different. It is a matter for regret that such people have never experienced the therapeutic leverage of friendship.

In summary, some agreement by investigators of friendship is found on these points: it is between two persons; it embraces persons whole; it is always in some degree *a priori*; it accepts the other in the same terms as the self; it functions reciprocally to nurture whole persons. The reader is invited to notice how our contributors converge and diverge on these basic points.

THREE KINDS OF FRIENDSHIP

Aristotle

Aristotle here distinguishes three kinds of friendship, naming them friendships of pleasure, of utility, and of character. In the first, some quality of the other—his wit, for example—affords us pleasure; in the second, the other is useful toward the attainment of a goal of ours; in the third it is the other person in himself that we love.

Notice the resemblances between the first two forms and a certain disparity in the third. Pleasure and utility partition *the other, they split him up into pieces, directing themselves to some while ignoring others. The friendship of character, on the other hand, encompasses the other in his totality. If we concevive of persons as indivisible wholes, then by the first two forms it is not to persons that we are related. This consideration will lead such a thinker as Martin Buber to withhold the term friendship from the first two forms.*

For Aristotle as for Plato, friendship is a form of love in the mode of Eros. It has been noted that Eros is sometimes thought to be unable to account for friendship, since friendship is a reciprocity among equals, while Eros is always directed to superior value. Plato's theory of Eros-friendship appears in the selection from the Lysis, *and should be compared with Aristotle's account (Chap. 7, below). According to Aristotle's principle of equalization, when the greater is more loved than he loves, then a "proportion" exists which is "in a sense" an equality. This principle contains a number of difficulties from which the* Lysis *is exempt. For one, Aristotle speaks of the love of the superior for the inferior as the lesser love, but as Eros aims always aloft, downward love is impossible, not merely diminished. And we need only think of the situation of father and child to be prompted toward a conviction that the lesser's (the child's) need is greater, in which case Aristotle's principle appears to result in distributive injustice.*

After what we have said, a discussion of friendship would naturally follow, since it is a virtue or implies virtue, and is besides most necessary with a view to living. For without friends no one would choose to live, though he had all other goods; even rich men and those in possession of office and of dominating power are thought to need friends most of all; for

From *Nichomachean Ethics*, Bk. VIII, chaps. 1–8. *The Basic Works of Aristotle*, ed. Richard McKeon (New York: Random House, 1941), pp. 1060–1068. Reprinted by permission of Random House.

what is the use of such prosperity without the opportunity of beneficence, which is exercised chiefly and in its most laudable form towards friends? Or how can prosperity be guarded and preserved without friends? The greater it is, the more exposed is it to risk. And in poverty and in other misfortunes men think friends are the only refuge. It helps the young, too, to keep from error; it aids older people by ministering to their needs and supplementing the activities that are failing from weakness; those in the prime of life it stimulates to noble actions—'two going together'—for with friends men are more able both to think and to act. Again, parent seems by nature to feel it for offspring and offspring for parent, not only among men but among birds and among most animals; it is felt mutually by members of the same race, and especially by men, whence we praise lovers of their fellowmen. We may see even in our travels how near and dear every man is to every other. Friendship seems too to hold states together, and lawgivers to care more for it than for justice; for unanimity seems to be something like friendship, and this they aim at most of all, and expel faction as their worst enemy; and when men are friends they have no need of justice, while when they are just they need friendship as well, and the truest form of justice is thought to be a friendly quality.

But it is not only necessary but also noble; for we praise those who love their friends, and it is thought to be a fine thing to have many friends; and again we think it is the same people that are good men and are friends.

Not a few things about friendship are matters of debate. Some define it as a kind of likeness and say like people are friends, whence come the sayings 'like to like', 'birds of a feather flock together', and so on; others on the contrary say 'two of a trade never agree'. On this very question they inquire for deeper and more physical causes, Euripides saying that 'parched earth loves the rain, and stately heaven when filled with rain loves to fall to earth', and Heraclitus that 'it is what opposes that helps' and 'from different tones comes the fairest tune' and 'all things are produced through strife'; while Empedocles, as well as others, expresses the opposite view that like aims at like. The physical problems we may leave alone (for they do not belong to the present inquiry); let us examine those which are human and involve character and feeling, e.g. whether friendship can arise between any two people or people cannot be friends if they are wicked, and whether there is one species of friendship or more than one. Those who think there is only one because it admits of degrees have relied on an inadequate indication; for even things different in species admit of degree. We have discussed this matter previously.

The kinds of friendship may perhaps be cleared up if we first come to know the object of love. For not everything seems to be loved but only the lovable, and this is good, pleasant, or useful; but it would seem to be that by which some good or pleasure is produced that is useful, so that it is the good and the useful that are lovable as ends. Do men love, then, *the* good, or what is good for *them*? These sometimes clash. So too with regard to the pleasant. Now it is thought that each loves what is good for himself, and that the good is without qualification lovable, and what is good for each man is lovable for him; but each man loves not what is good for him but what seems good. This however will make no difference; we shall just have to say that this is 'that which seems lovable'. Now there are three grounds on which people love; of the love of lifeless objects we do not use the word 'friendship'; for it is not mutual love, nor is there a wishing of good to the other (for it would surely be ridiculous to wish wine well; if one wishes anything for it, it is that it may keep, so that one may have it one-self); but to a friend we say we ought to wish what is good for his sake. But to those who thus wish good we ascribe only goodwill, if the wish is not reciprocated; goodwill when it *is* reciprocal being friendship. Or must we add 'when it is recognized'? For many people have goodwill to those whom they have not seen but judge to be good or useful; and one of these might return this feeling. These people seem to bear goodwill to each other; but how could one call them friends when they do not know their mutual feelings? To be friends, then, they must be mutually recognized as bearing goodwill and wishing well to each other for one of the aforesaid reasons.

Now these reasons differ from each other in kind; so, therefore, do the corresponding forms of love and friendship. There are therefore three kinds of friendship, equal in number to the things that are loveable; for with respect to each there is a mutual and recognized love, and those who love each other wish well to each other in that respect in which they love one another. Now those who love each other for their utility do not love each other for themselves but in virtue of some good which they get from each other. So too with those who love for the sake of pleasure; it is not for their character that men love readywitted people, but because they find them pleasant. Therefore those who love for the sake of utility love for the sake of what is good for *themselves*, and those who love for the sake of pleasure do so for the sake of what is pleasant to *themselves*, and not in so far as the other is the person loved but in so far as he is useful or pleasant. And thus these friendships are only incidental; for it is not as being the man he is that the loved person is loved, but as providing some good or pleasure. Such friendships, then, are easily dissolved, if the parties do not remain like themselves; for if the one party is no longer pleasant or useful the other ceases to love him.

Now the useful is not permanent but is always changing. Thus when the motive of the friendship is done away, the friendship is dissolved, inasmuch as it existed only for the ends in question. This kind of friend-ship seems to exist chiefly between old people (for at that age people pur-sue not the pleasant but the useful) and, of those who are in their prime or young, between those who pursue utility. And such people do not live much with each other either; for sometimes they do not even find each other pleasant; therefore they do not need such companionship unless they are useful to each other; for they are pleasant to each other only in so far as they rouse in each other hopes of something good to come. Among such friendships people also class the friendship of host and guest. On the other hand the friendship of young people seems to aim at pleasure; for they live under the guidance of emotion, and pursue above all what is pleasant to themselves and what is immediately before them; but with increasing age their pleasures become different. This is why they quickly become friends and quickly cease to be so; their friendship changes with the object that is found pleasant, and such pleasure alters quickly. Young people are amorous too; for the greater part of the friendship of love depends on emotion and aims at pleasure; this is why they fall in love and quickly fall out of love, changing often within a single day. But these people do wish to spend their days and lives together; for it is thus that they attain the purpose of their friendship.

Perfect friendship is the friendship of men who are good, and alike in virtue; for these wish well alike to each other *qua* good, and they are good in themselves. Now those who wish well to their friends for their sake are most truly friends; for they do this by reason of their own nature and not incidentally; therefore their friendship lasts as long as they are good—and goodness is an enduring thing. And each is good without qualification and to his friend, for the good are both good without qualification and useful to each other. So too they are pleasant; for the good are pleasant both without qualification and to each other, since to each his own activities and others like them are pleasurable, and the actions of the good *are* the same or like. And such a friendship is as might be expected permanent, since there meet in it all the qualities that friends should have. For all friendship is for the sake of good or of pleasure—good or pleasure either in the abstract or such as will be enjoyed by him who has the friendly feeling—and is based on a certain resemblance; and to a friendship of good men all the qualities we have named belong in virtue of the nature of the friends themselves; for in the case of this kind of friendship the other qualities also[1] are alike in both friends, and that which is good without qualification is also without qualification pleasant, and these are the most lovable qualities. Love and friendship therefore are found most and in their best form between such men.

But it is natural that such friendships should be infrequent; for such men are rare. Further, such friendship requires time and familiarity; as the proverb says, men cannot know each other till they have 'eaten salt together'; nor can they admit each other to friendship or be friends till each

[1] i. e. absolute pleasantness, relative goodness, and relative pleasantness, as well as absolute goodness.

has been found lovable and been trusted by each. Those who quickly show the marks of friendship to each other wish to be friends, but are not friends unless they both are lovable and know the fact; for a wish for friendship may arise quickly, but friendship does not.

This kind of friendship, then, is perfect both in respect of duration and in all other respects, and in it each gets from each in all respects the same as, or something like what, he gives; which is what ought to happen between friends. Friendship for the sake of pleasure bears a resemblance to this kind; for good people too *are* pleasant to each other. So too does friendship for the sake of utility; for the good are also useful to each other. Among men of these inferior sorts too, friendships are most permanent when the friends get the same thing from each other (e. g. pleasure), and not only that but also from the same source, as happens between ready-witted people, not as happens between lover and beloved. For these do not take pleasure in the same things, but the one in seeing the beloved and the other in receiving attentions from his lover; and when the bloom of youth is passing the friendship sometimes passes too (for the one finds no pleasure in the sight of the other, and the other gets no attentions from the first); but many lovers on the other hand are constant, if familiarity has led them to love each other's characters, these being alike. But those who exchange not pleasure but utility in their amour are both less truly friends and less constant. Those who are friends for the sake of utility part when the advantage is at an end; for they were lovers not of each other but of profit.

For the sake of pleasure or utility, then, even bad men may be friends of each other, or good men of bad, or one who is neither good nor bad may be a friend to any sort of person, but for their own sake clearly only good men can be friends; for bad men do not delight in each other unless some advantage come of the relation.

The friendship of the good too and this alone is proof against slander; for it is not easy to trust any one's talk about a man who has long been tested by oneself; and it is among good men that trust and the feeling that 'he would never wrong me' and all the other things that are demanded in true friendship are found. In the other kinds of friendship, however, there is nothing to prevent these evils arising.

For men apply the name of friends even to those whose motive is utility, in which sense states are said to be friendly (for the alliances of states seem to aim at advantage), and to those who love each other for the sake of pleasure, in which sense children are called friends. Therefore we too ought perhaps to call such people friends, and say that there are several kinds of friendship—firstly and in the proper sense that of good men *qua* good, and by analogy the other kinds; for it is in virtue of something good and something akin to what is found in true friendship that they are friends, since even the pleasant is good for the lovers of pleasure. But these two kinds of friendship are not often united, nor do the same people become friends for the sake of utility and of pleasure; for things that are only incidentally connected are not often coupled together.

Friendship being divided into these kinds, bad men will be friends for the sake of pleasure or of utility, being in this respect like each other, but good men will be friends for their own sake, i. e. in virtue of their goodness. These, then, are friends without qualification; the others are friends incidentally and through a resemblance to these.

As in regard to the virtues some men are called good in respect of a state of character, others in respect of an activity, so too in the case of friendship; for those who live together delight in each other and confer benefits on each other, but those who are asleep or locally separated are not performing, but are disposed to perform, the activities of friendship; distance does not break off the friendship absolutely, but only the activity of it. But if the absence is lasting, it seems actually to make men forget their friendship; hence the saying 'out of sight, out of mind'. Neither old people nor sour people seem to make friends easily; for there is little that is pleasant in them, and no one can spend his days with one whose company is painful, or not pleasant, since nature seems above all to avoid the painful and to aim at the pleasant. Those, however, who approve of each other but do not live together seem to be well-disposed rather than actual friends. For there is nothing so characteristic of friends as living together (since while it is people who are in need that desire benefits, even those who are supremely happy desire to spend their days together; for solitude suits such people least of all); but people cannot live together if they are not pleasant and do not enjoy the same things, as friends who are companions seem to do.

The truest friendship, then, is that of the good, as we have frequently said; for that which is without qualification good or pleasant seems to be lovable and desirable, and for each person that which is good or pleasant to him; and the good man is lovable and desirable to the good man for both these reasons. Now it looks as if love were a feeling, friendship a state of character; for love may be felt just as much towards lifeless things, but mutual love involves choice and choice springs from a state of character; and men wish well to those whom they love, for their sake, not as a result of feeling but as a result of state of character. And in loving a friend men love what is good for themselves; for the good man in becoming a friend becomes a good to his friend. Each, then, both loves what is good for himself, and makes an equal return in goodwill and in pleasantness; for friendship is said to be equality, and both of these are found most in the friendship of the good.

Between sour and elderly people friendship arises less readily, inasmuch as they are less good-tempered and enjoy companionship less; for these are thought to be the greatest marks of friendship and most productive of it. This is why, while young men become friends quickly, old men do not; it is because men do not become friends with those in whom they do not delight; and similarly sour people do not quickly make friends either. But such men may bear goodwill to each other; for they wish one another well and aid one another in need; but they are hardly *friends* because they do not spend their days together nor delight in each other, and these are thought the greatest marks of friendship.

One cannot be a friend to many people in the sense of having friendship of the perfect type with them, just as one cannot be in love with many people at once (for love is a sort of excess of feeling, and it is the nature of such only to be felt towards one person); and it is not easy for many people at the same time to please the same person very greatly, or perhaps even to be good in his eyes. One must, too, acquire some experience of the other person and become familiar with him, and that is very hard. But with a view to utility or pleasure it is possible that many people should please one; for many people are useful or pleasant, and these services take little time.

Of these two kinds that which is for the sake of pleasure is the more like friendship, when both parties get the same things from each other and delight in each other or in the same things, as in the friendships of the young; for generosity is more found in such friendships. Friendship based on utility is for the commercially minded. People who are supremely happy, too, have no need of useful friends, but do need pleasant friends; for they wish to live with *some one* and, though they can endure for a short time what is painful, not one could put up with it continuously, nor even with the Good itself if it were painful to him; this is why they look out for friends who are pleasant. Perhaps they should look out for friends who, being pleasant, are also good, and good for them, too; for so they will have all the characteristics that friends should have.

People in positions of authority seem to have friends who fall into distinct classes; some people are useful to them and others are pleasant, but the same people are rarely both; for they seek neither those whose pleasantness is accompanied by virtue nor those whose utility is with a view to noble objects, but in their desire for pleasure they seek for ready-witted people, and their other friends they choose as being clever at doing what they are told, and these characteristics are rarely combined. Now we have said that the *good* man *is* at the same time pleasant and useful; but such a man does not become the friend of one who surpasses him in station, unless he is surpassed also in virtue; if this is not so, he does not establish equality by being proportionally exceeded in both respects. But people who surpass him in both respects are not so easy to find.

However that may be, the aforesaid friendships involve equality; for the friends get the same things from one another and wish the same things for one another, or exchange one thing for another, e. g. pleasure for utility; we have said, however, that they are both less truly friendships and less permanent. But it is from their likeness and their unlikeness to the same thing that they are thought both to be and not to be friendships. It is by their likeness to the friendship of virtue that they seem to be friendships (for one of them involves pleasure and the other utility, and these characteristics belong to the friendship of virtue as well); while it is because the friendship of virtue is proof against slander and permanent, while these quickly change (besides differing from the former in many other respects), that they appear *not* to be friendships; i. e. it is because of their unlikeness to the friendship of virtue.

But there is another kind of friendship, viz. that which involves an inequality between the parties, e. g. that of father to son and in general of elder to younger, that of man to wife and in general that of ruler to subject. And these friendships differ also from each other; for it is not the same that exists between parents and children and between rulers and subjects, nor is even that of father to son the same as that of son to father, nor that of husband to wife the same as that of wife to husband. For the virtue and the function of each of these is different, and so are the reasons for which they love; the love and the friendship are therefore different also. Each party, then, neither gets the same from the other, nor ought to seek it; but when children render to parents what they ought to render to those who brought them into the world, and parents render what they should to their children, the friendship of such persons will be abiding and excellent. In all friendships implying inequality the love also should be proportional, i. e. the better should be more loved than he loves, and so should the more useful, and similarly in each of the other cases; for when the love is in proportion to the merit of the parties, then in a sense arises equality, which is certainly held to be characteristic of friendship.

But equality does not seem to take the same form in acts of justice and in friendship; for in acts of justice what is equal in the primary sense is that which is in proportion to merit, while quantitative equality is secondary, but in friendship quantitative equality is primary and proportion to merit secondary. This becomes clear if there is a great interval in respect of virtue or vice or wealth or anything else between the parties; for then they are no longer friends, and do not even expect to be so. And this is most manifest in the case of the gods; for they surpass us most decisively in all good things. But it is clear also in the case of kings; for with them, too, men who are much their inferiors do not expect to be friends; nor do men of no account expect to be friends with the best or wisest men. In such cases it is not possible to define exactly up to what point friends can remain friends; for much can be taken away and friendship remain, but when one party is removed to a great distance, as God is, the possibility of friendship ceases. This is in fact the origin of the question whether friends really wish for their friends the greatest goods, e. g. that of being gods; since in that case their friends will no longer be friends to them, and therefore will not be good things for them (for friends *are* good things). The answer is that if we were right in saying that friend wishes good to friend for his sake, his friend must remain the sort of being he is, whatever that may be; therefore it is for him only so long as he remains a man that he will wish the greatest goods. But perhaps not *all* the greatest goods; for it is for himself most of all that each man wishes what is good.

Most people seem, owing to ambition, to wish to be loved rather than to love; which is why most men love flattery; for the flatterer is a friend in an inferior position, or pretends to be such and to love more than he is loved; and being loved seems to be akin to being honoured, and this is what most people aim at. But it seems to be not for its own sake that people choose honour, but incidentally. For most people enjoy being honoured by those in positions of authority because of their hopes (for they think that if they want anything they will get it from them; and therefore they delight in honour as a token of favour to come); while those who desire honour from good men, and men who know, are aiming at confirming their own opinion of themselves; they delight in honour, therefore, because they believe in their own goodness on the strength of the judgement of those who speak about them. In being loved, on the other hand, people delight for its own sake; whence it would seem to be better than being honoured, and friendship to be desirable in itself. But it seems to lie in loving rather than in being loved, as is indicated by the delight mothers take in loving; for some mothers hand over their children to be brought up, and so long as they know their fate they love them and do not seek to be loved in return (if they cannot have both), but seem to be satisfied if they see them prospering; and they themselves love their children even if these owing to their ignorance give them nothing of a mother's due. Now since friendship depends more on loving, and it is those who love their friends that are praised, loving seems to be the characteristic virtue of friends, so that it is only those in whom this is found in due measure that are lasting friends, and only their friendship that endures.

It is in this way more than any other that even unequals can be friends; they can be equalized. Now equality and likeness are friendship, and especially the likeness of those who are like in virtue; for being steadfast in themselves they hold fast to each other, and neither ask nor give base services, but (one may say) even prevent them; for it is characteristic of good men neither to go wrong themselves nor to let their friends do so. But wicked men have no steadfastness (for they do not remain even like to themselves), but become friends for a short time because they delight in each other's wickedness. Friends who are useful or pleasant last longer; i. e. as long as they provide each other with enjoyments or advantages. Friendship for utility's sake seems to be that which most easily exists between contraries, e. g. between poor and rich, between ignorant and learned; for what a man actually lacks he aims at, and one gives something else in return. But under this head, too, we might bring lover and beloved, beautiful and ugly. This is why lovers sometimes seem ridiculous, when they demand to be loved as they love; if they are equally lovable their claim can perhaps be justified, but when they have nothing lovable about them it is ridiculous. Perhaps, however, contrary does not even aim at contrary by its own nature, but only incidentally, the desire being for what is intermediate; for that is what is good, e. g. it is good for the dry not to become wet but to come to the intermediate state, and similarly with the hot and in all other cases. These subjects we may dismiss; for they are indeed somewhat foreign to our inquiry.

THE CONGENIALITY OF EXCELLENCES

Plato

The inquiry here is directed at the meaning of friendship under Eros, and Socrates offers it in the principle of the congeniality of excellences.

Critics of Eros often center upon friendship, charging that Eros renders it inexplicable. This is so, they say, because Eros aims only upward, from deficiency to sufficiency, while true friendship is a horizontal relation of reciprocity between equals. Does not Socrates acknowledge in the Lysis *that the good person, like the god, is sufficient unto himself and needs no friends?*

But this contention rests upon a hasty understanding of Eros and a careless reading of the Lysis. *What Socrates actually says is that the good man, in so far as he is good, is sufficient unto himself. And the burden of his previous interrogation of Lysis was to show that no man can be good in everything, but only in limited specifics. Lysis is deficient at chariot driving, weaving, and estate management (for examples), but sufficient at reading, writing, and lyre playing.*

Thus Socrates uses Lysis to represent the condition of all men. At best an individual is deficient in many things, sufficient in the few which constitute his personal destiny. In so far as he is good he has no need of friends, but in so far as he is deficient he has need. On this model equality and reciprocity appear, each man needing the other's excellences which are different from his own.

The "congeniality" of excellences, offered by Socrates at the end of the dialogue as the principle of friendship, is the contention "excellences attract one another," which is to say that a man loves the excellences of others no less than his own. But is Socrates unaware that in practical fact men oftenest respond to others' excellences with envy and resentment? No, for Socrates offers as the condition for the love of others that a man must first know himself and live in truth to himself; he must be manifesting that excellence which is his own.

I dare say, Lysis, I said, that your father and mother love you very much.
Certainly, he said.
And they would wish you to be perfectly happy.
Yes.

From the *Lysis. The Dialogues of Plato*, trans. B. Jowett, 3rd ed. (Oxford University Press, 1892), Vol. 1, pp. 54–58 and 73–74. Reprinted by permission of Oxford University Press.

But do you think that any one is happy who is in the condition of a slave, and who cannot do what he likes?

I should think not indeed, he said.

And if your father and mother love you, and desire that you should be happy, no one can doubt that they are very ready to promote your happiness.

Certainly, he replied.

And do they then permit you to do what you like, and never rebuke you or hinder you from doing what you desire?

Yes, indeed, Socrates; there are a great many things which they hinder me from doing.

What do you mean? I said. Do they want you to be happy, and yet hinder you from doing what you like? for example, if you want to mount one of your father's chariots, and take the reins at a race, they will not allow you to do so—they will prevent you?

Certainly, he said, they will not allow me to do so.

Whom then will they allow?

There is a charioteer, whom my father pays for driving.

And do they trust a hireling more than you? and may he do what he likes with the horses? and do they pay him for this?

They do.

But I dare say that you may take the whip and guide the mule-cart if you like;—they will permit that?

Permit me! indeed they will not.

Then, I said, may no one use the whip to the mules?

Yes, he said, the muleteer.

And is he a slave or a free man?

A slave, he said.

And do they esteem a slave of more value than you who are their son? And do they entrust their property to him rather than to you? and allow him to do what he likes, when they prohibit you? Answer me now: Are you your own master, or do they not even allow that?

Nay, he said; of course they do not allow it.

Then you have a master?

Yes, my tutor; there he is.

And is he a slave?

To be sure; he is our slave, he replied.

Surely, I said, this is a strange thing, that a free man should be governed by a slave. And what does he do with you?

He takes me to my teachers.

You do not mean to say that your teachers also rule over you?

Of course they do.

Then I must say that your father is pleased to inflict many lords and masters on you. But at any rate when you go home to your mother, she will let you have your own way, and will not interfere with your happiness; her wool, or the piece of cloth which she is weaving, are at your disposal: I am sure that there is nothing to hinder you from touching her wooden spathe, or her comb, or any other of her spinning implements.

Nay, Socrates, he replied, laughing; not only does she hinder me, but I should be beaten, if I were to touch one of them.

Well, I said, this is amazing. And did you ever behave ill to your father or your mother?

No, indeed, he replied.

But why then are they so terribly anxious to prevent you from being happy, and doing as you like?—keeping you all day long in subjection to another, and, in a word, doing nothing which you desire; so that you have no good, as would appear, out of their great possessions, which are under the control of anybody rather than of you, and have no use of your own fair person, which is tended and taken care of by another; while you, Lysis, are master of nobody, and can do nothing?

Why, he said, Socrates, the reason is that I am not of age.

I doubt whether that is the real reason, I said; for I should imagine that your father Democrates, and your mother, do permit you to do many things already, and do not wait until you are of age: for example, if they want anything read or written, you, I presume, would be the first person in the house who is summoned by them.

Very true.

And you would be allowed to write or read the letters in any order which you please, or to take up the lyre and tune the notes, and play with the fingers, or strike with the plectrum, exactly as you please, and neither father nor mother would interfere with you.

That is true, he said.

Then what can be the reason, Lysis, I said, why they allow you to do the one and not the other?

I suppose, he said, because I understand the one, and not the other.

Yes, my dear youth, I said, the reason is not any deficiency of years, but a deficiency of knowledge; and whenever your father thinks that you are wiser than he is, he will instantly commit himself and his possessions to you.

I think so.

Aye, I said; and about your neighbour, too, does not the same rule hold as about your father? If he is satisfied that you know more of housekeeping than he does, will he continue to administer his affairs himself, or will he commit them to you?

I think that he will commit them to me.

Will not the Athenian people, too, entrust their affairs to you when they see that you have wisdom enough to manage them?

Yes.

And oh! let me put another case, I said: There is the great king, and he has an eldest son, who is the Prince of Asia;—suppose that you and I go to him and establish to his satisfaction that we are better cooks than his son, will he not entrust to us the prerogative of making soup, and putting in anything that we like while the pot is boiling, rather than to the Prince of Asia, who is his son?

To us, clearly.

And we shall be allowed to throw in salt by handfuls, whereas the son will not be allowed to put in as much as he can take up between his fingers?

Of course.

Or suppose again that the son has bad eyes, will he allow him, or will he not allow him, to touch his own eyes if he thinks that he has no knowledge of medicine?

He will not allow him.

Whereas, if he supposes us to have a knowledge of medicine, he will allow us to do what we like with him—even to open the eyes wide and sprinkle ashes upon them, because he supposes that we know what is best?

That is true.

And everything in which we appear to him to be wiser than himself or his son he will commit to us?

That is very true, Socrates, he replied.

Then now, my dear Lysis, I said, you perceive that in things which we know every one will trust us,—Hellenes and barbarians, men and women, —and we may do as we please about them, and no one will like to interfere with us; we shall be free, and masters of others; and these things will be really ours, for we shall be benefited by them. But in things of which we have no understanding, no one will trust us to do as seems good to us—they will hinder us as far as they can; and not only strangers, but father and mother, and the friend, if there be one, who is dearer still, will also hinder us; and we shall be subject to others; and these things will not be ours, for we shall not be benefited by them. Do you agree?

He assented.

And shall we be friends to others, and will any others love us, in as far as we are useless to them?

Certainly not.

Neither can your father or mother love you, nor can anybody love anybody else, in so far as they are useless to them?

No.

And therefore, my boy, if you are wise, all men will be your friends and kindred, for you will be useful and good; but if you are not wise, neither father, nor mother, nor kindred, nor any one else, will be your friends. And in matters of which you have as yet no knowledge, can you have any conceit of knowledge?

That is impossible, he replied.

And you, Lysis, if you require a teacher, have not yet attained to wisdom.

True.

And therefore you are not conceited, having nothing of which to be conceited.

Indeed, Socrates, I think not.

When I heard him say this, I turned to Hippothales, and was very nearly making a blunder, for I was going to say to him: That is the way, Hippothales, in which you should talk to your beloved, humbling and lowering him, and not as you do, puffing him up and spoiling him. But I saw that he was in great excitement and confusion at what had been said, and I remembered that, although he was in the neighbourhood, he did not want to be seen by Lysis; so upon second thoughts I refrained.

May not the truth be rather, as we were saying just now, that desire is the cause of friendship; for that which desires is dear to that which is desired at the time of desiring it? and may not the other theory have been only a long story about nothing?

Likely enough.

But surely, I said, he who desires, desires that of which he is in want?

Yes.

And that of which he is in want is dear to him?

True.

And he is in want of that of which he is deprived?

Certainly.

Then love, and desire, and friendship would appear to be of the natural or congenial. Such, Lysis and Menexenus, is the inference.

They assented.

Then if you are friends, you must have natures which are congenial to one another?

Certainly, they both said.

And I say, my boys, that no one who loves or desires another would ever have loved or desired or affected him, if he had not been in some way congenial to him, either in his soul, or in his character, or in his manners, or in his form.

Yes, yes, said Menexenus. But Lysis was silent.

Then, I said, the conclusion is, that what is of a congenial nature must be loved.

It follows, he said.

Then the lover, who is true and no counterfeit, must of necessity be loved by his love.

Lysis and Menexenus gave a faint assent to this; and Hippothales changed into all manner of colours with delight.

Here, intending to revise the argument, I said: Can we point out any difference between the congenial and the like? For if that is possible, then I think, Lysis and Menexenus, there may be some sense in our argument about friendship. But if the congenial is only the like, how will you get rid of the other argument, of the uselessness of like to like in as far as they are like; for to say that what is useless is dear, would be absurd? Suppose, then, that we agree to distinguish between the congenial and the like—in the intoxication of argument, that may perhaps be allowed.

Very true.

And shall we further say that the good is congenial, and the evil uncongenial to every one? Or again that the evil is congenial to the evil, and the good to the good; and that which is neither good nor evil to that which is neither good nor evil?

 *FRIENDSHIP AT A DISTANCE*

Ralph Waldo Emerson

Friends ought to live together, Aristotle argues, because they take greatest delight in the company of others, and because the activity of friendship ceases with distance.

To the contrary, according to Emerson. We scarcely exaggerate his thesis if we say that true friendship requires distance, lest we "desecrate noble and beautiful souls by intruding on them."

Emerson prizes restraint and discretion, despising the motives of ferrety, prying eyes. The reader may simply conclude that Emerson prefers solitude to friendship. But Emerson wants to remind us that in physical solitude we are not alone. Our friend is active within us, his virtues serving as models for our emulation. As the hues of the opal will not be seen if the eye is too near, so too the greatness of a man.

Let us buy our entrance to this guild by a long probation. Why should we desecrate noble and beautiful souls by intruding on them? Why insist on rash personal relations with your friend? Why go to his house, or know his mother and brother and sisters? Why be visited by him at your own? Are these things material to our covenant? Leave this touching and clawing. Let him be to me a spirit. A message, a thought, a sincerity, a glance from him, I want, but not news, nor pottage. I can get politics and chat and neighborly conveniences from cheaper companions. Should not the society of my friend be to me poetic, pure, universal and great as nature itself? Ought I to feel that our tie is profane in comparison with yonder bar of cloud that sleeps on the horizon, or that clump of waving grass that divides the brook? Let us not vilify, but raise it to that standard. That great defying eye, that scornful beauty of his mien and action, do not pique yourself on reducing, but rather fortify and enhance. Worship his superiorities; wish him not less by a thought, but hoard and tell them all. Guard him as thy counterpart: Let him be to thee for ever a sort of beautiful enemy, untamable, devoutly revered, and not a trivial conveniency to be soon outgrown and cast aside. The hues of the opal, the light of the diamond, are not to be seen if the eye is too near. To my friend I write a letter and from him I receive a letter. That seems to you a little. It suffices me. It is a spiritual gift, worthy of him to give and of me to receive. It profanes no-

From "Friendship" by Ralph Waldo Emerson. In *Centenary Edition, The Complete Works of Ralph Waldo Emerson* (Boston: Houghton Mifflin Company), *Essays, First Series*, pp. 209–211. Reprinted by permission of Houghton Mifflin Company.

body. In these warm lines the heart will trust itself, as it will not to the tongue, and pour out the prophecy of a godlier existence than all the annals of heroism have yet made good.

THE EAGLE'S LOFTY SOLITUDE

Arthur Schopenhauer

Steer clear of fools is Schopenhauer's advice, for social intercourse is a process of leveling down. The good dancer or tennis player is diminished by an inferior partner, and in social intercourse with inferiors the only part of yourself which shows is "that of which you have least reason to be proud."

The deeper meaning of Schopenhauer's theme is that the growth toward human greatness is the progressive move toward solitude. Take for example an idea—let us say an idea of the meaning of Christianity. So long as we have given it no thought of our own, the idea we have of Christianity is the commonplace one, the one that is "in the air," the one that is "everyone's." But as soon as we have begun to work at it ourselves our idea becomes separated from common opinion, and the more we work at it the more uncommon it becomes. (Thus the views of our leading theologians will be sure to astonish the man in the pew on Sunday morning.)

Now extend the illustration from a single idea to one's life as a whole. The individual who works with himself and grows in the direction of personal excellence moves at the same time toward uniqueness, and this, Schopenhauer observes, is to sentence oneself to solitude. For to communicate requires common ground, and the worthy individual has left commonness behind. The rule then is: the greater one's nature, the lesser is the possibility of friendship.

Schopenhauer stresses that the man of worth has a sharp eye for the follies and vulgarities of other men. Must we not ask him whether such a man does not also possess an exceptional eye for other men's virtues—a power by which the opportunities of valuable friendship are multiplied?

It is astonishing how easily and how quickly similarity, or difference of mind and disposition, makes itself felt between one man and another as soon as they begin to talk; every little trifle shows it. When two people of totally different natures are conversing, almost everything said by the one will, in a greater or less degree, displease the other, and in many cases produce positive annoyance; even though the conversation turn upon the most out-of-the way subject, or one in which neither of the parties has any real interest. People of similar nature, on the other hand, immediately

From *Essays of Arthur Schopenhauer*, trans. T. Bailey Saunders (New York: A. L. Burt, n.d.), pp. 142–146 and 148–149. Reprinted by permission of A. L. Burt, Publishers.

come to feel a kind of general agreement; and if they are cast very much in the of same mold, complete harmony or even unison will flow from their intercourse.

This explains two circumstances. First of all, it shows why it is that common, ordinary people are so sociable and find good company wherever they go. Ah! those good, dear, brave people. It is just the contrary with those who are not of the common run; and the less they are so, the more unsociable they become; so that if, in their isolation, they chance to come across some one in whose nature they can find even a single sympathetic chord, be it never so minute, they show extraordinary pleasure in his society. For one man can be to another only so much as the other is to him. Great minds are like eagles, and build their nest in some lofty solitude.

Secondly, we are enabled to understand how it is that people of like disposition so quickly get on with one another, as though they were drawn together by magnetic force—kindred souls greeting each other from afar. Of course the most frequent opportunity of observing this is afforded by people of vulgar tastes and inferior intellect, but only because their name is legion; while those who are better off in this respect and of a rarer nature, are not often to be met with: they are called rare because you can seldom find them.

Take the case of a large number of people who have formed themselves into a league for the purpose of carrying out some practical object; if there be two rascals among them, they will recognize each other as readily as if they bore a similar badge, and will at once conspire for some misfeasance or treachery. In the same way, if you can imagine—*per impossible*—a large company of very intelligent and clever people, among whom there are only two blockheads, these two will be sure to be drawn together by a feeling of sympathy, and each of them will very soon secretly rejoice at having found at least one intelligent person in the whole company. It is really quite curious to see how two such men, especially if they are morally and intellectually of an inferior type, will recognize each other at first sight; with what zeal they will strive to become intimate; how affably and cheerily they will run to greet each other, just as though they were old friends—it is all so striking that one is tempted to embrace the Buddhist doctrine of metempsychosis and presume that they were on familiar terms in some former state of existence. . . .

No man can see "over his own height." Let me explain what I mean.

You cannot see in another man any more than you have in yourself; and your own intelligence strictly determines the extent to which he comes within its grasp. If your intelligence is of a very low order, mental qualities in another, even though they be of the highest kind, will have no effect at all upon you; you will see nothing in their possessor except the meanest side of his individuality—in other words, just those parts of his character and disposition which are weak and defective. Your whole estimate of the man will be confined to his defects, and his higher mental qualities will no more exist for you than colors exist for those who cannot see.

Intellect is invisible to the man who has none. In any attempt to criticise another's work, the range of knowledge possessed by the critic is as essential a part of his verdict as the claims of the work itself.

Hence intercourse with others involves a process of leveling down. The qualities which are present in one man, and absent in another, cannot come into play when they meet; and the self-sacrifice which this entails upon one of the parties, calls forth no recognition from the other.

Consider how sordid, how stupid, in a word, how vulgar most men are, and you will see that it is impossible to talk to them without becoming vulgar yourself for the time being. Vulgarity is in this respect like electricity; it is easily distributed. You will then fully appreciate the truth and propriety of the expression, "to make yourself cheap;" and you will be glad to avoid the society of people whose only possible point of contact with you is just that part of your nature of which you have least reason to be proud. So you will see that, in dealing with fools and blockheads, there is only one way of showing your intelligence—by having nothing to do with them. That means, of course, that when you go into society, you may now and then feel like a good dancer who gets an invitation to a ball, and on arriving, finds that every one is lame—with whom is he to dance? . . .

Men are like children, in that, if you spoil them, they become naughty.

Therefore it is well not to be too indulgent or charitable with any one. You may take it as a general rule that you will not lose a friend by refusing him a loan, but that you are very likely to do so by granting it; and, for similar reasons, you will not readily alienate people by being somewhat proud and careless in your behavior; but if you are very kind and complaisant toward them, you will often make them arrogant and intolerable, and so a breach will ensue.

There is one thing that, more than any other, throws people absolutely off their balance—the thought that you are dependent upon them. This is sure to produce an insolent and domineering manner toward you. There are some people, indeed, who become rude if you enter into any kind of relation with them; for instance, if you have occasion to converse with them frequently upon confidential matters, they soon come to fancy that they can take liberties with you, and so they try to transgress the laws of politeness. This is why there are so few with whom you care to become more intimate, and why you should avoid familiarity with vulgar people. If a man comes to think that I am more dependent upon him than he is upon me, he at once feels as though I had stolen something from him; and his endeavor will be to have his vengeance and get it back. The only way to attain superiority in dealing with men, is to let it be seen that you are independent of them.

And in this view it is advisable to let every one of your acquaintance—whether man or woman—feel now and then that you could very well dispense with their company. This will consolidate friendship. Nay, with most people there will be no harm in occasionally mixing a grain of disdain with your treatment of them; that will make them value your friendship all the more. *Chi non istima vien stimato*, as a subtle Italian proverb has it— to disregard is to win regard. But if we really think very highly of a person, we should conceal it from him like a crime. This is not a very gratifying thing to do, but it is right. Why, a dog will not bear being treated too kindly, let alone a man! . . .

As paper-money circulates in the world instead of real coin, so, in the place of true esteem and genuine freindship, you have the outward appearance of it—a mimic show made to look as much like the real thing as possible.

On the other hand, it may be asked whether there are any people who really deserve the true coin. For my own part, I should certainly pay more respect to an honest dog wagging his tail than to a hundred such demonstrations of human regard.

True and genuine friendship presupposes a strong sympathy with the weal and woe of another—purely objective in its character and quite disinterested; and this in its turn means an absolute identification of self with the object of friendship. The egoism of human nature is so strongly antagonistic to any such sympathy, that true friendship belongs to that class of things—the sea-serpent, for instance—with regard to which no one knows whether they are fabulous or really exist somewhere or other.

Still, in many cases, there is a grain of true and genuine friendship in the relations of man to man, though generally, of course, some secret personal interest is at the bottom of them—some one among the many forms that selfishness can take. But in a world where all is imperfect, this grain of true feeling is such an ennobling influence that it gives some warrant for calling those relations by the name of friendship, for they stand far above the ordinary friendships that prevail among mankind. The latter are so constituted that, were you to hear how your dear friends speak of you behind your back, you would never say another word to them.

Apart from the case where it would be a real help to you if your friend were to make some considerable sacrifice to serve you, there is no better means of testing the genuineness of his feeling than the way in which he receives the news of a misfortune that has just happened to you. At that moment the expression of his features will either show that his one thought is that of true and sincere sympathy for you; or else the absolute composure of his countenance, or the passing trace of something other than sympathy, will confirm the well-known maxim of La Rochefoucauld: *Dans l'adversité de nos meilleurs amis, nous trouvons toujours quelque chose qui ne nous deplait pas.** Indeed, at such a moment, the ordinary so-called

---

*In our best friends' misfortune, we always find something that doesn't displease us.

friend will find it hard to suppress the signs of a slight smile of pleasure. There are few ways by which you can make more certain of putting people into a good humor than by telling them of some trouble that has recently befallen you, or by unreservedly disclosing some personal weakness of yours. How characteristic this is of humanity!

Distance and long absence are always prejudicial to friendship, however disinclined a man may be to admit it. Our regard for people whom we do not see—even though they be our dearest friends—gradually dries up in the course of years, and they become abstract notions; so that our interest in them grows to be more and more intellectual—nay, it is kept up only as a kind of tradition; while we retain a lively and deep interest in those who are constantly before our eyes, even if they be only pet animals. This shows how much men are limited by their senses, and how true is the remark that Goethe makes in "Tasso" about the dominant influence of the present moment:

"Die Gegenwart ist eine mächtige Gottin."†

"Friends of the house" are very rightly so called; because they are friends of the house rather than of its master; in other words, they are more like cats than dogs.

Your friends will tell you that they are sincere; your enemies are really so. Let your enemies' censure be like a bitter medicine, to be used as a means of self-knowledge.

A friend in need, as the saying goes, is rare. Nay, it is just the contrary; no sooner have you made a friend than he is in need, and asks you for a loan.

†The present is a mighty goddess.

THE FRIEND AS THOU

Martin Buber

Against those who see friendship as emerging from comradeship or fellow-feeling, Martin Buber insists upon friendship's utter uniqueness. Friendship is a relation between persons serving to encourage unique personhood, while every collective induces the lapse of individuality, submerging persons within the group. Moreover all relations which take people piecemeal (Aristotle's "friendship of pleasure" and "friendship of utility" for examples) are antithetical to the nature of friendship. For friendship accepts the other en toto, as a whole—which is to say as a person, a "Thou" rather than an "it." And in so doing it is opposed, Buber says, "by almost everything that is commonly understood as specifically modern." In other words modern life is depersonalization (equated by Buber with dehumanization), and within it friendship stands as the sole sanctuary for the preservation and nurture of personhood.

... It is usual to ascribe what takes place between men to the social realm, thereby blurring a basically important line of division between two essentially different areas of human life. I myself, when I began nearly fifty years ago to find my own bearings in the knowledge of society, making use of the then unknown concept of the interhuman, made the same error. From that time it became increasingly clear to me that we have to do here with a separate category of our existence, even a separate dimension, to use a mathematical term, and one with which we are so familiar that its peculiarity has hitherto almost escaped us. Yet insight into its peculiarity is extremely important not only for our thinking, but also for our living.

We may speak of social phenomena wherever the life of a number of men, lived with one another, bound up together, brings in its train shared experiences and reactions. But to be thus bound up together means only that each individual existence is enclosed and contained in a group existence. It does not mean that between one member and another of the group there exists any kind of personal relation. They do feel that they belong together in a way that is, so to speak, fundamentally different from every possible belonging together with someone outside the group. And there do arise, especially in the life of smaller groups, contacts which frequently favour the birth of individual relations, but, on the other hand, fre-

From *The Knowledge of Man: Selected Essays*, trans. Maurice Friedman and Ronald Gregor Smith, ed. Maurice Friedman (New York: Harper and Row, 1965), pp. 72–81. Reprinted by permission of Harper and Row, Publishers, Incorporated.

254 PHILOSOPHIES OF LOVE: Friendship

quently make it more difficult. In no case, however, does membership in a group necessarily involve an existential relation between one member and another. It is true that there have been groups in history which included highly intensive and intimate relations between two of their members—as, for instance, in the homosexual relations among the Japanese Samurai or among Doric warriors—and these were countenanced for the sake of the stricter cohesion of the group. But in general it must be said that the leading elements in groups, especially in the later course of human history, have rather been inclined to suppress the personal relation in favour of the purely collective element. Where this latter element reigns alone or is predominant, men feel themselves to be carried by the collectivity, which lifts them out of loneliness and fear of the world and lostness. When this happens—and for modern man it is an essential happening—the life between person and person seems to retreat more and more before the advance of the collective. The collective aims at holding in check the inclination to personal life. It is as though those who are bound together in groups should in the main be concerned only with the work of the group and should turn to the personal partners, who are tolerated by the group, only in secondary meetings.

The difference between the two realms became very palpable to me on one occasion when I had joined the procession through a large town of a movement to which I did not belong. I did it out of sympathy for the tragic development which I sensed was at hand in the destiny of a friend who was one of the leaders of the movement. While the procession was forming, I conversed with him and with another, a goodhearted 'wild man', who also had the mark of death upon him. At that moment I still felt that the two men really were there, over against me, each of them a man near to me, near even in what was most remote from me; so different from me that my soul continually suffered from this difference, yet by virtue of this very difference confronting me with authentic being. Then the formations started off, and after a short time I was lifted out of all confrontation, drawn into the procession, falling in with its aimless step; and it was obviously the very same for the two with whom I had just exchanged human words. After a while we passed a café where I had been sitting the previous day with a musician whom I knew only slightly. The very moment we passed it the door opened, the musician stood on the threshold, saw me, apparently saw me alone, and waved to me. Straightway it seemed to me as though I were taken out of the procession and of the presence of my marching friends, and set there, confronting the musician. I forgot that I was walking along with the same step; I felt that I was standing over there by the man who had called out to me, and without a word, with a smile of understanding, was answering him. When consciousness of the facts returned to me, the procession, with my companions and myself at its head, had left the café behind.

The realm of the interhuman goes far beyond that of sympathy. Such simple happenings can be part of it as, for instance, when two strangers exchange glances in a crowded streetcar, at once to sink back again into the convenient state of wishing to know nothing about each other. But also every casual encounter between opponents belongs to this realm, when it affects the opponent's attitude—that is, when something, however imperceptible, happens between the two, no matter whether it is marked at the time by any feeling or not. The only thing that matters is that for each of the two men the other happens as the particular other, that each becomes aware of the other and is thus related to him in such a way that he does not regard and use him as his object, but as his partner in a living event, even if it is no more than a boxing match. It is well known that some existentialists assert that the basic factor between men is that one is an object for the other. But so far as this is actually the case, the special reality of the interhuman, the fact of the contact, has been largely eliminated. It cannot indeed be entirely eliminated. As a crude example, take two men who are observing one another. The essential thing is not that the one makes the other his object, but the fact that he is not fully able to do so and the reason for his failure. We have in common with all existing beings that we can be made objects of observation. But it is my privilege as man that by the hidden activity of my being I can establish an impassable barrier to objectification. Only in partnership can my being be perceived as an existing whole.

The sociologist may object to any separation of the social and the interhuman on the ground that society is actually built upon human relations, and the theory of these relations is therefore to be regarded as the very foundation of sociology. But here an ambiguity in the concept 'relation' becomes evident. We speak, for instance, of a comradely relation between two men in their work, and do not merely mean what happens between them as comrades, but also a lasting disposition which is actualized in those happenings and which even includes purely psychological events such as the recollection of the absent comrade. But by the sphere of the interhuman I mean solely actual happenings between men, whether wholly mutual or tending to grow into mutual relations. For the participation of both partners is in principle indispensable. The sphere of the interhuman is one in which a person is confronted by the other. We call its unfolding the dialogical.

In accordance with this, it is basically erroneous to try to understand the interhuman phenomena as psychological. When two men converse together, the psychological is certainly an important part of the situation, as each listens and each prepares to speak. Yet this is only the hidden accompaniment to the conversation itself, the phonetic event fraught with meaning, whose meaning is to be found neither in one of the two partners nor in both together, but only in their dialogue itself, in this 'between' which they live together.

BEING AND SEEMING

The essential problem of the sphere of the interhuman is the duality of being and seeming.

Although it is a familiar fact that men are often troubled about the impression they make on others, this has been much more discussed in moral philosophy than in anthropology. Yet this is one of the most important subjects for anthropological study.

We may distinguish between two different types of human existence. The one proceeds from what one really is, the other from what one wishes to seem. In general, the two are found mixed together. There have probably been few men who were entirely independent of the impression they made on others, while there has scarcely existed one who was exclusively determined by the impression made by him. We must be content to distinguish between men in whose essential attitude the one or the other predominates.

This distinction is most powerfully at work, as its nature indicates, in the interhuman realm—that is, in men's personal dealings with one another.

Take as the simplest and yet quite clear example the situation in which two persons look at one another—the first belonging to the first type, the second to the second. The one who lives from his being looks at the other just as one looks at someone with whom he has personal dealings. His look is 'spontaneous', 'without reserve'; of course he is not uninfluenced by the desire to make himself understood by the other, but he is uninfluenced by any thought of the idea of himself which he can or should awaken in the person whom he is looking at. His opposite is different. Since he is concerned with the image which his appearance, and especially his look or glance, produces in the other, he 'makes' this look. With the help of the capacity, in greater or lesser degree peculiar to man, to make a definite element of his being appear in his look, he produces a look which is meant to have, and often enough does have, the effect of a spontaneous utterance—not only the utterance of a psychical event supposed to be taking place at that very moment, but also, as it were, the reflection of a personal life of such-and-such a kind.

This must, however, be carefully distinguished from another area of seeming whose ontological legitimacy cannot be doubted. I mean the realm of 'genuine seeming', where a lad, for instance, imitates his heroic model and while he is doing so is seized by the actuality of heroism, or a man plays the part of a destiny and conjures up authentic destiny. In this situation there is nothing false; the imitation is genuine imitation and the part played is genuine; the mask, too, is a mask and no deceit. But where the semblance originates from the lie and is permeated by it, the interhuman is threatened in its very existence. It is not that someone utters a lie, falsifies some account. The lie I mean does not take place in relation to particular facts, but in relation to existence itself, and it attacks interhuman existence as such. There are times when a man, to satisfy some stale conceit, forfeits the great chance of a true happening between I and Thou.

Let us now imagine two men, whose life is dominated by appearance, sitting and talking together. Call them Peter and Paul. Let us list the different configurations which are involved. First, there is Peter as he wishes to appear to Paul, and Paul as he wishes to appear to Peter. Then there is Peter as he really appears to Paul, that is, Paul's image of Peter, which in general does not in the least coincide with what Peter wishes Paul to see; and similarly there is the reverse situation. Futher, there is Peter as he appears to himself, and Paul as he appears to himself. Lastly, there are the bodily Peter and the bodily Paul. Two living beings and six ghostly appearances, which mingle in many ways in the conversation between the two. Where is there room for any genuine interhuman life?

Whatever the meaning of the word 'truth' may be in other realms, in the interhuman realm it means that men communicate themselves to one another as what they are. It does not depend on one saying to the other everything that occurs to him, but only on his letting no seeming creep in between himself and the other. It does not depend on one letting himself go before another, but on his granting to the man to whom he communicates himself a share in his being. This is a question of the authenticity of the interhuman, and where this is not to be found, neither is the human element itself authentic.

Therefore, as we begin to recognize the crisis of man as the crisis of what is between man and man, we must free the concept of uprightness from the thin moralistic tones which cling to it, and let it take its tone from the concept of bodily uprightness. If a presupposition of human life in primeval times is given in man's walking upright, the fulfilment of human life can only come through the soul's walking upright, through the great uprightness which is not tempted by any seeming because it has conquered all semblance.

But, one may ask, what if a man by his nature makes his life subservient to the images which he produces in others? Can he, in such a case, still become a man living from his being, can he escape from his nature?

The widespread tendency to live from the recurrent impression one makes instead of from the steadiness of one's being is not a 'nature'. It originates, in fact, on the other side of interhuman life itself, in men's dependence upon one another. It is no light thing to be confirmed in one's being by others, and seeming deceptively offers itself as a help in this. To yield to seeming is man's essential cowardice, to resist it is his essential courage. But this is not an inexorable state of affairs which is as it is and must so remain. One can struggle to come to oneself—that is, to come to confidence in being. One struggles, now more successfully, now less, but never in vain, even when one thinks he is defeated. One must at times pay dearly for life lived from the being; but it is never too dear. Yet is there not bad being, do weeds not grow everywhere? I have never known a young person who seemed to me irretrievably bad. Later indeed it becomes more and more difficult to penetrate the increasingly tough layer which has settled down on a man's being. Thus there arises the false perspective of the seemingly fixed 'nature' which cannot be overcome. It is false; the foreground is deceitful; man as man can be redeemed.

Again we see Peter and Paul before us surrounded by the ghosts of the semblances. A ghost can be exorcized. Let us imagine that these two find it more and more repellent to be represented by ghosts. In each of them the will is stirred and strengthened to be confirmed in their being as what they really are and nothing else. We see the forces of real life at work as they drive out the ghosts, till the semblance vanishes and the depths of personal life call to one another.

PERSONAL MAKING PRESENT

By far the greater part of what is today called conversation among men would be more properly and precisely described as speechifying. In general, people do not really speak to one another, but each, although turned to the other, really speaks to a fictitious court of appeal whose life consists of nothing but listening to him. Chekhov has given poetic expression to this state of affairs in *The Cherry Orchard,* where the only use the members of a family make of their being together is to talk past one another. But it is Sartre who has raised to a principle of existence what in Chekhov still appears as the deficiency of a person who is shut up in himself. Sartre regards the walls between the partners in a conversation as simply impassable. For him it is inevitable human destiny that a man has directly to do only with himself and his own affairs. The inner existence of the other is his own concern, not mine; there is no direct relation with the other, nor can there be. This is perhaps the clearest expression of the wretched fatalism of modern man, which regards degeneration as the unchangeable nature of *Homo sapiens* and the misfortune of having run into a blind alley as his primal fate, and which brands every thought of a break-through as reactionary romanticism. He who really knows how far our generation has lost the way of true freedom, of free giving between I and Thou, must himself, by virtue of the demand implicit in every great knowledge of this kind, practise directness—even if he were the only man on earth who did it—and not depart from it until scoffers are struck with fear, and hear in his voice the voice of their own suppressed longing.

The chief presupposition for the rise of genuine dialogue is that each should regard his partner as the very one he is. I become aware of him, aware that he is different, essentially different from myself, in the definite, unique way which is peculiar to him, and I accept whom I thus see, so that in full earnestness I can direct what I say to him as the person he is. Perhaps from time to time I must offer strict oppositon to his view about the subject of our conversation. But I accept this person, the personal bearer of a conviction, in his definite being out of which his conviction has grown—even though I must try to show, bit by bit, the wrongness of this very conviction. I affirm the person I struggle with: I struggle with him as his partner, I confirm him as creature and as creation, I confirm him who is opposed to me as him. who is over against me. It is true that it now depends on the other whether genuine dialogue, mutuality in speech arises between us. But if I thus give to the other who confronts me his legitimate standing as a man with whom I am ready to enter into dialogue, then I may trust him and suppose him to be also ready to deal with me as his partner.

But what does it mean to be 'aware' of a man in the exact sense in which I use the word? To be aware of a thing or a being means, in quite general terms, to experience it as a whole and yet at the same time without reduction or abstraction, in all its concreteness. But a man, although he exists as a living being among living beings and even as a thing among things, is nevertheless something categorically different from all things and all beings. A man cannot really be grasped except on the basis of the gift of the spirit which belongs to man alone among all things, the spirit as sharing decisively in the personal life of the living man, that is, the spirit which determines the person. To be aware of a man, therefore, means in particular to perceive his wholeness as a person determined by the spirit; it means to perceive the dynamic centre which stamps his every utterance, action, and attitude with the recognizable sign of uniqueness. Such an awareness is impossible, however, if and so long as the other is the separated object of my contemplation or even observation, for this wholeness and its centre do not let themselves be known to contemplation or observation. It is only possible when I step into an elemental relation with the other, that is, when he becomes present to me. Hence I designate awareness in this special sense as 'personal making present'. . . .

If we want to do today's work and prepare tomorrow's with clear sight, then we must develop in ourselves and in the next generation a gift which lives in man's inwardness as a Cinderella, one day to be a princess. Some call it intuition, but that is not a wholly unambiguous concept. I prefer the name 'imagining the real', for in its essential being this gift is not a looking at the other, but a bold swinging—demanding the most intensive stirring of one's being—into the life of the other. This is the nature of all genuine imagining, only that here the realm of my action is not the all-possible, but the particular real person who confronts me, whom I can attempt to make present to myself just in this way, and not otherwise, in his wholeness, unity, and uniqueness, and with his dynamic centre which realizes all these things ever anew.

Let it be said again that all this can only take place in a living partnership, that is, when I stand in a common situation with the other and expose myself vitally to his share in the situation as really his share. It is true that my basic attitude can remain unanswered, and the dialogue can die in seed. But if mutuality stirs, then the interhuman blossoms into genuine dialogue.

PART *VI*
Fellow Feeling

FELLOW FEELING: UNIVERSAL BOND OF HUMANKIND

Tyrant, killer, and prostitute; communist, socialist, and capitalist; housewife, lawyer, and artist; black, yellow, and white—beneath the panorama of human diversity lies common ground in every person's basic humanity. It is in this ground that fellow feeling ("brotherhood" and "sympathy" are frequent synonyms) is to be sought. By "fellow feeling" we mean a deep-lying *affirmation* which is felt by every person for every person on the sole basis of their shared humanity.

By no means does fellow feeling deny the negations, the rivalries, jealousies, and hatreds which men's differences so evidently arouse. But it insists that somewhere beneath or mixed with the negative feelings must be the germ at least of a positive one, for to hate a man is impossible without an interest in him. Let the reader test himself. How does he respond to the good fortune or recognized achievement of someone he knows? Probably he must admit (with the rest of us) that often he responds to such news with twinges of resentment, with the wish that the honor were his and not the other's. But if he probes himself further he may also discover a degree of what we call "vicarious" pleasure or "reflected glory." There is an objective basis for such feelings in the recognition that every worthy manifestation by any man is a mark of the humanity of which we ourselves are a part. That human history includes a Homer, a Shakespeare, an Isaac Newton, is legitimate cause for a measure of pride in us all. Here is fellow feeling. It is the recognition of ourselves in every other human being, and of them in us. And it is the affirmation of our species which is manifested in our self-affirmation. This is why Aristotle saw no selfishness in pride (as distinguished from vanity); the proud man bespeaks the dignity and worth, not of himself merely, but of the species.

Each individual is both unique and universal—so say the basic doctrines of Hinduism, Buddhism, and ancient Stoicism; so says the Christian principle of the brotherhood of man under the Fatherhood of God. These doctrines become concrete when we understand them as systematic attempts to explain a sort of immediate experience which itself is clear and certain—the experience of fellow feeling. And today, when Yale psychologist-critic Kenneth Kenniston (for example) envisions a truly pluralistic society in which differences are not merely tolerated but enjoyed and actively encouraged, he is presupposing a fellow feeling which can be strengthened enough to override the insecurities and defenses which differences commonly evoke.

But how can we account for our rampant jealousies, hatreds, and envies? How does it happen that one man's success is thought to be at everyone else's expense? The quickest answer brands fellow feeling illusory. It comes from the doctrine of psychological egoism, which contends that an individual can know only himself and care only for himself. But egoism has lately been hit by several discoveries, notably from the field of developmental psychology. It appears that the insularity of the individual which egoism affirms is a condition which we perhaps *grow into*, but it is not the situation in which we start. As infants and children each of us is in fact much more social than individual, acquiring his ideas, feelings, and yes, his very identity, from others—his family and teachers, and through them his community. It also appears that many among us never grow beyond this dependent *altruism* to become persons in their own right. Listen carefully to a loud proponent of psychological egoism and you will likely find that he adheres to a religion, a morality, and perhaps a politics which were imbibed with his mother's milk and are nothing of his own. By his *orthodoxy*, by his penchant for the *commonplaces* of thought and feeling, he is the living refutation of the egoism he espouses.

But the genuineness or spuriousness of fellow feeling is not the only issue concerning it. If all men were to be convinced tomorrow of its reality, by no means would they agree on its value. In fellow feeling we relate affirmatively to the tyrant and the criminal. But this does not answer the question, *should* we. And what of our nation's enemies? Marine Corps boot camp is calculatingly designed to extinguish the recruit's fellow feeling for those he must eventually kill.

Leaving aside war and immorality, does an unconditional love dampen the striving for excellence? To be loved simply because we are human beings—doesn't this conduce to complacency? Where is the incentive to growth? More strongly still, some critics believe that a love of man's commonness generates a "herd" or "mass" morality which despises any kind of exceptionality—and excellence is always exceptional (see Plato's criticism of democracy, Book VIII, *The Republic*, or its updating in Ortega y Gasset's *The Revolt of the Masses*).

Such are some of the issues which are raised by skeptics and opponents of fellow feeling. The selections which follow are written by thinkers who are in varying degree proponents, and here as well the issues are many. The readings will serve their purpose if they lead, prod, and provoke the reader toward his own conclusions.

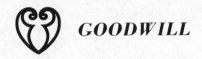

GOODWILL

Aristotle

Aristotle here seeks to distinguish "goodwill" from friendship, contending that the former is the ground out of which the latter emerges. As defined by Aristotle, goodwill falls somewhere between our categories of comradeship and fellow feeling. It is a positive regard for the value of others which may extend "towards people whom one does not know." While Aristotle does not suggest its existence as a universal subterranean bond among humankind (the meaning of fellow feeling), such extension appears ideally possible in view of the absence of a principle of exclusion.

What has been "said already" (see the selection) is that goodwill is a positive regard for the value of others which, when reciprocated, and when known to be felt by both parties, becomes friendship. Notice that goodwill is conditional, responding to "some excellence and worth" in another. But since Aristotle insists that it can extend to people whom one does not know, this excellence and worth must be presumptive. Here is a suggestion that the love of excellence is love of that which every human being has and which, then, can be presumed. It is potential *excellence—the unique* daimon *within each individual which it is his responsibility to actualize. Here we find the ground on which Eros, the love of excellence, can be universalized.*

Goodwill is a friendly sort of relation, but is not *identical* with friendship; for one may have goodwill both towards people whom one does not know, and without their knowing it, but not friendship. This has indeed been said already. But goodwill is not even friendly feeling. For it does not involve intensity or desire, whereas these accompany friendly feeling; and friendly feeling implies intimacy while goodwill may arise of a sudden, as it does towards competitors in a contest; we come to feel goodwill for them and to share in their wishes, but we would not *do* anything with them; for, as we said, we feel goodwill suddenly and love them only superficially.

Goodwill seems, then, to be a beginning of friendship, as the pleasure of the eye is the beginning of love. For no one loves if he has not first been delighted by the form of the beloved, but he who delights in the form of another does not, for all that, love him, but only does so when he also longs for him when absent and craves for his presence; so too it is not possible for people to be friends if they have not come to feel goodwill for each

From *The Basic Works of Aristotle*, ed. Richard McKeon (New York: Random House, 1941), p. 1083. Reprinted by permission of Random House, Inc.

other, but those who feel goodwill are not for all that friends; for they only *wish* well to those for whom they feel goodwill, and would not do anything with them nor take trouble for them. And so one might by an extension of the term friendship say that goodwill is inactive friendship, though when it is prolonged and reaches the point of intimacy it becomes friendship— not the friendship based on utility nor that based on pleasure; for goodwill too does not arise on those terms. The man who has received a benefit bestows goodwill in return for what has been done to him, but in doing so is only doing what is just; while he who wishes some one to prosper because he hopes for enrichment through him seems to have goodwill not to him but rather to himself, just as a man is not a friend to another if he cherishes him for the sake of some use to be made of him. In general, goodwill arises on account of some excellence and worth, when one man seems to another beautiful or brave or something of the sort, as we pointed out in the case of competitors in a contest.

SYMPATHY AS A SOCIAL EMERGENT

Herbert Spencer

British philosopher Herbert Spencer (1820–1903) applied evolutionary principles—Darwinian and Lamarckian—to the whole of existence. Like physiological traits, feelings come into being within evolutionary process and are furthered or extinguished by natural selection. Such is the case with sympathy—the ability to feel "ideally" what another feels actually by observing the sounds and motions by which he expresses his feeling.

Sympathy is not part of man's original equipment, but arises when changing conditions bring individuals into close and continuous presence of one another. The gregarious "habit" is acquired, within which sympathetic emotions arise, prove useful (in coordinating community labors, for example), and are retained by the evolutionary process. Moreover Spencer (and Darwin) saw moral development here, for sympathy is certain to increase with sociation and intellectual development (which recognizes species-wide interests), leading at last to the abolition of war and the attainment of a final social "equilibrium."

Today this "moral optimism" is thrown in question (if not refuted outright) by interim historical developments. Ours is characterized as an age of alienation, which at bottom means the curtailment of the capacity for sympathetic bonding. But this malaise comes late in man's evolutionary development. It is in advanced cultures, it seems, that the phenomemon of alienation takes root and spreads. Hence the contention that sympathy necessarily increases with evolutionary development is cast in doubt.

Darwin and Spencer thought of sympathy as entirely positive and life-affirming, but Scheler points to a significant ambiguity in the concept. "One may rejoice at another's joy and also repine at it; grieve at his sorrow, and also gloat upon it" (The Nature of Sympathy, *Part I, Chap. 8).* *In this case sympathies (or fellow feelings) may also be life destroying, and by the Spencerian argument for increase with sociation the life-de-destroying feelings will grow together with the positive feelings.*

In the Darwin-Spencer account, man begins as isolated and individual and grows into sociation and sympathy. But sociology and psychology today offer strong evidence to the contrary. According to the genetic theory of Emile Durkheim, George Herbert Mead, Max Scheler and many

From *The Principles of Psychology* by Herbert Spencer, 3rd ed. (London: Williams and Norgate, 1881), vol. 2, pp. 560–568. Reprinted by permission of Williams and Norgate, Publishers.

others, he is social from the beginning, progressively individuating himself as he grows. Here sympathy appears as an original *capacity which is likely to be lost in the course of personal and historical development.*

Recognizing the truth that sociality, while in some cases negatived by the wants of the species, becomes in other cases naturally established as furthering the preservation of the species, we have now to consider what mental traits accompany sociality—what feeling it implies and cultivates.

Sociality can begin only where, through some slight variation, there is less tendency than usual for the individuals to disperse widely. The off-spring of the same parents, naturally kept together during their early days, may have their proneness to stay together maintained for a longer time —they may tend to part only at a somewhat later age. If the family profits by this slight modification, dispersion will in subsequent generations be more and more postponed, until it ceases entirely. That slight variations of mental nature sufficient to initiate this process may be fairly assumed, all our domestic animals show us: differences in their characters and likings are conspicuous.

Sociality having thus commenced, and survival of the fittest tending ever to maintain and increase it, it will be further strengthened by the inherited effects of habit. The perception of kindred beings, perpetually seen, heard, and smelt, will come to form a predominant part of consciousness— so predominant a part that absence of it will inevitably cause discomfort. We have but to observe how the caged bird wants to escape, and how the dog, melancholy while chained up, is in ecstasies when liberated, to be re-minded that every kind of perceptive activity habitual to a race implies a correlative desire, and a correlative discomfort if that desire is not satis-fied. Even during an individual life, as men around us continually show, a trick or habit of quite a special and trivial kind comes to have a correspond-ing longing which is with difficulty resisted. Clearly, then, in a species to which gregariousness is advantageous, the desire to be together will, gen-eration after generation, be fostered by the habit of being together. How strong this desire does become we see in domestic animals. Horses left alone are often depressed in consequence, and show themselves eager for companionship. A lost sheep is manifestly unhappy until it again finds the flock. The strength of the desire is, indeed, such that in the absence of members of their own species, gregarious animals will form companion-ships with members of other species.

Without further evidence we may safely infer that among creatures led step by step into gregariousness, there will little by little be established a pleasure in being together—a pleasure in the consciousness of one another's presence—a pleasure simpler than, and quite distinct from, those higher ones which it makes possible. It is a pleasure of like grade with that displayed by the dog on getting off the high road into a field, where the mere sight of grass and contact of the feet with it produce a delight showing itself in scouring around. In the one case, as in the other, there is a set of nervous structures correlated with a set of external conditions. The presence of the external conditions is needful for the exercise of the structures. In the absence of the conditions there arises a craving, and, when the conditions are supplied, a corresponding gratification.

From the mental states produced in a gregarious animal by the *presence* of others like itself, we pass to the mental states produced in it by the *actions* of others like itself. The transition is insensible; for consciousness of the presence rarely exists apart from consciousness of the actions. Here, however, we may limit ourselves to actions that have marked significance.

As indicated above, an advantage gained by gregariousness which is probably the first, and remains among many creatures the most important, is the comparative safety secured by earlier detection of enemies. The emotion of fear expresses itself in movements of escape, preceded and accompanied, it may be, by sounds of some kind. Members of a herd simultaneously alarmed by a distant moving object or by some noise it makes—simultaneously making the movements and sounds accompanying alarm—severally see and hear these as being made by the rest at the same time that they are themselves making them, and at the same time that there is present the feeling which prompts them. Frequent repetition inevitably establishes an association between the consciousness of fear and the consciousness of these signs of fear in others—the sounds and movements cannot be perceived without there being aroused the feeling habitually joined with them when they were before perceived. Hence it inevitably happens that what is called the natural language of fear becomes, in a gregarious race, the means of exciting fear in those to whom no fearful object is perceptible. The alarmed members of a flock, seen and heard by the rest, excite in the rest the emotion they are displaying; and the rest, prompted by the emotion thus sympathetically excited, begin to make like movements and sounds. Evidently the process thus initiated must, by inheritance of the effects of habit, furthered by survival of the fittest, render organic a quick and complete sympathy of this simple kind. Eventually a mere hearing of the sound of alarm peculiar to the species, will by itself arouse the emotion of alarm. For the meaning of this sound becomes known not only in the way pointed out but in another way. Each is conscious of the sound made by itself when in fear; and the hearing of a like sound, tending to recall the sound made by itself, tends to arouse the accompanying feeling.

Hence the panics so conspicuous among gregarious creatures. Motions alone often suffice. A flock of birds towards which a man approaches will quietly watch for a while; but when one flies, those near it, excited by its movements of escape, fly also; and in a moment the rest are in the air.

The same happens with sheep. Long they stand stupidly gazing, but when one runs, all run; and so strong is the sympathetic tendency among them that they will severally go through the same movement at the same spot—leaping where there is nothing to be leapt over. Commonly along with these motions of alarm there are sounds of alarm, which may similarly be observed to spread. Rooks on the ground no sooner hear the loud caw of one that suddenly rises, than they join in chorus as they rise.

Beyond sympathetic fear, thus readily established in gregarious animals because from hour to hour causes of fear act in common on many, and because the signs of fear are so conspicuous, there are sympathetic feelings of other kinds established after a kindred manner. Creatures living together are simultaneously affected by surrounding conditions of a favourable kind; are therefore liable to be simultaneously thrown into pleasurable states; are therefore habitually witnesses of the sounds and movements accompanying such states, in others as well as in themselves; and hence, in a way like that above explained, are apt to have pleasurable feelings sympathetically excited.

Lambs in the spring show us that the friskiness of one is a cause of friskiness in those near it—if one leaps, others leap. Among horses, pleasurable excitement spreads, as every hunting-field shows. A pack of dogs, too, takes up the cry when a leader begins to give tongue. In the poultry-yard kindred facts may be noticed. Early in the day that quacking of the ducks which is significant of satisfaction, comes and goes in chorus: when one sets the example, the rest follow. The like happens with geese and with fowls. Gregarious birds in a wild state furnish further illustrations. In a rookery the cawing rises into bursts of many voices, and then almost dying away, again suddenly spreads sympathetically; and the like holds with the screamings of parrots and macaws.

This sympathy is most variously exhibited by that most intelligent of the gregarious animals which come under daily observation—the dog. Beyond sympathetic cries of excitement among dogs when chasing their prey in company, there is the sympathetic barking which every quarrel in the streets sets up, and which, under another form, is sometimes so annoying in the night; and there is also the sympathetic howling to be heard from dogs kept together in a kennel. Here, again, the feelings that are communicated from one to another, are feelings often simultaneously produced in many by a common cause. Able, however, as the dog is to perceive more complex and less conspicuous marks of feeling, it displays a degree and variety of sympathy considerably beyond this. Having long had men as well as members of their own species for companions, dogs have acquired tendencies to be sympathetically excited by manifestations of human feeling. I do not refer simply to the fact that sometimes a dog will howl sympathetically when he hears singing, and will even occasionally follow the voice up the gamut; for this is but a slight modification of the effect produced in him by the sounds other dogs make. But I refer to the fact that some dogs are sympathetically affected by the silent manifestations of pain and pleasure in those they are attached to—will stand with drooping tail and grave wistful gaze when the face and attitude of a master show depression, and will display joy on seeing a smile.

Here we are naturally introduced to the truth that the degree and range of sympathy depend on the clearness and extent of representation. A sympathetic feeling is one that is not immediately excited by the natural cause of such a feeling, but one that is mediately excited by the presentation of signs habitually associated with such a feeling. Consequently, it pre-supposes ability to perceive and combine these signs, as well as ability to represent their implications, external or internal, or both. So that there can be sympathy only in proportion as there is power of representation.

For this reason it is that among inferiour gregarious animals the range of sympathy is so narrow. The signs of pleasure when it becomes great, and the signs of fear, which is the most common pain, alone arouse in them fellow-feelings. With other emotions there is no sympathy; either because the signs of them are comparatively inconspicuous, or because the causes of them do not act simultaneously on all. A ewe that has lost her lamb, does not by her manifestations of feeling excite like feelings in other ewes; first, for the reason that her bleat does not differ much from the bleat caused by simple discomfort; second, for the reason that other ewes have not habitually had such slight modifications of bleat associated in themselves with the pains produced by loss of offspring; and third, for the reason that what other manifestations come from the bereaved ewe in the shape of motions and facial modifications, are inappreciable to the rest, and could not be mentally combined even if they were appreciable. There have neither been the requisite experiences, nor does there exist such power of representation as could combine the experiences, did they exist, into the needful antecedent to the feeling.

Hence increase of intelligence is one condition, though by no means the sole condition, to increase in extent of sympathy. Because they lack intelligence, herbivorous creatures, though their habits in scarcely any ways check the growth of sympathy, nevertheless remain unsympathetic in all directions save those above described. While the dog, trained by the habits of his species in the perception of more complex and varied appearances, has gained a considerably greater breadth of sympathy, notwithstanding that restraint which the predatory life puts on its extension.

One further group of general considerations must be set down. The genesis of sympathy implying in the first place the presence of other beings, and implying in the second place subjection to influences simultaneously operating on these other beings, and calling forth marks of feeling from them; it results that sympathy is cultivated by all relations among individuals which fulfil these conditions. Of such relations we have thus far recognized but one—the relation which gregariousness implies. But there are two others—the sexual relation and the parental relation. These co-operate in various degrees; and the most marked effects are produced where they both act along with simple sociality. A paragraph may be given to each.

The sexual relation can be expected to further the development of sympathy in a considerable degree, only if it has considerable permanence. Where the rearing of offspring is so carried on as to keep the parents together during the interval required for bringing up a single brood, and still more where it is so carried on as to keep them together during the rearing of successive broods, there are maintained the conditions under which arise certain sympathetic excitations beyond those entailed by gregariousness alone. As, in their common relation to progeny, parents are liable to have certain pleasurable and painful feelings frequently called out from them by the same cause at the same time in marked ways, they will become sympathetic in respect of such feelings; and in so far as such feelings are in part made up of more general feelings, expressed by more general signs, they will become relatively sympathetic in respect of the more general feelings. Birds furnish instances of the fulfilment of these conditions followed by production of these results. The contrast between polygamous birds, the males of which take no shares in rearing the offspring, and monogamous birds, the males of which take large shares in rearing them, supplies significant evidence. Where the male joins in feeding the young after they are hatched, as among our hedge birds, there is sympathy in fear, when the offspring are in danger; and probably in other feelings not so conspicuous. Among the martins and swifts, the male often feeds the female during incubation; and here we perceive in the simultaneous twittering of groups sitting on the eaves, or in the simultaneous screaming as they fly about together in the evening, and there is a more active sympathy than among barn-door fowls. Most marked, however, is the contrast in the poultry-yard between fowls and pigeons. The same pair of pigeons bring up successive broods, the female while sitting is fed by the male, and the male takes an unusual share in feeding the young: furnishing them with partially-macerated food from his crop. Here, and especially among the variety named doves, the sympathy is so great as to furnish familiar metaphors.

Fellow-feeling is also cultivated in each parent by its direct relations to progeny. Feeling having this origin is so intimately mingled with the parental feeling, which is a primitive and much simpler one, that the two cannot be clearly distinguished. But since parent and offspring are by their intimate relation often exposed to common causes of pleasure and pain, there must be a special exercise of sympathy between them, or rather, of sympathy in the parent towards the offspring; for the offspring, being but partially developed, cannot so interpret the natural language as to make the effects reciprocal. It will habitually happen that the signs of satisfaction consequent on abundance of food, will be shown by offspring and parent together, as well as kindred signs consequent on genial warmth; and the marks of discomfort, say from inclemency, as well as those of alarm from danger, will be frequently simultaneous. Hence there are furnished the conditions under which specialities of sympathy can arise.

These brief indications of an extensive class of facts, will make it adequately clear that there are three causes of sympathy, due respectively to the three relations—between members of a species, between male and female, and between parent and offspring. Co-operating as these causes do in various ways and degrees, according as the circumstances of the species determine one or other set of habits as most conducive to survival, it is inferable that where the circumstances allow co-operation of all the causes, the effects are likely to be the greatest. Among inferior animals, co-operation of all the causes is not frequent: rooks supplying us with one of the few instances easily observable. And even where all the causes co-operate the effect producible depends on the accompanying degree of intelligence; since the capacity for being sympathetically affected, implies the capacity for having an ideal feeling of some kind aroused by perception of the sounds and motions implying a real feeling of the same kind in another.

FELLOW FEELING AS ORIGINAL HUMAN UNITY

Max Scheler

Scheler here offers a most provocative claim. He says that we can enter into the experience of others without ever having had that particular quality of experience before. This means that the lives of others can serve "to effect a real enlargement of our own lives and to transcend the limitations of our own actual experience." The avenue by which this is achieved is fellow feeling.

Most theories of communication limit our knowledge of others to experience which we have previously had in ourselves. From the other's gestures we recall our feeling when on some earlier occasion we ourselves made similar gestures, and we infer the same feeling in him. Or his gesture evokes a feeling in us which we "project" upon him.

Such theories presuppose that each of us is locked within himself and devoid of immediate touch with others. This supposition fills Scheler with impatience, for it fails to understand the nature of the person. Each person is both a unique individual and a part of universal humankind. His uniqueness is an achievement, and outcome of a process of growth. In the process of intellectual development, for example, one rises to a unique conception of the meaning of "freedom," or "love." But he begins with the common meaning. In the same way each of us begins as "common humanity" and grows toward uniqueness. But the common humanity remains within us and affords direct access to others. When the other manifests a feeling which we ourselves have not had he activates (through fellow feeling) within us what has until now been a dormant potential.

Now true fellow-feeling is wholly functional througout: there is no reference to the state of one's own feelings. In commiserating with B, the latter's state of feeling is given as located entirely in B himself: it does not filter across into A, the commiserator, nor does it produce a corresponding or similar condition in A. It is merely 'commiserated with,' not undergone by A as a real experience. It may seem extraordinary that we should be able to feel the emotional states of others, and really 'suffer' over them; that the result of rejoicing *with* them should be, *not* that we are joyful on their account, for this would then be simply our own joy, but that we are

From *The Nature of Sympathy* by Max Scheler, trans. Peter Heath, with a general introduction to Max Scheler's works by W. Stark (Yale University Press, 1954), pp. 41–50. Reprinted by permission of Routledge and Kegan Paul, Ltd., London.

able to *savour* their joy without thereby needing to get into a joyful mood ourselves; but this is just what happens in the phenomenon of *genuine* fellow-feeling. Whereas the causation or infective propagation of analogous feeling-states in ourselves by reason of their presence in others, is no true fellow-feeling at all, but merely seems to be so because of a misapprehension.

In my essay on 'Self-deception' I have dealt with yet another type of case, where again there is no authentic fellow-feeling present, but this time because there is a sort of identification with the other person. It is to some extent the opposite of the previous case. I have in mind the situation in which our own life acquires a tendency to dissipate itself in a vicarious re-enactment of the doings of one or more other people; where we are so *caught up*, as it were, in the other's changing moods and interests that we no longer seem to lead a life of our own; or where our own life largely consists in a series of reactions to such material content as becomes available, *at second hand*, through the other person's experience. Here we react to what actually touches him, as though touched by it ourselves; not because of any illusion or hallucination concerning the priority of the individual feelings, but simply because we are leading *his* life and not our own, while remaining quite unaware of the vicarious relationship by which this process is effected. The distinctive element in this sort of case lies above all in the attitude to one's own self and the evaluation of one's own interests, acts of will, conduct, and indeed one's very existence. This attitude and assessment are now no more than derivative, being determined by the changing *regard* in which the other person holds or might hold us, and which he may demonstrate. We think well of ourselves in finding favour with him, and badly when we do not. Our very acts and decisions are determined by the implicit demands inherent *in his conception of us*. Now this picture he has of us is not, as it normally is, a *result* of our own spontaneous life and activity, which we then receive back at second hand, rejoicing, for example, to find him endorsing it. On the contrary, what happens is that his life and activity becomes entirely dependent on his fluctuating opinion of us. This produces a purely reactive style of life having, on the account alone, a low moral value.

Such a reactive attitude towards society is characteristic of the abnormally *vain* man, who—in contrast to the proud type, is utterly in thrall to the notice and opinion of other people; it is only *as* one who is seen, marked and attended to that he has any sense of his moral reality, and his own personality, wishes and feelings are completely hidden from him by the 'personage' he enacts. It is also characteristic, though in a very different fashion, of a type I should describe as the mental *parasite*. This human species lives, mentally, entirely on those around him, or on a *single* member of his acquaintance, in the sense that he partakes of the latter's experiences as his own, not merely echoing the other's thoughts and opinions, but thinking and uttering them on his own account, and sharing his moods likewise. It is a consciousness of internal emptiness and nullity, which gives rise to this type of personality; a vacuity which drives him out of 'himself,' and hence to fill his empty belly with the experience of others. And this passive type finally passes into the far more dangerous active form of the disposition: that of the spiritual *vampire*, the hollowness of whose existence, coupled with a passionate quest for experience, drives him to a limitless *active* penetration into the inmost reaches of the other's self; unlike the passive type, he does not fasten on a single individual, but always on one after another, so as to live a life of his own in their experiences, and fill the void within. Strindberg has given a masterly description of the type in his play *The Dance of Death*. It is also common for certain psychoses to exhibit a variant form of the general attitude here outlined; I refer to that excessive deference in attitude, thought and action, towards the 'spectator' and the impression supposedly made upon him, which is so especially noticeable in *hysteria*. Here the presence of an onlooker immediately upsets the patient's natural self-possession, his consciousness of himself being replaced by the *image* of himself as seen by the onlooker, and as judged by the latter's standards of preference. He speaks, acts and conducts himself by reference to this image and on the spur of the moods it evokes—refusing to eat, for instance, or even committing suicide in some cases. It would be a mistake to describe this, as many psychiatric textbooks do, simply as 'excessive vanity,' 'play-acting' or 'coquetry' on the part of the patient. For those who affect such attitudes are conscious, not only of the picture they present, but also that it is *they* who present it; they oscillate between this picture and an awareness of themselves as they really are. For the hysterical patient, however, the picture has come to life; the image of what he might be has come, for him, to *displace* what he actually is. Preoccupied as he is with the other person, the real course of his receptive, expressive and active life is actuated by variations in the fully-formed image supposedly seen there, depending on whatever authoritative version of it may have caught his fancy at the time; though he does not consciously set out to produce such variations in the image, for the sake of a pleasurable reaction thereto. Such a patient therefore, will not be content, like the still normal 'prima donna' type, to put on a stricken air so as to make others feel sorry for him, or a gay one to cheer them up; instead, he will implement the wished-for calamity by *actually* staging one, will actually kill himself, actually get into a state of wild hilarity, etc., but all still entirely for the benefit of the spectator and depending on his presence. The vain man, the play-actor and the coquette do not act thus, for they have not lost their capacity for self-awareness and merely vacillate between their own true condition and the image of themselves as others see them.

All such sub-species of this general type consist of forms which have nothing to do with fellow-feeling proper, seeing that the conditions for this, the consciousness and feeling of being oneself, of leading one's own life and thus of being 'separate' from others, are only apprehended here in a degenerate form. For this reason, too, their *ethical value is negative*, however much they may be mistaken for refinements of fellow-feeling or even for love. There is certainly nothing to prevent such attitudes from leading to actions of great benefit to the other person. All these people are capable of acts of what is commonly called 'sacrifice'. But in fact that is merely what they look like. For a man who neither leads his own life nor finds it worth living cannot sacrifice himself for another. He simply does not possess the one thing needful for sacrifice, namely a life of his own. Such neglect of self may have the quality of being useful and well-intentioned towards others, or it may be damaging and malevolent—as in the case of pure villainy, which may render the villain quite forgetful of his own advantage and even reckless of damage to himself; but even where the process begins in goodwill, it is an almost invariable rule in such cases, that it *ends in hatred*, and the more so, the more the agent persists in throwing himself *away* in this spurious fashion, for it is the very opposite of really meritorious self-*devotion*. Without a certain self-awareness and self-respect, acquired at first hand, and not derived from the effect produced on others, it is not possible to live morally. But the more our self-respect is impaired in the process referred to, the harder do we struggle to retain it, and the sterner grows the conflict between this endeavour and the countervailing tendency to lapse into absorption in another person. Figuratively speaking, although the 'slave' has voluntarily delivered himself into the bondage of living another's life rather than his own, he comes at last to chafe against his fetters, and to rise up against his 'master.' And so the expense of spirit which at first resembled love turns necessarily to hatred, as a final means of self-assertion.[1]

A peculiar mixture of genuine fellowship with subservience of this type is to be found in the relationship of 'patriarchal' authority between parents and children, or master and man. Its characteristic feature is the *mixture* of authority and considerate or indulgent fellow-feeling in the superior towards his subordinate, and, in the latter, a submissive deference to the life and will of the master, together with a genuinely solicitous fellow-feeling for him. The Russian appellation of 'Little Father' expresses this very strikingly.

But let us return to the genetic theories of fellow-feeling, and to the point made earlier, that in true unalloyed commiseration and rejoicing there is no state of sorrow or joy in oneself. This phenomenological fact is a stumbling-block for all those theories which undertake to explain the fact of fellow-feeling, without reverting, as before, to 'inference' or 'automatic

[1] This process often finds expression in an 'ambivalent' oscillation between love and hatred, in which hatred always sets in when self-abandonment has gone too far, to be again transformed into love, once the personal self has been reinstated. The fear of love, so-called, is in fact the fear of 'throwing oneself away.'

illusion.' For they do so by asserting that perception of the symptoms and occasioning circumstances of joy or sorrow in another person either has the effect of *immediately* evoking the *reproduction* of a similar joy or sorrow previously experienced in oneself, or else that it does so *indirectly* by way of a tendency to imitate the symptoms so perceived. Let us disregard the second alternative and confine ourselves to the reproduction of past states of feeling. Lipps, like Störring, makes all fellow-feeling consequent on a prior reproduction of feeling, and assumes that, given such a reproduction, which would necessarily present the feelings in question as having been previously felt to be my own, there is a further process of 'empathy' by which they are then carried over into the other person. In so doing he recognizes a problem which Störring disregards. For in fact we do at least have the impression that in fellow-feeling the other's emotions are in some sense 'given.' Störring does not explain this impression at all. While in view of all I have previously said about his theory of empathy, Lipps explains it wrongly. For it follows from what has already been shown that a genetic theory is irrelevant here, since the other person's state of mind is directly grasped *in* the expressive phenomenon itself—without any sort of projective 'empathy.' But this raises the question whether such a reproduction of one's own joy or sorrow does or can play any part whatever in genuine fellow-feeling.

Let us first consider those cases where such reproduction undoubtedly does occur. Everybody must have had the experience of going in serious trouble to someone and telling this interested relative or friend of his distress. And he may well have noticed how the adviser in question, instead of entering into his visitor's circumstances, takes the latter's tale as an opportunity for indulging in a spate of reminiscence about *himself*, as to how a very similar thing once happened to him, and what he then did about it. 'Yes,' they say, 'that's life all over: I once had pretty well the same thing happen to me.' Somewhat put out, we draw our friend's attention to the fact that here the circumstances are 'rather different'; we do our utmost to divert the rapt historian's gaze from his own career to our present troubles. But all too often he calmly goes on with his tale. Again, we have all met people who temper the quantity and direction of their interest according to what has given *them* most joy or sorrow in their own lives. But is such an obtrusion of one's own experience, even though it be reproduced quite automatically *without* any act of recall, any more authentic as a case of fellow-feeling than the previous one, seeing that it again involves a diversion of interest from the other person back to oneself? I do not think so. This genetic theory does nothing to account for positive unalloyed fellow-feeling, which is a genuine *out-reaching* and entry into the other person and his individual situation, a true and authentic *transcendence* of one's self; it merely explains some of the casual empirical circumstances associated with the working of fellow-feeling, and these are more liable to disturb and detract from it, than to produce or promote it. In so far as our own reproduced experiences may intervene between our fellow-feeling and the other person's state of mind, the purely positive character of the feeling is veiled in an obscuring medium originating in the particular state of our psychophysical organization at the time. This genetic association-theory overlooks the very existence of *pure* fellow-feeling as such, just as it ignores the possibility of pure remembering (independent of the memory-image, as Bergson has effectively shown[2]), and of a pure intuition indivisible into sensory constituents. To add a further point, the experience reproduced, for instance the grief or anguish felt in pitying a person afflicted by these states, would have to be a *genuine* feeling (though less intense than the original state). For it is not supposed to be a question of remembering a feeling one has possessed or shared, but of actually reproducing it, so that there really is a new feeling present, albeit a weaker one. Thus, to pity a drowning man, I should have to be stricken for a moment with fear like his own; to have pity for someone in pain, I should need to feel a twinge of it myself. But the purer and truer the fellow-feeling, the less does this happen; the more it does occur, the closer we approach to a condition of emotional infection, which actually does consist in such a reproduction of feelings, either directly or by virtue of the tendency to echo the expression of feeling in others; and the effect of this is to *lower* the moral value of the attitude accordingly.

This theory is at fault in yet another respect. For it entails that our fellow-feeling must necessarily be confined to processes and incidents in other people's experience such as *we have already met with ourselves*. But this conclusion is as little in accord with the facts as the corresponding view, that we can only understand what we have actually been through ourselves. We can have a lively and immediate participation in joy or sorrow, can share with others their appreciation of value, and can even enter into another person's commiseration for a third party, without ever having sampled that particular quality of experience before. A person who has never felt mortal terror can still understand and envisage it, just as he can also share in it. It is a futile evasion to argue that for this we must at least have had real experience of the 'elements' of the state or value in question, such as those comprised in fear, or in some sort of 'death-like feeling', in the present case. For what sort of 'elements' are these? How far must we descend in search of those mental particles which the atomistic psychology believes to be constituent of experience? And on what principle or rule are these 'elements' to be compounded, if we do not already have some idea of what the end-product is to be, namely mortal terror? Are we to go on shuffling these elements in imagination, until they happen to fit the case? Such a game would be most unlikely to come out.

[2]Henri Bergson: *Matter and Memory* (authorized translation by N. M. Paul and W. Scott Palmer), London, Macmillan, 1911.

Certainly, the variety of emotional tones within the compass of a species such as man, is no less *finite* however large it may be, than the limited number of basic colours he is able to perceive. Nevertheless, it is quite wrong to suppose that these basic colours must necessarily be encountered in actual perception and sensation, before they can be visualized' at all; the fact is that this intrinsic limitation of range holds *equally* good throughout for *all* modes of colour-awareness alike, whether in perception, in judgement, or in the use of imagery (in memory, fantasy, etc.); it is only because of the biologically purposive character of the order in which these acts are brought into use, that we usually begin by perceiving qualities in sensation, on receipt of an external stimulus, before they are presénted in imagery.[3] It is exactly the same in the present case. Given the range of emotional qualities of which man is intrinsically capable, and from which alone his own actual feelings are built up, he has an *equally innate* capacity for comprehending the feelings of others, even though he may never on any occasion have encountered such feelings (or their ingredients) in himself, as real unitary experiences.

Moreover, this applies increasingly, the more such feelings ascend from the sensory level, through the vital, to the spiritual plane. It is only for *sensory* feelings ('feeling-sensations') that reproduction is required, in order to be sure of understanding and participating in them. Thus it is scarcely possible for a normal person to acquire a real understanding of a perverse sensual pleasure and impossible for him to share in it, any more than he can in the enjoyment of pain. It is equally difficult to partake in the enthusiasm of the Japanese for consuming raw fish; and difficult even, for a man of culture to summon up a genuine sympathetic enjoyment in the pleasures of the populace, such as their taste for rowdy music, for instance. The varieties of sensory pleasure and pain in animals are also largely alien to us, and fellow-feeling is no longer operative in such cases. Nevertheless, so far as the various modes of *vital feeling* are concerned, understanding and fellow-feeling are able to range throughout the *entire* animate universe, even though they rapidly fall off in respect of specific qualities as we descend the organic scale. The mortal terror of a bird, its sprightly or dispirited moods, are intelligible to us and awaken our fellow-feeling, despite our total inability to penetrate those of its sensory feelings which depend on its particular sensory organization. Again, the very people whose sensuous enjoyments are unintelligible and uncongenial to the person of culture, are perfectly comprehensible to him in respect of their vital emotions, and awaken his wholehearted interest therein. While the understanding and sharing of *mental*, and still more of *spiritual* feel-

---

[3]It has not yet been established for certain whether those born blind have any conception of colour.

ings, is completely independent of all such gulfs between the contingent personal backgrounds of individuals. Jesus' despair in Gethsemane can be understood and shared regardless of our historical, racial and even human limitations. And for every candid heart which steeps itself in that desolation it operates, not as a reminder or revival of personal sufferings, great or small, but as the revelation of a new and greater suffering hitherto *undreamed* of.

Only so are we enabled, by understanding, emotional reproduction and fellow-feeling for other people's circumstances, values and standards (fellow-feeling plus evaluation), to effect a real *enlargement* of our own lives and to *transcend* the limitations of our own actual experience; thereby reconciling the appearance of both such fields of actual experience under that *governing* master-concept of life in all its fullness, vouchsafed to the open-hearted through a sympathetic understanding of value and circumstance in the present and the past. According to the theories we are rejecting, we are supposed, firstly, to be necessarily confined in the prison of our own casual experiences, in all their individual, racial and historical heterogeneity, so that the objects of our understanding and sympathy would represent merely a *selection* from such experience as *we* have actually had. Thus an age could only understand and sympathize with those aspects of a bygone epoch which were familiar from its own experience. 'Wha's like us?' would become an axiom for the historian, and the habit of analogical comparison with the present day, which is really a grave abuse of history, would be enthroned as the basic principle of historical method. The idea of an inner *moral unity of mankind* over and above the actual contacts of its members, would likewise become a pure fiction. A second conclusion would necessarily follow from such a view: that though fellow-feeling so often seems to affect our volition and action, and even the entire course of our inner life, setting it right, for instance, by inducing us to abandon a plan or renounce decisions already made lest they should prove detrimental to others, this would merely be an illusory effect, since such sympathy could only extend to matters for which our own life hitherto had furnished the material. Fellow-feeling and its objects, being merely epiphenomenal to what has actually been experienced, would have no hope of ever exerting any *real effective* influence on its present course of development. And now let us confront this view with a case like that of Buddha's conversion. A man who, having grown up amid luxury and splendour and all the amenities of life, was led by the sight of a few instances of poverty and sickness to discern and respond to all the pain and misery of the world, so that his whole life thereafter took an entirely different course. Or again, we may take an example from Tolstoi's story *Master and Servant* which tells how the master's mean little heart is *opened*, after lifelong closure, in the act of his first experience of pure sympathy at the sight of his servant perishing of cold;

and this not only for the limited feeling of the moment, but for everything to which he had hitherto been blind, neglectful or obtuse in his own life.[4]

But we have no need of such exalted examples. We can perceive in our daily lives a rhythmic alternation between the closed and the open viewpoint, between self-regarding aloofness and sympathetic interest in the lives of other people. We may notice how our flow of sympathy is by no means dependent on variations in the external stimuli, but fluctuates widely in spite of them. Thus it often fails us when confronted with the fact and the evidence of intense suffering, and then often without any such powerful inducement, some trifle may open all our soul to human joys and sorrows for days and weeks on end, as if a light were suddenly shone, or a window opened, in a darkened room. It is brought home to us here with especial clarity, how fellow-feeling differs, in the *autonomy* of its functioning, from states of mind occasioned by factors external to ourselves.

[4]Jacob Wassermann's novel *Christian Wahnschaffe*, gives a masterly portrayal of a man addicted to selfish enjoyment and a slave to the conventions of his station and class, who slowly learns, by repeated acquaintance with human distress and misery, to open his heart to the other side of life and society (tr. by Ludwig Lewisohn as *The World's Illusion*, Rahway, N.J., 1921, re-issued by Allen and Unwin, 1929).

 **SYMPATHY AND THE
EMERGENCE OF SELF**

George Herbert Mead

"The self, as that which can be an object to itself, is essentially a social structure, and it arises in social experience" (Mind, Self and Society, *Part III, Chap. 18).*

*With this thesis Mead gives overwhelming importance to sympathetic feelings, for it is upon them that the very formation of self depends. Our first impressions of self come to us through the eyes of others, the result of taking the attitudes of others towards us. Our ability to do this arises from the language of gestures for which Mead's illustration is the dog-fight. "The act of each dog becomes the stimulus to the other dog for his response. There is then a relationship between these two; and as the act is responded to by the other dog, it, in turn, undergoes change. The very fact that the dog is ready to attack another becomes a stimulus to the other dog to change his own position or his own attitude. He has no sooner done this than the change of attitude in the second dog in turn causes the first dog to change his attitude. We have here a conversation of gestures" (*Mind, Self and Society, *Part II, Chap. 7).*

The gesture becomes a "significant symbol" when it implicity arouses in the individual making it the same response it arouses (or is intended to arouse) in the individual to whom it is addressed. It is this capacity of identical response which Mead calls sympathy, and on which the formation of self rests. The self emerges as an organization of others' attitudes toward itself.

George Herbert Mead (1863-1931) was a major figure in American pragmatism. His theory of the social genesis of self continues to exercise great influence in psychology, social science, and (through John Dewey) American education.

The term "sympathy" is an ambiguous one, and a difficult one to interpret. I have referred to an immediate attitude of care, the assistance of one individual by another, such as we find expecially in the relations among lower forms. Sympathy comes, in the human form, in the arousing in one's self of the attitude of the individual whom one is assisting, the taking the attitude of the other when one is assisting the other. A physician may simply carry through an operation in an objective fashion without any sympathetic

From *Mind, Self and Society from the Standpoint of a Social Behaviorist*, ed. Charles W. Morris (University of Chicago Press, 1934), pp. 298-303. Reprinted by permission of The University of Chicago Press.

attitude toward the patient. But in an attitude which is sympathetic we imply that our attitude calls out in ourselves the attitude of the person we are assisting. We feel with him and we are able so to feel ourselves into the other because we have, by our own attitude, aroused in ourselves the attitude of the person whom we are assisting. It is that which I regard as a proper interpretation of what we ordinarily call "imitation," and "sympathy," in the vague, undefined sense which we find in our psychologies, when they deal with it at all.

Take, for example, the attitude of parents to the child. The child's tone is one of complaint, suffering, and the parent's tone is one that is soothing. The parent is calling out in himself an attitude of the child in accepting that consolation. This illustration indicates as well the limitation of sympathy. There are persons with whom one finds it difficult to sympathize. In order to be in sympathy with someone, there must be a response which answers to the attitude of the other. If there is not a response which so answers, then one cannot arouse sympathy in himself. Not only that, but there must be co-operation, a reply on the part of the person sympathized with, if the individual who sympathizes is to call out in himself this attitude. One does not put himself immediately in the attitude of the person suffering apart from one's own sympathetic attitude toward him. The situation is that of a person assisting the other, and because of that calling out in himself the response that his assistance calls out in the other. If there is no response on the part of the other, there cannot be any sympathy. Of course, one can say that he can recognize what such a person must be suffering if he could only express it. He thereby puts himself in the place of another who is not there but whom he has met in experience, and interprets this individual in view of the former experience. But active sympathy means that the individual does arouse in another the response called out by his assistance and arouses in himself the same response. If there is no response, one cannot sympathize with him. That presents the limitation of sympathy as such; it has to occur in a co-operative process. Nevertheless, it is in the foregoing sense that one person identifies himself with another. I am not referring to an identification in the Hegelian sense of an Ego, but of an individual who perfectly naturally arouses a certain response in himself because his gesture operates on himself as it does on the other.

To take a distinctively human, that is, self-conscious, social attitude toward another individual, or to become aware of him as such, is to identify yourself sympathetically with him, by taking his attitude toward, and his role in, the given social situation, and by thus responding to that situation implicitly as he does or is about to do explicitly; in essentially the same way you take his attitude toward yourself in gestural conversation with him, and are thus made self-conscious. Human social activities depend very largely upon social co-operation among the human individuals who carry them on, and such co-operation results from the taking by these individuals of social attitudes toward one another. Human society endows the human individual with a mind; and the very social nature of that mind requires him to put himself to some degree in the experiential places of, or to take the attitudes of, the other individuals belonging to that society and involved with him in the whole social process of experience and behavior which that society represents or carries on.

I wish now to utilize this mechanism in dealing with religion and the economic process. In the economic field the individual is taking the attitude of the other in so far as he is offering something to the other and calling out in reply a response of giving in the individual who has a surplus. There must be a situation in which the individual brings forward his own object as something that is valuable. Now, from his point of view it is not valuable, but he is putting himself in the attitude of the other individual who will give something in return because he can find some use for it. He is calling out in himself the attitude of the other in offering something in return for what he offers; and although the object has for the individual no direct value, it becomes valuable from the point of view of the other individual into whose place the first individual is able to put himself.

What makes this process so universal is the fact that it is a dealing with surpluses, dealing with that which is, so to speak, from the point of view of the individual without value. Of course, it gets a value in the market and then one assesses it from the point of view of what one can get for it, but what makes it a universal thing is that it does not pass into the individual's own direct use. Even if he takes something that he can use and trades that, he has to regard it as something he is going to get rid of in order to get something still more valuable; it has to be something he is not going to use. The immediate value of our owning a thing directly is the use to which we put it, its consumption; but in the economic process we are dealing with something that is immediately without value. So we set up a universal sort of a process. The universality is dependent upon this fact that each person is bringing to the market the things he is not going to use. He states them in terms of the abstraction of money by means of which he can get anything else. It is this negative value that gives the universality, for then it can be turned over to anybody who can give something in return which can be used.

In the primitive community where everybody is related to everybody else, a surplus as such has no meaning. The things are distributed in accordance with definite custom; everybody shares the surplus. Wealth does not exist under such conditions at all. There are certain returns given to the artisan, but they are not returns put into the form that can be expended for any goods which he wants to get in return for something he does not want. The setting-up, then, of the media of exchange is something that is highly abstract. It depends upon the ability of the individual to put himself in the place of the other to see that the other needs what he does not himself need, and to see that what he himself does not need is something that another does need. The whole process depends on an identification of one's self with the other, and this cannot take place among living forms in which there is not a capacity for putting one's self in the place of the other through communicating in a system of gestures which constitute language. Here are then two phases in which universal societies, although highly abstract societies, do actually exist, and what I have been presenting is the import from the psychological standpoint of these universal societies and their tendencies to complete themselves. One cannot complete the process of bringing goods into a market except by developing means of communication. The language in which that is expressed is the language of money. The economic process goes right on tending to bring people closer together by setting up more and more economic techniques and the language mechanism necessary to these procedures.

The same is true in a somewhat different sense from the point of view of the universal religions. They tend to define themselves in terms of communities, because they identify themselves with the cult in the community, but break out beyond this in the missionary movement, in the form of propagandists. The religion may be of a relatively primitive sort, as in Mohammedanism, or in the more complex forms of Buddhism and Christianity; but it inevitably undertakes to complete the relations involved in the attitude of saving other people's souls, of helping, assisting, other people. It develops the missionary who is a physician, those who are artisans, those who set up processes in the community which will lead to the attachment to the very things involved in the religious attitude. We see it first of all in the monasteries of Europe, where the monks undertook to set themselves up as the artisans. They illustrate the tendency of religion to complete itself, to complete the community which previously existed in an abstract form. Such is the picture that I wanted to present as one of the valuable interpretative contributions of such a view of the self as here developed.

Prevention of war/genocide

1. *exposing as D. Ellsberg*
2. *society nurtures violence*
3. *increase education on peace*
4. *Consensual signature before war/sta*
5. *apparatus that control apparatus*
6. *Sports/olympic approach — to disclaim energy*
7. *look for the enemy and star US*